University Centre at
Blackburn
College

Telephone: 01254 292165

Please return this book on or before the last date shown

Edinburgh Critical Guides to Literature
Series Editors: Martin Halliwell, University of Leicester and
Andy Mousley, De Montfort University

Published Titles:
Gothic Literature, Andrew Smith
Canadian Literature, Faye Hammill
Women's Poetry, Jo Gill
Contemporary American Drama, Annette J. Saddik
Shakespeare, Gabriel Egan
Asian American Literature, Bella Adams
Children's Literature, M. O. Grenby
Contemporary British Fiction, Nick Bentley
Renaissance Literature, Siobhan Keenan

Forthcoming Titles in the Series:
Restoration and Eighteenth-Century Literature, Hamish Mathison
Contemporary American Fiction, David Brauner
Victorian Literature, David Amigoni
Crime Fiction, Stacy Gillis
Modern American Literature, Catherine Morley
Scottish Literature, Gerard Carruthers
Modernist Literature, Rachel Potter
Medieval Literature, Pamela King
Women's Fiction, Sarah Sceats
African American Literature, Jennifer Terry
Contemporary British Drama, David Lane
Contemporary Poetry, Nerys Williams

Contemporary British Fiction

Nick Bentley

Edinburgh University Press

For Karla

© Nick Bentley, 2008

Transferred to digital print 2013

Edinburgh University Press Ltd
22 George Square, Edinburgh

Typeset in 11.5/13 Monotype Ehrhardt
by Servis Filmsetting Ltd, Stockport, Cheshire
Printed and bound by CPI Group (UK) Ltd, Croydon, CR0 4YY

A CIP record for this book is available from the British Library

ISBN 978 0 7486 2419 5 (hardback)
ISBN 978 0 7486 2420 1 (paperback)

Contents

Series Preface

The study of English literature in the early twenty-first century is host to an exhilarating range of critical approaches, theories and historical perspectives. 'English' ranges from traditional modes of study such as Shakespeare and Romanticism to popular interest in national and area literatures such as the United States, Ireland and the Caribbean. The subject also spans a diverse array of genres from tragedy to cyberpunk, incorporates such hybrid fields of study as Asian American literature, Black British literature, creative writing and literary adaptations, and remains eclectic in its methodology.

Such diversity is cause for both celebration and consternation. English is varied enough to promise enrichment and enjoyment for all kinds of readers and to challenge preconceptions about what the study of literature might involve. But how are readers to navigate their way through such literary and cultural diversity? And how are students to make sense of the various literary categories and periodisations, such as modernism and the Renaissance, or the proliferating theories of literature, from feminism and marxism to queer theory and eco-criticism? The Edinburgh Critical Guides to Literature series reflects the challenges and pluralities of English today, but at the same time it offers readers clear and accessible routes through the texts, contexts, genres, historical periods and debates within the subject.

Martin Halliwell and Andy Mousley

Acknowledgements

I would like to thank Andy Mousley and Martin Halliwell for their helpful editorial advice and their patience, and Jackie Jones, Máiréad McElligott and James Dale at Edinburgh University Press. Thanks to Keele University for allowing me a period of research leave, which was partly used in writing the book. I would also like to thank several of my colleagues with whom I have taught and had many stimulating and informative discussions on texts and issues relevant to this book, including Bella Adams, David Amigoni, Steven Barfield, Annika Bautz, Fred Botting, Robert Duggan, Scott McCracken, Roger Pooley, Amber Regis, Sharon Ruston, Helen Stoddart, Barry Taylor, Philip Tew and Kate Walchester. I would also like to thank Karla Smith for proofreading the book and the discussions we have had on its subject matter.

Teaching contemporary British fiction has shaped my thinking about the subject over the last few years, and I would like to thank the many students I have had the privilege to work with at Birmingham University, the Open University, Wedgwood Memorial College and, especially, Keele University.

Some of the material in this book has appeared in different form in academic journals. Reworked versions of sections of Chapters 1 and 5 have appeared in *Textual Practice*, and of Chapter 5 in *Postgraduate English*. Thanks to the editors at both these journals for giving permission for this material to be represented here.

Finally, I would like to thank my family for the continued love and support they have given me throughout the writing of this book.

Chronology

Date	Historical and Cultural Events	Publication of Novels
1975	Margaret Thatcher becomes Conservative Party Leader; Sex Discrimination Bill	David Lodge, *Changing Places*; Sam Selvon, *Moses Ascending*
1976	James Callaghan takes over from Harold Wilson as Prime Minister; Race Relations Act; Notting Hill riots; punk rock begins in Britain	Emma Tennant, *Hotel de Dream*
1977	Silver Jubilee of Elizabeth II	Angela Carter, *The Passion of New Eve*; John Fowles, *Daniel Martin*
1978	New Wave influences British Rock and Pop	Beryl Bainbridge, *Young Adolf*; A. S. Byatt, *The Virgin in the Garden*; Ian McEwan, *The Cement Garden*

Date	Historical and Cultural Events	Publication of Novels
1979	'Winter of Discontent'; Margaret Thatcher elected as Conservative Prime Minister	Angela Carter, *The Bloody Chamber*; John Le Carré, *Smiley's People*
1980	Riots in Bristol; Ronald Reagan elected President of US	Graham Swift, *The Sweet Shop Owner*
1981	British Nationality Bill; riots in Birmingham, Bristol, Liverpool, London, and Manchester	Alasdair Gray, *Lanark*; Salman Rushdie, *Midnight's Children*; Graham Swift, *Shuttlecock*
1982	The Falklands War between Britain and Argentina	Pat Barker, *Union Street*
1983	Conservatives re-elected; Neil Kinnock takes over leadership of the Labour Party from Michael Foot	Salman Rushdie, *Shame*; Graham Swift, *Waterland*; Fay Weldon, *The Lives and Loves of a She Devil*
1984	The Miner's Strike; IRA bombing of Conservative Party Conference in Brighton	Martin Amis, *Money: A Suicide Note*; J. G. Ballard, *Empire of the Sun*; Julian Barnes, *Flaubert's Parrot*; Angela Carter, *Nights at the Circus*; Alasdair Gray, *1982 Janine*
1985	Riots in London and Birmingham	Peter Ackroyd, *Hawksmoor*; A. S. Byatt, *Still Life*; John Fowles, *A Maggot*; Doris Lessing, *The Good Terrorist*; Jeanette Winterson, *Oranges Are Not the Only Fruit*

Date	Historical and Cultural Events	Publication of Novels
1986	Wapping Print Workers' Strike	Kingsley Amis, *The Old Devils*
1987	Conservatives re-elected; 'Black Monday' – Stock Market Crash; storms cause heavy damage across Britain	V. S. Naipaul, *The Enigma of Arrival*; Ian McEwan, *The Child in Time*; Jeanette Winterson, *The Passion*
1988	Reform of the Education System; rave culture – Summer of Love	Doris Lessing, *The Fifth Child*; Salman Rushdie, *The Satanic Verses*
1989	The Fall of the Berlin Wall; revolutions in Eastern Europe; end of the Cold War; 'Poll Tax' in Scotland; fatwa issued against Salman Rushdie	Martin Amis, *London Fields*; Julian Barnes, *A History of the World in 10½ Chapters*; Janice Galloway, *The Trick is to Keep Breathing*; Kazuo Ishiguro, *The Remains of the Day*; Jeanette Winterson, *Sexing the Cherry*
1990	'Poll Tax' in England and Wales; 'Poll Tax' riots in London; John Major takes over as Conservative Leader; President Mandela released from prison in South Africa; human gene experimentation began	A. S. Byatt, *Possession: A Romance*; Hanif Kureishi, *The Buddha of Suburbia*

Date	Historical and Cultural Events	Publication of Novels
1991	'First' Gulf War; end of apartheid in South Africa	Martin Amis, *Time's Arrow*; Pat Barker, *Regeneration*; Angela Carter, *Wise Children*; Caryl Phillips, *Cambridge*; Jane Rogers, *Mr Wroe's Virgins*; Iain Sinclair, *Downriver*
1992	Conservatives re-elected; Major's government forced to devalue the pound	Alasdair Gray, *Poor Things*; Nick Hornby, *Fever Pitch*; Ian McEwan, *Black Dogs*; Adam Thorpe, *Ulverton*; Jeanette Winterson, *Written on the Body*
1993	Stephen Lawrence murder; Bill Clinton elected President of US	Pat Barker, *The Eye in the Door*; Irvine Welsh, *Trainspotting*
1994	Tony Blair becomes Leader of the Labour Party; Church of England ordains first women priests	Jonathan Coe, *What a Carve Up!*; James Kelman, *How Late it Was, How Late*; A. L. Kennedy, *Now That You're Back*; Iain Sinclair, *Radon Daughters*
1995	Britpop at its height	Martin Amis, *The Information*; Pat Barker, *The Ghost Road*; Helen Fielding, *Bridget Jones's Diary*; Nick Hornby, *High Fidelity*; Hanif Kureishi, *The Black Album*; Salman Rushdie, *The Moor's Last Sigh*

Date	Historical and Cultural Events	Publication of Novels
1996	IRA bombs in London Docklands and Manchester	Beryl Bainbridge, *Every Man for Himself*; A. S. Byatt, *Babel Tower*; Seamus Deane, *Reading in the Dark: A Novel*; John King, *The Football Factory*; Graham Swift, *Last Orders*
1997	Tony Blair elected as Labour Prime Minister; death of Princess Diana; the devolution process for Scotland and Wales begins	Bernard MacLaverty, *Grace Notes*
1998	Northern Ireland Peace Agreement	Julian Barnes, *England, England*; Alan Hollinghurst, *The Swimming Pool Library*; Ian McEwan, *Amsterdam*; Courttia Newland, *The Scholar*
1999	NATO military involvement in the War in Yugoslavia	Courttia Newland, *Society Within*
2000	George W. Bush elected President of US	Kazuo Ishiguro, *When We Were Orphans*; Will Self, *How the Dead Live*; Zadie Smith, *White Teeth*; Jeanette Winterson, *The.PowerBook*
2001	Labour re-elected; riots in Oldham, Bradford, Leeds and Burnley; 11 September attacks on the World Trade Center in New York and the Pentagon	Jonathan Coe, *The Rotters' Club*; Niall Griffiths, *Sheepshagger*; Nick Hornby, *How To Be Good*; Ian McEwan, *Atonement*; Iain Sinclair, *Landor's Tower*; Ali Smith, *Hotel World*

Date	Historical and Cultural Events	Publication of Novels
2002	US and British troops invade Afghanistan	Will Self, *Dorian*; Sarah Waters, *Fingersmith*
2003	Invasion of Iraq by US and British troops; Saddam Hussein's regime toppled; troops remain in Iraq	Martin Amis, *Yellow Dog*; Monica Ali, *Brick Lane*; J. G. Ballard, *Millennium People*
2004	Civil Partnership Act	Jonathan Coe, *The Closed Circle*; Alan Hollinghurst, *The Line of Beauty*; Andrea Levy, *Small Island*; David Mitchell, *Cloud Atlas*; Iain Sinclair, *Dining on Stones*
2005	7 July bomb attacks on London's transport system	Julian Barnes, *Arthur and George*; Diana Evans, *26a*; Ian McEwan, *Saturday*; Salman Rushdie, *Shalimar the Clown*; Zadie Smith, *On Beauty*
2006		Monica Ali, *Alentejo Blue*; J. G. Ballard, *Kingdom Come*; Will Self, *The Book of Dave*
2007	Gordon Brown takes over from Tony Blair as Prime Minister	Ian McEwan, *On Chesil Beach*

Introduction

This book is an introduction to British fiction written in the last thirty years or so and is aimed primarily at readers who are studying the subject or have a general interest in the area. Each of the sections takes a particular theme or trend identifiable in the period, and each chapter selects three novels that explore some aspect of that theme. I have worked with the assumption that readers will have already read the novels discussed in each chapter. As with most books of this type, it is not expected to be read cover to cover, and chapters and sections can be read independently. There is inevitably an amount of overlap and because of the range of issues they discuss some of the novels could have been included in different chapters.

Before proceeding, the category of *contemporary* fiction needs to be clarified both with respect to this book and the wider understanding of the term in literary studies. What do we mean when we describe certain literature as contemporary? In one sense the very idea of the contemporary in literature is problematic in that the term in common usage refers to the immediate present, and once a book is published it inevitably becomes part of a literary history. In this book, contemporary refers to the period 1975–2005. The first date is chosen for reasons that will be explained in a moment, the latter date is simply related to the year in which the latest references to fiction appear. The fact that this period of literary history tends

to be called 'contemporary' has to do with the way in which literature is periodized generally in literary studies. Until fairly recently,
literature of the second half of the twentieth century tended to be
called post-war literature, referring to the Second World War as the
starting point for this literary-historical category. There are a
number of problems with this nomenclature, one of which is that
there have now been a number of wars in which Britain has been
involved. Secondly, the period is becoming too large for the post-
war categorization to be useful. It seems to make more sense now to
split this category into an earlier and later period.

Contemporary fiction, then, tends to be defined as the period
from the mid-1970s to the present. This is somewhat of an arbitrary
division, but has precedents in a number of recent books.[1] The main
factor in choosing 1975 is that it is the year that saw the election
of Margaret Thatcher as the leader of the Conservative Party
and marks a key moment of transition in the politics of Britain, and
by extension the social, economic and cultural climate. From the
end of the Second World War, a politics of consensus was established in Britain whereby an unwritten cross-party agreement
accepted the basic systems of the government, such as the welfare
state and a mixed economy of state owned and private industry.
This represented a balance of socialist and capitalist policies that
was based broadly on the economic theories of John Maynard
Keynes.[2] Thatcherite monetarist policies, which aimed to disman-
tle the framework of state owned industry, to break the power of the
Trades Unions and to significantly reform the main bodies of the
Welfare State, effectively ended this consensus and signalled a
period in which British politics became an ideological stand-off
between clearly demarcated Left and Right wings. In hindsight,
then, the mid-to-late seventies heralded a period of political, social
and cultural change that divides some of the fundamental characteristics of contemporary Britain from the end of the Second World
War onwards. The novel is traditionally a form of literature that has
responded symbiotically with social and political movements and
fiction in the contemporary period has continued in that vein.

Another problem concerning the coverage of this book is how to
define the term British, or rather how to decide which writers have
been or want to be labelled with a national tag that in some sense

determines the way in which their work is read. Salman Rushdie, for example, was born in India, moved to Pakistan at a young age then moved to Britain, and at the time of writing lives in New York. It is somewhat problematic, therefore, to call him straightforwardly British. He has, however, most often been categorized in those terms and even though the novel discussed in depth in this book is mainly set in Pakistan it does not seem unreasonable to include him in a book about recent British fiction. The decision of which writers and which of their novels to include was a difficult one, but generally I have tried to offer a representative range by choosing texts that are recognized as being part of an emerging canon of contemporary British fiction. I have not included writers from the Republic of Ireland – contemporary Irish literature warrants a book in its own right – despite many Irish novelists, such as John Banville, having a direct relationship with contexts and themes in British writing.

One of the target readerships for this book is students of litera-ture in higher education studying courses in contemporary fiction, so I have tried to include several writers that tend to be found on uni-versity and college syllabuses. I have, however, tried to cover some less canonical writers such as Courttia Newland and, to a certain extent, Iain Sinclair.[3] The issue of canonicity will be addressed in the conclusion, and the particular difficulties associated with iden-tifying a canon of contemporary British fiction, given that the range of novels being produced in this field is, by definition, continually increasing. In the Student Resources section at the end of the book I have included a list of further recommended fiction that fits well with the main themes of each chapter. This list is not meant to be exhaustive, but offers a good representation of other novels that address similar themes to the ones analyzed.

Before moving on to discuss individual writers and novels, it would be useful to have a sense of some of the important contexts informing them. In what follows I give a brief overview of some of these over the last thirty years (and where relevant longer), and provide some examples of their influence in the fiction of the period. This is divided into five sections: (1) Politics; (2) Class; (3) Gender and Sexuality; (4) Postcolonialism, Multiculturalism and National Identity; and (5) Youth and Subcultures.

POLITICS

If we take a long view of the political history of Britain from the mid seventies to the middle of the first decade of the twenty-first century then it is a story of the move from a politics of ideological opposition to one of broad consensus between the major political parties. In the winter of 1978–79, the Labour government faced a series of industrial relations crises that saw some of the bigger Trade Unions campaigning for higher wage deals. The so-called 'winter of discontent' resulted in power cuts, rubbish piling up on London streets and a serious rift between British labour and those who had traditionally represented their interests in parliament. This stand-off continued to dog Left wing and Labour politics until the mid-1990s.

It was partly due to the turmoil on the Left of British politics that Margaret Thatcher's Conservative government gained power in the 1979 general election. This heralded a series of economic and social policies that radically challenged some of the foundations of the British system as it had been established by the first Labour government in the period after the end of the Second World War. The development of Thatcherism rested fundamentally on policies that shifted responsibility for social welfare from the state to the individual. On the surface Thatcherism produced an ideology of individual success and the accumulation of wealth. Thatcher famously stated in an interview with *Woman's Own* magazine that 'There is no such thing as society', and this off-the-cuff remark came to represent the focus on individualism at the heart of Thatcherism.[4] State services such as the National Health Service became the targets for so-called rationalization, which in practice meant the loss of many jobs and the imposition of management teams charged with the job of cutting down the national health bill as much as possible. As part of this outlook Britain was stripped of its nationalized assets in a series of sell-offs of companies such as British Rail, British Telecom, British Gas and British Petroleum, which saw similar 'rationalizations', and the accumulation of large profits by some of those who bought up the under-priced shares.

Culturally, these policies revealed new fears of the two nations idea of Britain. On the one hand there was a rise in the unembarrassed spectacle of conspicuous consumption in certain quarters that saw the rise of the so-called Yuppies (young and upwardly mobile). Equally it saw a high rise in unemployment due especially to the shift from older primary industries such as coal, steel and shipbuilding. This led to the development of an impoverished working class, and consequently to the development of resistance movements amongst many sections of the population that were excluded from, or refused to buy into, the new culture of individualism. The lack of a viable political opposition to the Tories, meant that popular political movements such as the Miner's Strike and the Campaign against the Poll Tax took to the streets, often ending in scenes of violence where a police force began to take on the look of a government-led militia. In 1981 in particular, there were a series of spontaneous riots in some of the underprivileged inner city areas of Britain who took the brunt of the economic policies pursued by Thatcherism, and often fuelled by claims of racist intimidation by the police. Such riots were seen in St. Paul's in Bristol in 1980, Chapeltown in Leeds, Handsworth in Birmingham, Toxteth in Liverpool, Moss Side in Manchester and Brixton in London. Part of the Thatcherite agenda was to break the power of the Unions, who some felt were holding British companies to ransom with the threat of industrial action for increasing pay rises. This policy culminated in the bitter Miner's Strike of 1984–85, in which the National Union of Mineworkers led by Arthur Scargill attempted to challenge the attempt by the Conservatives to close several collieries. The striking miners were eventually defeated by the overwhelming forces of the state resulting in the decimation of many mining communities, especially in Wales and the north of England.

The ideological entrenchment of the 1980s gradually gave way to a form of consensus politics in the mid to late 1990s, mainly due to the reform of the Labour Party led initially by Neil Kinnock and continued by John Smith and Tony Blair which resulted in 'New Labour', a reworking of the party that claimed to hold on to traditional Labour values, whilst at the same time accepting many of the policies that the Tories had introduced in the 1980s. The resulting victory of Labour in the 1997 election under Blair meant that British politics had, as perhaps always, been fought out on the issue of which party most successfully presented itself as representing the centre ground. Culturally, however, there was a marked shift in the late 1990s where conspicuous consumption came to be viewed as somewhat passé and a new politics of conscience, often centred on environmental issues, began to replace the left-wing politics of the previous generation (not to say that those groups disappeared or that the economic problems that they were reacting against went away).

These political issues have been addressed in differing ways by contemporary novelists. Iain Sinclair, for example, has continued to produce fiction that is critical of the Thatcher government's policies. Jonathan Coe has been critical of both Thatcherism in his *What a Carve Up!* (1994) and New Labour in his 2004 novel *The Closed Circle* which includes a cameo of Tony Blair. Alan Hollinghurst's *The Line of Beauty* (2004) includes the other major political figure of the period; in one scene Margaret Thatcher appears at a party and dances with the novel's main character. Hollinghurst is more ambivalent in his treatment of Thatcher, nevertheless the narrative details the personal consequences of the kind of excess and lack of social responsibility her policies caused, a similar approach to that taken by Will Self in his novel *Dorian* (2002), set mainly in the 1980s.

One of the successes of the New Labour government was to begin the peace process in Northern Ireland, a situation that had dogged British politics since the end of the 1960s. The history of Northern Ireland over the past four decades is complex and has seen the most conspicuous acts of violence from both sides of the dispute on mainland Britain since, arguably, the Civil War. Certain notable events stand out and have been addressed in some of the fiction of the period. On Sunday, 30 January 1972, the British Army opened fire on a mostly peaceful demonstration of Irish Catholics in the Bogside area of Derry, resulting in the death of fourteen people. Bloody Sunday, as it came to be known, marked a transition in the relations between Irish Republicans and the British government and saw an escalation of violence by paramilitaries on both sides of the sectarian divide. The extension of the IRA's campaign to Britain in the mid-1970s resulted in several high profile bombings including the Birmingham pub bombings in 1974. In Jonathan Coe's novel *The Rotters' Club* (2001) two of the characters are present in 'The Tavern in the Town', one of the pubs targeted, when the bomb goes off, and Coe evokes the sense of outrage the event caused in Birmingham at the time, as well as the backlash against innocent Irish people then settled in England. The 'Troubles', as they came to be known, were effectively halted by the Irish Peace Process, ushered in by Blair's newly elected Labour government after 1997. This was part of a broader policy of devolution that saw the creation of the Welsh assembly and the Scottish parliament in the late 1990s, which although only having certain powers have formed a focus for debate on the issue of national identity amongst the separate countries of the United Kingdom. In Northern Ireland, the main literary response to the Troubles has been in drama, although the novels of Seamus Deane and Bernard MacLaverty are notable exceptions.[5] There has been a renaissance in Scottish writing in the last forty years or so with such notable figures as Janice Galloway, Alasdair Gray, James Kelman, A. L. Kennedy, Ali Smith, Alan Warner and Irvine Welsh.

There have been a number of key international events that have impacted on Britain over the last thirty years and have been used as source material for British writers. At the beginning of the period the ongoing Cold War between communism and capitalism led to the amassing of armaments by the Soviet Union and the US-led Western Powers. The anxieties caused cast a significant shadow over British culture, often articulated as fear for an impending, nuclear Third World War. This has formed a significant topic in fiction by writers such as Martin Amis, J. G. Ballard and Graham Swift, and most notably in the spy novel series produced by John le Carré.[6] The fall of the Berlin Wall in 1989, followed by the series of revolutions across Eastern Europe, effectively ended the Cold War. Again a number of novels have used these events as a backdrop. Ian McEwan's novel *Black Dogs* (1992), for example, takes the fall of the Berlin Wall as the starting point for an exploration of violence that goes back to the Second World War, and Zadie Smith's *White Teeth* (2000), a novel that maps the impact of certain key events during the period, has a passage that describes the mixed reaction by a number of characters to the events in Berlin in 1989.[7]

Perhaps the most significant event of the last thirty years or so, in terms of its consequences, was the attack on the World Trade Center and the Pentagon on 11 September 2001 and such a historic event was bound to find itself addressed in fiction written after that event. In Monica Ali's *Brick Lane* (2003), the event is observed on television by the main character, and the novel describes the impact it has on the multiethnic area in which the main character lives in East London.[8] Ian McEwan in his 2005 novel *Saturday*, uses the context of 9/11 in the observation early in the novel of an airliner on fire flying over London: 'Everyone agrees, airliners look different in the sky these days, predatory or doomed'.[9] The context of terrorism and the political and ethical questions it raises is also a key feature in J. G. Ballard's novels *Millennium People* (2003) and *Kingdom Come* (2006).[10] The consequences of 9/11 are still being played out in Afghanistan, Iraq and in acts of terrorism in Britain and other parts of the world, and it is likely that these will continue to produce subject matter for much fiction produced in Britain in the coming years.

CLASS

The ideological divisions of the 1980s and early 1990s represented by the political differences of the Labour and Conservative Parties were primarily based on issues of social class. The Labour Party, since its origins at the turn of the twentieth century, had traditionally strove to represent the interests of the British working class; whilst the Conservatives had developed in their long history from being the party of the landed aristocracy to being increasingly appealing to the middle classes (especially since the decline of the Liberal Party from the end of the First World War onwards). That is not to say, however, that class has always determined voting patterns. Not all eligible working-class voters necessarily support the Labour Party; the electoral successes of the Tories in 1979, 1983, 1987 and 1992 relied, in part, on a significant amount of support amongst the working class. Similarly, a large section of the middle classes, especially intellectuals, creative artists and professionals have tended to support left-wing political causes throughout the period.

    This leads to one of the problems with the terms of definition in which class has traditionally been understood. The division of society into the three broad economic classes of working, middle and upper relies heavily on social and economic theories developed by those on the Left, and in particular those influenced by Marxist theory (although Marx tended to identify just two classes: the ruling class and the proletariat, the former being an amalgamation of middle and upper classes). In Britain, these clear class divisions owed much to the legacy of the social problems of the 1930s imported into the very different world that began to emerge after the Second World War. The categorization of such a complex beast as the nature of social division is fraught with problems. There have been more recent attempts to offer classification of social groups in terms of economic wealth such as Thompson and Hickey's five level class model, however, this still retains an element of simplifying the situation.[11] Nevertheless, it is still useful, in certain circumstances, to identify social groups in terms of class, if only because it makes it easier to develop a sense of class consciousness from which political resistance movements may be formed.

One other problem with class as a system by which to categorize people, and one that is particularly relevant to the role of literature and fiction in society, is the shift that occurred in some quarters in the 1950s about the way class was understood. This shift, broadly speaking, involved a rethinking of class in cultural rather than economic terms. This process was led in Britain by cultural critics and writers such as Raymond Williams, Richard Hoggart, E. P. Thompson and Stuart Hall, and resulted in the emergence of what came to be known in universities as Cultural Studies. One of the premises behind this movement was that class could be identified as a cultural phenomenon, rather than purely along economic lines. Pioneering work by Hoggart on the cultural pursuits of the working class served to redefine the term itself, and similarly by Williams on literature and Thompson with respect to political and cultural movements historically.[12]

This shift has problematized the way in which class has been understood in the last forty years or so. For example, identifiable cultural pursuits and practices of the working class in the 1950s and into the 1960s such as popular music, film and television, football and 'pub' culture can hardly be claimed now as the pursuits of this section of society alone. The immense cultural shifts that have taken place since the fifties mean that the old categories of class are far more difficult to identify. This is not to say that the differences in wealth between the richest and poorest elements do not continue to have a significant effect on the way British society is organized, and the way people are represented in cultural terms. The recent media invention of the so-called 'chavs' is based on older class prejudices recycled in a new form that allows it to circulate in society without the charge of classism that it clearly relies on.

One recurring theme throughout the period from the 1950s onwards is the claim that Britain is becoming (or has become) a classless society. A series of Prime Ministers from both the major parties have made this claim from Macmillan in the 1950s, Thatcher in the 1980s through to Major and Blair in the 1990s and into the new century. This tends to be a political move that in some way bolsters the justification of a political agenda, rather than being based on actual statistics about the wealth distribution of people in Britain. There are, however, contexts in which the claim holds weight especially in the policies championed by the Thatcher government (and continued by New Labour) that contributed to this blurring of the lines between the classes, such as the move to increase home ownership and the rise in the number of people gaining a university education.

This continued debate and confusion over the subject of class has provided a rich source for much of the fiction produced during period covered by this book. The field is still dominated by what could be broadly called middle-class writers such as Monica Ali, Kingsley Amis, Martin Amis, J. G. Ballard, Julian Barnes, A. S. Byatt, Jonathan Coe, Margaret Drabble, Alan Hollinghurst, Nick Hornby, Kazuo Ishiguro, Ian McEwan, Jane Rogers, Salman Rushdie and Sarah Waters. There has been, however, a rise in the number of novels that are set in working-class locations or engage with working-class issues. The literary context for this again goes back to the 1950s (and earlier). That decade saw an increase in the number of novels that were concerned to record and represent working-class experience in fiction, a medium that had traditionally been the enclave of the middle classes. Writers such as Alan Sillitoe, Keith Waterhouse, John Braine and David Storey produced novels that were situated in working-class life and as writers could claim to be a part of that social group. The 'working-class' novel as it came to be known, has become a staple of

British fiction from the 1950s onwards, although, significantly the tag itself has become unfashionable. Writers such as Monica Ali, Pat Barker, Julie Burchill, Angela Carter, Alasdair Gray, James Kelman, John King, Courttia Newland, Zadie Smith, Alan Warner, Sarah Waters, Irvine Welsh and Jeanette Winterson have all produced novels that could be described as working-class in terms of the primary cultural setting. As can be seen from this list, however, what might in the 1950s have been described as working-class fiction tends to get identified more with other social categories such as gender, sexuality, ethnicity, national identity and youth.

GENDER AND SEXUALITY

In 1949, Simone de Beauvoir published *The Second Sex*, a text which can be identified as a founding moment of second wave feminism. One of the central theses of the book was summed up by the line, 'I am not born a woman I become one'.[13] This position recognized that although individuals are born as male or female, the development of masculinity and femininity is not determined at birth, but is learned through the process of socialization. Femininity and masculinity, therefore, are a series of artificial constructs or codes of behaviour that are maintained and reproduced by the dominant ideas and practices in society. It was also shown that the prevailing constructs of gender change historically. Identifying these codes as constructed and historically contingent, and not natural or essentialist, made it possible to argue for a resistance to the way in which society had conventionally demarcated roles for men and women. This fundamental proposition underpinning many of the ideas in new wave feminism allowed for the political campaigns during the 1960s and especially the seventies that coalesced under the banner of the Women's Liberation Movement. Feminism, however, was far from a monolithic movement and several, often competing, strands emerged in the later 1960s and 70s. In America, Betty Friedan, one of those involved in the development of the new wave, advocated a form of feminism based on equal rights for women and a sharing of the roles that society currently divided between the genders. In her important 1963 book,

The Feminine Mystique, she challenged the way in which women had been designated certain roles which kept them subjugated, and advocated the development of a society where women could enter into public and professional life on an equal footing with men. This form of feminism, however, tended to focus on women in middle-class and upper-class environments and developed into ideas that came to be referred to as liberal feminism. In Britain, feminist writers and activists were often closely associated with socialist political movements and tended to see women's rights as part of a wider social agenda that included class. Sheila Rowbotham, for example, tried to argue in an influential pamphlet published in 1968 'Women's Liberation and the New Politics', that women's liberation was an economic as well as cultural issue.[14] In the British context there was also a strong literary element to the Women's Liberation Movement including notable figures such as playwright Michelene Wandor and literary critic Germaine Greer.[15]

With respect to literary criticism, the feminist movement developed in the 1970s in two main directions: the first was led by critics such as Kate Millett and tended to identify sexist and often misogynist positions in male-authored literature of the past; the second by writers such as Sandra Gilbert, Susan Gubar, Ellen Moers and Elaine Showalter, who tried to establish an alternative canon of women's literature, a body of writing sometimes referred to as gynocriticism.[16] The influence of feminism on British fiction has been profound, to the extent that today, contemporary women novelists are just as likely to gain major literary awards and to be included on contemporary fiction syllabuses as men. This is certainly not the case if you look at any other period of British literature (with the possible exception of the Victorian novel). Many British women writers emerged (or were already established) in the late 1960s and 1970s who were keen to engage with feminist issues such as A. S. Byatt, Angela Carter, Margaret Drabble, Janice Galloway, Doris Lessing, Emma Tennant and Fay Weldon.

Alongside the Anglo-American tradition in feminist literary criticism, certain British novelists have been more influenced by the French feminists: Hélène Cixous, Luce Irigaray and Julia Kristeva. This body of work tended to engage more with poststructuralist theories of language. Hélène Cixous, for example, argues that the whole basis of Western language and philosophy has been based on 'dual, hierarchical systems' such as Activity/Passivity, Sun/Moon, Culture/Nature and Man/Woman that place the female in either a position of inferiority or invisibility: 'Either woman is passive or she does not exist'.[17] Her own writing seeks to rectify this imbalance by creating a new type of writing that combines literary creation with criticism in an attempt to represent female experience through the use of language and syntax. This experiment with writing and language, labelled *écriture féminine*, identifies gender difference in the very understanding of, and relationship between, words. This was not entirely new in a British context, as Virginia Woolf had speculated some years earlier on the way in which sentence structure could be gendered. In 'To Cambridge Women' she identifies what she calls a 'man's sentence' as 'unsuited for a woman's use', and implicitly advocates that women should try to develop a style of writing that distanced itself from the male tradition.[18] Contemporary British writers such as Jeanette Winterson and Janice Galloway have experimented with language in a way that evokes this kind of gendered writing.

One of the problems associated with this line of thinking, however, is that the kinds of sentence that are designated as female tend to be loose, rambling, resist making a firm point and value expression over logic. This, of course, could be construed as reproducing the very characteristics that had traditionally been associated with femininity in a patriarchal discourse. A different approach was the taking over by women of those characteristics normally associated with masculinity and a figure that we have already encountered looms large here. Margaret Thatcher has in many ways become an unlikely icon of this kind of feminism, unlikely because she openly disagreed with the main arguments put forward by feminists in the 1970s and 80s. She was, however, a visible example of the way in which women could achieve top positions of power in the 1980s. To do so, however, often involved her taking on what many regarded as masculine characteristics. This fact in itself, though, suggested that gender signification was independent of biological sex. To cite Thatcher as a feminist icon is misleading in many ways, as the make-up of parliament in the 1980s was overwhelmingly male, as was the demographic of the leading figures in British industry and public services. Nevertheless, a certain amount of the success of the arguments put forward by feminism in the 1980s and into the 1990s can be attributed to the fact that Britain had, for the first time in its history, a female Prime Minister.

The success that feminism achieved in the 1970s and 1980s in changing cultural perceptions of the accepted roles for men and women in society began to be more noticeable in the 1990s, to the extent that some cultural commentators and theorists began to talk of a *post*-feminist situation. The concept of post-feminism can be understood in two senses. Firstly, it can refer to the fact that most of the main aims of second wave feminism from the 1960s to the 1980s had been achieved and consequently were no longer relevant in the 1990s. Secondly, and in contradiction to this argument, post-feminism could refer to the sense that although successes had been achieved in equal rights, the most powerful and highly paid positions in Britain were still predominately occupied by men. This form of post-feminism recognized that the original objectives of the Women's Liberation Movement were still legitimate areas for political campaigning despite the successes that had already been achieved. Associated with the idea of post-feminism, the 1990s saw the rise of significant popular cultural movements and trends. One of these was the so-called 'ladette' culture, a form of social behaviour that advocated the pleasures and codes of practice that had previously been the enclave of young men, such as heavy drinking, clubbing, and active pursuance of sexual partners. This popular movement was led by phenomena such as the success of the Spice Girls, who presented themselves as a kind of post-feminist gang, who used sexuality on their own terms. The main spokesperson of the band, Geri Halliwell, a fan of Mrs Thatcher, advocated a culture where young women had the confidence to tell you what they 'really, really want', and were able to get it.

The successes of feminism also affected the way in which masculinity was re-assessed during the period. One of the original tenets of feminism was that men were as conditioned by prevailing gender codes as women; as Betty Friedan put it: 'Men weren't really the enemy – they were fellow victims suffering from an outmoded masculine mystique'.[19] In the 1980s the idea of the New Man began to circulate, which referred to a male (usually heterosexual) that was in touch with his feminine side and who broadly agreed with the idea of women's equality. Many male writers began to explore the new gender frameworks that were emerging due to the successes and visibility of feminism and how this had developed new definitions of masculinity. Writers such as Martin Amis and Julian Barnes in the 1980s and Nick Hornby, Tony Parsons and John King were interested in what constituted masculinity in the 1990s, and how that had changed since their fathers' generation.

The emergence of new genres of popular fiction given the provocative titles of chick lit and lad lit reflected this concern with the new parameters of femininity and masculinity and how individuals growing up in contemporary society are forced to negotiate these new constructs. Chick lit novelists like Helen Fielding and Jane Green produce coming of age narratives in which female protagonists attempt to find their place in the world, usually in heterosexual partnerships with men who appear to effortlessly combine the benefits of both older and newer forms of masculinity: new men, who are not too new.[20]

The years from the end of the 1960s also saw a sea change in attitudes towards homosexuality, which has also found its place in British fiction in the last quarter of the twentieth century. In many ways the Gay Liberation Movement that emerged in North America and Western Europe in the late 1960s ran parallel with the Women's Liberation Movement, and their interests and agendas often overlapped.

In a British context, the Sexual Offences Act of 1967 decriminalized homosexuality for consenting adults over the age of 21 in England and Wales.[21] However, continued inequalities in the law, everyday prejudice and acts of violence against homosexuals necessitated the formation and continuation of Gay and Lesbian rights movements in Britain in the 1970s and 1980s. One of the major international events that had influence in Britain was the riot at the Stonewall Inn, a lesbian and gay club in New York City, in May 1969. The riot was a response to the unjustified but repeated raids on the bar made by police during this period. These events served to bring to popular attention the injustices carried out against the gay and lesbian community generally, and served to strengthen resistance against this kind of prejudice in both Britain and the States. Various pieces of legislation have been passed from the sixties onwards that have, due in no small part to the efforts of sexual politics campaigners, redressed some of the inequalities in Britain with respect to homosexuality, most recently in Britain in the Civil Partnership Act of 2004, which grants same-sex couples the same rights and responsibilities as a civil marriage.

In terms of the theoretical approaches to sexuality, 'queer theory' developed amongst intellectuals in the late 1980s and 1990s and aimed to disrupt the way in which sexual and gender identities are constructed in society. Like French feminism, it was highly inflected with ideas from poststructuralist theory, and in particular the seminal work produced by Michel Foucault, *The History of Sexuality* (1976).[22] Part of the aim was to champion aspects of gay culture as a response to the sense in which it was still regarded as a form of tolerated deviance in many parts of mainstream culture. 'Queer' had previously been used as a term of abuse against homosexual men and women, but this body of theory reclaimed the word and gave it positive connotations. Theorists such as Teresa de Lauretis, Judith Butler and Eve Kosofsky Sedgwick produced important work in this field in the 1990s, the latter two in the area of literary studies.

Recent British fiction has been a rich source for the exploration of gay, lesbian and bisexual relationships, and as a cultural space in which to raise political and social issues around sexuality. The increasing acceptance of gay and lesbian fiction is in part a reflection of the successes of the Gay Rights Movement of the 1970s and 80s and there has been mainstream success for what a couple of decades ago would have been marginalized as gay fiction, for example in the work of Julie Burchill, Hanif Kureishi, Alan Hollinghurst, Adam Mars-Jones, Jeanette Winterson and Sarah Waters.

POSTCOLONIALISM, MULTICULTURALISM AND NATIONAL IDENTITY

On the 15 August 1947 the new sovereign nation of India was born as it gained independence from Britain. India was always the jewel in the crown of the British Empire and its loss represented a key moment in British history. Perhaps more importantly it signalled the beginning of the gradual dismantling of most of the Empire over the next fifty years or so. The legacy of colonialism has been one of the most far reaching influences both on the former colonies and also on Britain itself, both in terms of its position in the new world order after 1945, and also in the changing nature of its home population. The term postcolonialism has been coined to define this new state of affairs and a series of theories and discourses has arisen in many fields to explain and assess the impact of this enormous shift in the political organization of the world. Britain has continued to maintain links with many of the former colonies through the establishment of the Commonwealth, which is an association of many of the countries that used to be ruled by Britain. This continued association has also affected the pattern of migration and has been a significant feature of Britain's population demographic in the years following the Second World War.

From the 1950s onwards Britain has developed into a multicultural nation as groups of people moved from parts of the Caribbean, South East Asia and Africa (as well as other parts of the world) and settled in Britain, often in communities that gathered together in Britain's urban areas. This series of diasporas has changed the face of British society and culture in profound ways, but has not always been a smooth process. Many of the areas that the new arrivals settled in were often deprived, where the older populations were themselves suffering social and economic adversity. There has always been resistance in certain quarters to the development of communities from other parts of the world, often exacerbated by successive governments playing the so-called 'race card' – rhetoric designed to create unnecessary fear amongst the established British population with images of being invaded and swamped by immigrants. Enoch Powell, for example, in 1968 delivered his now infamous 'rivers of blood' speech warning against the dangers of immigration.[23] In reality, immigration has been gradual over the period, and in fact, people from minority ethnic groups have never made up more than 8 per cent of the British population.

Political attitudes to immigration have vacillated over the period, and tend to shift from the idea that wholesale assimilation into a sense of Britishness is the preferred outcome, to a model of multiculturalism, whereby immigrant communities retain a sense of their original cultures whilst adapting to the cultural make-up of Britain. In practice the immigrant experience tends to involve a mixture of assimilation and multiculturalism, which is often dependent on other issues such as class, gender and religion. Alongside this process there have been periods that have seen the increase in tensions between ethnic communities, most often seen in inner city areas, for example, in the riots that occurred in Brixton, Chapeltown, Toxteth, and Moss Side in the early 1980s, and in Bradford, Burnley and Oldham in the early 2000s. To blame these outbreaks of popular violence on issues of race alone is to overlook the range of complex factors related to class, social deprivation and community relations with figures of authority such as the police. Nevertheless, the grievances of groups that coalesce around ethnic identities and the presence of right-wing political parties such as the National Front in the 1970s and 1980s and the British National Party over the last two decades have exacerbated underlying tensions within such communities. As discussed in Chapters 2 and 5 (respectively), both Monica Ali's *Brick Lane* and Hanif Kureishi's *The Buddha of Suburbia* (1990) detail the kinds of racially motivated violence meted out to innocent members of ethnic minorities.

British literature has been a cultural space in which the experiences of immigrants and broader political issues associated with these experiences have been articulated. There has, necessarily, been a certain amount of negotiation of the tradition of the English novel involved here. One of the dilemmas of postcolonial fiction is the attitude the colonized writing takes towards the literary paradigms and values of the colonizing nation. As Edward Said has shown, literature is far from a neutral form of discourse in the processes that were involved in the building and maintaining of Empire. Said's model of orientalism shows how a range of discourses including literature served to define a 'positional superiority' of the West in relation to the peoples and cultures of the orient, and this theory can be applied to a range of colonized nations extending across the Empire.[24] One of the aims of postcolonial literature has been to readdress the way in which ethnic minorities have been constructed in British literature. In the context of this book, this has found particular resonance in the development of what has come to be called 'Black British' fiction. It needs to be stressed at the outset that there are obvious problems with lumping together a range of very different writers such as Monica Ali, Hanif

Kureishi, Courttia Newland, Caryl Phillips, Salman Rushdie and Zadie Smith under such a heading. Nevertheless the novels they have produced have addressed, in different ways, issues associated with the multiethnic nature of contemporary Britain. One of the ways in which this has been achieved is through attention to language. For the postcolonial writer, as Bill Ashcroft, Gareth Griffiths and Helen Tiffin have noted, English is in one sense the language of the oppressor and many of the writers mentioned above have been forced to negotiate this fact. In Salman Rushdie's *Shame* (1983) for example, the narrator speaks of 'this Angrezi [English] in which I am forced to write' whilst Zadie Smith has one of her characters note that 'only the immigrants speak Queen's English these days'.[25]

One of the other key factors affecting national identity is the devolution of power within Britain, especially in the years since 1997. Scotland has its own parliament, Wales and Northern Ireland have their own assemblies all with a certain amount of legislative power. The new sense of national identity that these political changes have wrought, did not, of course, begin in 1997, and in some ways devolution was in response to the strong sense of separateness from England felt by many in those nations. The issues raised by colonial and postcolonial identity could, therefore, be extended to include the nations within the United Kingdom. To a certain extent, writers from Scotland, Wales and Northern Ireland have found themselves to be in a similar 'postcolonial' position in that distinct national literatures have sought to distinguish themselves from both English and the imposition of a homogenous 'British' culture. In a Scottish context, writers such as James Kelman and Irvine Welsh have foregrounded the use of types of Scottish vernacular to distance the narrative from any collective sense of a British identity. Take, for example, the following passage from James Kelman's *How Late it Was, How Late* (1994):

There wasnay much he could do, there wasnay really much he could do at all. No the now anyway. Nayn of it was down to him.[26]

Here, the disruption of conventional syntax and the use of words to convey dialect corresponds with one of the aims of postcolonial writing as identified by Ashcroft, Griffiths and Tiffin: 'The crucial function of language as a medium of power demands that postcolonial writing define itself by seizing the language of the centre and re-placing it in a discourse fully adapted to the colonized space'.[27] In Kelman's case, demotic language is used to distance the text, linguistically and culturally from English, whilst re-placing it in a Scottish context. Writing, in this way becomes political in its very syntax and word choice. This issue has also been dealt with in the context of some recent Welsh and Northern Irish writing. Niall Griffiths, for example, addresses the idea of contemporary Welshness in his novel *Sheepshagger* (2001), the title of which aggressively reverses one of the ways in which the English (in particular) have prejudiced and mocked the Welsh. Much contemporary fiction, then, has been keen to engage with the shifting positions of national identity over the last thirty years and I will return to this issue in Chapter 5, especially in the discussion of the representation of Englishness in Julian Barnes's novel *England, England* (1998).

The complexity of the internal make-up of the United Kingdom in addition to its engagement with a series of other national identities has made the issue of ethnicity extremely complex in contemporary Britain. As Richard Bradford notes, 'It would seem that within these islands the permutations upon identity, separateness, conflict and division are almost without limit'.[28] Certain ideas arising from postcolonial theory, however, have been useful in attempting to analyse these differences. One of these is Homi Bhabha's concept of hybridity and what he calls the third space.[29] Hybridity refers to the way in which two or more cultures combine in colonial and postcolonial relationships, but in doing so, refuse to privilege any one of the constituent parts. Thereby, the power relationship assumed in typical hierarchies between the colonized and the colonizer are avoided. This can be taken at the level of racial identity, whereby children of 'mixed-race' marriages could be described as hybrid, but more importantly in a cultural sense, whereby the idea of a 'third space' identifies a location of culture that rejects the binary oppositional framework in which race and the idea of ethnic origin has often operated. The third space is a new hybrid, but also contains the sense of the dual heritages that have contributed to its formation.

A second theory that has proved useful in this context is Stuart Hall's concept of new ethnicities. Hall identifies two trends in the historical development of racial politics, the first being when 'black' became an important signifier of cultural identity and allowed for a politics of resistance against racism in Britain. This involved challenging the use of black stereotypes in mainstream literature and culture, a process that gained ground from the 1950s onwards. It also championed the development of what became recognized as 'Black British' art and literature. The second context developed from the first and recognized that, in practice, there is a range of marginalized positions, a fact that complicates the idea of a unified 'black' subject in opposition to a 'white' subject. In 'New Ethnicities', Hall writes of the need to recognize that, ' "black" is essentially a politically and culturally *constructed* category', and that 'the immense diversity and differentiation of the historical and cultural experience of black subjects [. . .] inevitably entails a weakening or fading of the notion [of] "race" '.[30] This leads to what Hall identifies as a range of new ethnicities that not only relate to issues of race but also to class, gender, sexuality and youth. In addition, the 'black' subject is itself subject to a variety of different positions and particular histories. As Hall notes, it is no longer accurate or useful to talk of monolithic categories of race such as black and white when in practice much of Britain's ethnicity is made up of a series of identities that negotiate each of these categories.

A number of writers who have immigrated to Britain from former colonies or are the children of such immigrants have been producing novels since the 1950s that have articulated this experience, and have to differing degrees addressed some of the issues raised by Bhabha and Hall. The list is a long one, but includes such writers as Sam Selvon, Edward Brathwaite, V. S. Naipaul, Wilson Harris, Salman Rushdie, Hanif Kureishi, Courttia Newland, Zadie Smith and Monica Ali.

YOUTH AND SUBCULTURES

One significant theme in contemporary British fiction is the representation of youth and the experience of growing up in Britain. The coming of age narrative, or the *Bildungsroman* has been a staple of the British novel since the birth of the form in the early eighteenth century, and it is a form that aids the combination of a narrative plot line with the description of the social and cultural environments through which the main protagonist moves. Formally, either through the use of first-person or third-person narratives, the coming of age story allows for the workings of society to be described as if from a fresh perspective, and through the technique of defamiliarization, a cultural critique can be produced of some of the practices of contemporary society encountered for the first time by the protagonist.

In this book there are several novels that engage with the *Bildungsroman* form, although in some cases a parody of the nineteenth century model is often produced, for example, in the fantastic adventures experienced by the central character in Angela Carter's *The Passion of New Eve* (1977). Other examples discussed in this book include, Monica Ali's *Brick Lane*, Jeanette Winterson's *Oranges Are Not the Only Fruit* (1985), Nick Hornby's *Fever Pitch* (1992), Ian McEwan's *Atonement* (2001), A. S. Byatt's *Possession: A Romance* (1990), Hanif Kureishi's *The Buddha of Suburbia* and Julian Barnes's *England, England*, whilst Zadie Smith's *White Teeth* and Alasdair Gray's *Poor Things* (1992) also include coming of age narratives within their broader framework.

Within the genre of the *Bildungsroman* a more specific trend in fiction has developed since the 1950s that could be described as subcultural fiction. These are novels that set out to explore the inner world of certain youth cultures that have their own codes of practice, fashion and artistic styles and are usually identified by a particular style of music. This kind of fiction can perhaps be traced to one novel produced in the late 1950s, Colin MacInnes's *Absolute Beginners* (1959), which set out to describe, through the eyes of its teenage hero, the emerging youth cultures of the later half of the 1950s that included Teds, jazz fans (both traditional and modern) and the emergence of a group of sharp-dressed teenagers that later came to be known as Mods.[31] Within this framework, MacInnes explored postwar British society in terms of the legacies of Empire and the emergence of new ethnic subcultures in London, culminating in a fictional account of the actual 'race' riots in Notting Hill in 1958.

MacInnes's book set the model for a development of similar sub-cultural fictions throughout the 1960s and 1970s including Nik Cohn's rock'n'roll fiction and Richard Allen and Stewart Home's series of Skinhead novels.[32] In the 1980s and 1990s this trend continued through a range of different youth subcultures, especially in the 'club culture' narratives of the late eighties. These texts explored the world of alternative subcultural spaces such as illegal raves and gatherings and the use of drugs and other forms of criminality. The writers in this genre that emerged during this period include Irvine Welsh and Nicholas Blincoe.[33] Perhaps the most well known of these novels is Welsh's *Trainspotting* (1993) which dealt with the heroin-charged drug scene in Edinburgh in the late 1980s and early 1990s. The main characters in the novel, Renton, Sick-Boy and Begbie, represent a kind of subcultural manifestation of Thatcher's Britain in that they are imbued with a selfish self-preservation that is an inverted reflection of the Yuppie culture of the period. This is made evident in Renton's decision to betray the rest of the group at the end of the novel. Within this narrative, Welsh is able to produce a critique of the society that has influenced contemporary working-class life in Scotland especially for youth from deprived areas of Edinburgh.

The representation of youth subcultures in fiction has fed off work done in cultural studies. The British New Left in the 1950s became increasingly interested in the sociological and political factors behind the rise of youth culture, although tended on the whole to produce negative images of youth as followers of an Americanized 'shiny barbarism', a term coined by Richard Hoggart, one of the members associated with this group.[34] Stuart Hall and Paddy Whannel's book *The Popular Arts* (1964) took a more open view of the place of popular cultural forms in the early 1960s including television, fashion and pop music styles.[35] Much work done by the Contemporary Centre for Cultural Studies at Birmingham University centred on youth culture, with sociologists and cultural commentators such as Phil Cohen, Paul Willis, Angela McRobbie, Jenny Garber and Gary Clarke.[36] Dick Hebdige's seminal 1979 book *Subcultures: The Meaning of Style* introduced an analysis based on semiotics to the study of subcultural fashions, and in particular the *bricolage* style adopted by the then new phenomenon of punk.[37]

Subcultural influences can be seen to affect several characters in the novels discussed in this book, including the younger characters in Zadie Smith's *White Teeth* and Monica Ali's *Brick Lane*, and perhaps most significantly in Hanif Kureishi's *The Buddha of Suburbia*, which in part, takes the transition of subcultural styles from hippies to glam rock to punk as one of the narrative threads in the novel.

A NOTE ON THEORY

One of the key contexts in which contemporary fiction is studied at university is in relation to what has been seen as the explosion of literary and cultural theory from the 1950s onwards. For most of the early twentieth century and after the war, literary criticism was a mixture of author-centred criticism, which tended to determine the meaning of texts through reference to the author's life, and literary-historical criticism, which tried to place an author's text with respect to the literary period in which they were working. In the mid-twentieth century, this was accompanied by a series of approaches that were gathered under the heading of formalism. This included Russian formalism, which generally adopted a linguistic approach to literature and was interested in what gave literature its literariness. This loose grouping includes such figures as Mikhail Bakhtin and Viktor Skhlovsky and introduced concepts such as heteroglossia and defamiliarization.[38] In an American context, critics like Cleanth Brooks, William Wimsatt and Monroe Beardsley developed a different kind of formalism. Brooks was interested in the way poetry worked by setting up linguistic oppositions and paradoxes, whilst Wimsatt and Beardsley rejected the author's intention as a useful source for trying to determine the meaning of a text, and encouraged an approach that concentrated on the organization of the words on the page and how meaning was produced independently from the author.[39] This New Criticism distinguished itself from author-centred approaches as did two influential British literary theorists in the mid decades of the twentieth century, I. A. Richards and F. R. Leavis. Richards encouraged a form of analysis that had allegiances with the American New Critics and advocated 'practical criticism' which involved the 'close reading' of texts.[40] The New Critics and Richards tended to focus on poetry, as their attention to detail could be sustained more easily with relatively shorter texts. F. R. Leavis, on the other hand, wrote significantly on the English novel. Leavis imbued literary criticism not only with an evaluative critical faculty, but also with a sense of morality. He made bold claims for the novel arguing that in the greatest examples of the form it produced a philosophical and ethical investigation into the human condition, and that criticism of such novels necessitated a corresponding seriousness from the critic.[41]

Each of these approaches has relevance in the practical analysis of contemporary British fiction, however, from the 1960s onwards, this fairly straightforward range of critical positions exploded in a number of different directions too numerous to cover in detail here. For the study of contemporary British fiction it is a great advantage to know a little of the following 'schools' or loose groupings of literary and critical theory: Marxism, feminism (and post-feminism), structuralism, poststructuralism (including deconstruction), reader–response criticism, postmodernism, queer theory, postcolonialism, ecology and theories developed from cultural studies. The following chapters will introduce some of the main points related to these theories as and when they are relevant to the particular novels under discussion. Many of the writers covered in this book, such as Martin Amis, Julian Barnes, A. S. Byatt and Salman Rushdie, have a knowledge of the recent developments in literary and cultural theory and often refer to these ideas in their novels. There are a number of very good introductions and guides to literary theory and in the reading list at the end of this book there is a list of the most useful.

SUMMARY OF KEY POINTS

- Both 'contemporary' and 'British' are problematic categories that need to be addressed when discussing the fiction produced over the last thirty years.

- Sexual politics, including feminism and gay and lesbian rights movements, have had an influential effect on British fiction.
- The break up of the Empire and the multicultural nature of contemporary Britain have provided a rich source of subject matter for fiction.
- Much of contemporary British fiction has been interested in the role of youth and subcultures as distinct forms of identity.
- Questions of class, gender, ethnicity and age often interrelate in contemporary British fiction.

NOTES

1. See, for example, James Acheson and Sarah C. E. Ross (eds), *The Contemporary British Novel* (Edinburgh: Edinburgh University Press, 2005); Richard Bradford, *The Novel Now: Contemporary British Fiction* (Malden, MA: Blackwell, 2007); Jago Morrison, *Contemporary Fiction* (London: Routledge, 2003); Philip Tew, *The Contemporary British Novel* (London: Continuum, 2004).
2. John Maynard Keynes, *The General Theory of Employment, Interest, and Money* (Amherst, NY: Prometheus Books, [1936] 1997).
3. Iain Sinclair is a British writer who would certainly be part of any emerging canon of contemporary British literature, however, perhaps because of the perceived difficulty of his fiction, he does not appear on many undergraduate courses.
4. Douglas Keay, 'Aids, Education and the Year 2000', in *Women's Own* 31 October 1987, pp. 8–10.
5. Seamus Deane, *Reading in the Dark: A Novel* (London: Jonathan Cape, 1996); Bernard MacLaverty, *Grace Notes* (London: Jonathan Cape, 1997).
6. See Martin Amis, *Einstein's Monsters* (London: Jonathan Cape, 1987); J. G. Ballard *Empire of the Sun* (London: Gollancz, 1984); Graham Swift, *Waterland* (London: Picador, [1984] 1992); and John le Carré, *Smiley's People* (London: Hodder and Stoughton, 1980).

7. Ian McEwan *Black Dogs* (London: Jonathan Cape, 1992); Zadie Smith, *White Teeth* (Harmondsworth: Penguin, [2000] 2001).

8. Monica Ali, *Brick Lane* (London: Black Swan, [2003] 2004), pp. 365–8.

9. Ian McEwan, *Saturday* (London: Jonathan Cape, 2005), p. 16.

10. J. G. Ballard, *Millennium People* (London: Flamingo, 2003); and *Kingdom Come* (London: Fourth Estate, 2006).

11. See William Thompson and Joseph Hickey, *Society in Focus* (Boston, MA: Pearson, 2002).

12. See, for example, the following seminal texts in the foundation of British Cultural Studies: Richard Hoggart, *The Uses of Literacy* (Harmondsworth: Penguin, [1957] 1958); Raymond Williams, *Culture and Society 1780–1950* (London: Hogarth, [1957] 1987), and *The Long Revolution* (London: Chatto and Windus, 1961); and E. P. Thompson, *The Making of the English Working-Class* (Harmondsworth: Penguin, [1963] 1968).

13. Simone de Beauvoir, *The Second Sex*, ed. and trans. H. M. Parshley (London: Jonathan Cape, [1949] 1953).

14. Sheila Rowbotham, *Women's Liberation and the New Politics* (London: Virago, [1970] 1983).

15. Germaine Greer, *The Female Eunuch* (London: MacGibbon & Kee, 1970).

16. Kate Millett, *Sexual Politics* (New York: Doubleday, 1970); Sandra Gilbert and Susan Gubar, *The Madwoman in the Attic: The Woman Writer and the Nineteenth-Century Literary Imagination* (New Haven, CT: Yale University Press, 1979); Elaine Showalter, *A Literature of Their Own: British Women Novelists from Bronte to Lessing* (Princeton, NJ: Princeton University Press, 1977); Ellen Moers, *Literary Women* (London: Women's Press, 1978).

17. Hélène Cixous, 'The Newly Born Woman', in *Literary Theory: An Anthology*, 2nd edn, ed. Julie Rivkin and Michael Ryan (Malden, MA: Blackwell, 2004), pp. 348–54, p. 348

18. Virginia Woolf, 'To Cambridge Women', in *Literature in the Modern World: Critical Essays and Documants,* 2nd edn, ed. Dennis Walder (Oxford: Oxford University Press, 2004), pp. 91–6, p. 95.

19. Betty Friedan, *The Christian Science Monitor*, 1 April 1974; see also *The Feminine Mystique* (Harmondsworth: Penguin, 1963).

20. Helen Fielding, *Bridget Jones's Diary* (London: Picador, 1996); Jane Green, *Straight Talking* (Harmondsworth: Penguin, [1997] 2002), *Jemima J: A Novel About Ugly Ducklings and Swans* (Harmondsworth: Penguin, 1998).

21. Homosexuality remained illegal in Scotland until the Criminal Justice (Scotland) Act 1980, and in Northern Ireland until the Homosexual Offences (Northern Ireland) Order 1982.

22. Michel Foucault, *The History of Sexuality, Volume I*, trans. Robert Hurley (London: Penguin, [1976] 1990).

23. Enoch Powell, *Freedom and Reality* (Farnham: Elliot Right Way Books, 1969).

24. Edward Said, *Orientalism: Western Conceptions of the Orient* (Harmondsworth: Penguin, [1978] 1991).

25. Salman Rushdie, *Shame* (London: Picador, [1983] 1984), p. 38.

26. James Kelman, *How Late It Was, How Late* (London: Secker and Warburg, 1994), p. 29.

27. Bill Ashcroft, Gareth Griffiths and Helen Tiffin, *The Empire Writes Back: Theory and Practice in Post-Colonial Literatures* (London: Routledge, 1989), p. 38.

28. Bradford, *The Novel Now*, p. 160.

29. Homi K. Bhabha, *The Location of Culture* (London: Routledge, 1994).

30. Stuart Hall, 'New Ethnicities' in *Stuart Hall: Critical Dialogues in Cultural Studies*, ed. David Morley and Kuan-Hsing Chen (London: Routledge, 1996), pp. 441–9, p. 443.

31. Colin MacInnes, *Absolute Beginners* (Harmondsworth: Penguin, [1959] 1964).

32. Nik Cohn, *Pop* (London: Weidenfeld & Nicolson, 1969); Richard Allen, *Suedehead* (London: New English Library, 1971); Stewart Home, *Pure Mania* (Edinburgh: Polygon, 1989).

33. Irvine Welsh, *Trainspotting* (London: Secker & Warburg, 1993); Nicholas Blincoe, *Acid Casuals* (London: Serpent's Tail, 1995).

34. Hoggart, *The Uses of Literacy*, p. 193

35. Stuart Hall and Paddy Whannel, *The Popular Arts* (London: Pantheon, 1964).

36. Phil Cohen, 'Subcultural Conflict and Working-Class Community', in *The Subcultures Reader*, ed. Ken Gelder and Sarah Thornton (London: Routledge, 1997), pp. 90–9; John Willis, *Learning to Labour* (Aldershot: Saxon House, 1977); Angela McRobbie and Jenny Barber, 'Girls and Subcultures: An Explanation', in *Resistance Through Rituals: Youth Subcultures in Postwar Britain*, ed. Stuart Hall and Tony Jefferson (Birmingham: Hutchinson, 1975), pp. 209–22; Gary Clarke, 'Defending Ski-Jumpers: A Critique of Theories of Youth Subcultures', in Gelder, *The Subcultures Reader*, pp. 175–80

37. Dick Hebdige, *Subcultures: The Meaning of Style* (London: Routledge, 1979)

38. M. M. Bakhtin, 'Discourse in the Novel', in *The Dialogic Imagination: Four Essays by M.M.Bakhtin*, ed. and trans. Carl Emerson and Michael Holquist (Austin, TX: University of Texas Press, 1981), pp. 259–422; Viktor Shklovsky, 'Art as Technique', in *Literary Theory: An Anthology*, 2nd edn, ed. Julie Rivkin and Michael Ryan (Malden, MA: Blackwell, 2004), pp. 15–21.

39. Cleanth Brooks, *The Well-Wrought Urn: Studies in the Structure of Poetry* (New York: Harcourt, Brace and World, 1947); W. K. Wimsatt Jr, *The Verbal Icon* (Lexington, KY: University of Kentucky Press, 1954).

40. I. A. Richards, *Practical Criticism: A Study of Literary Judgment* (New York: Harcourt, Brace and World, [1929] 1967).

41. See, for example, F. R. Leavis *The Great Tradition* (London: Chatto and Windus, 1947).

CHAPTER I

Narrative Forms: Postmodernism and Realism

M ost periods of literary history reveal a set of writers who engage with the dominant literary modes and styles of the previous generation. Some of these writers see themselves as continuers of tradition, others as radical innovators, and some as a mixture of both. The formal characteristics of the British novel in the contemporary period have much to do with the debates around literary form that were established in the 1950s and 1960s, and which were themselves engaging with the debates of the 1920s and 1930s. The British literary environment in the 1950s had been largely influenced by what was perceived as a reaction to pre-war modernism. Writers that emerged during this period, such as Kingsley Amis, John Braine, William Cooper, Alan Sillitoe, C. P. Snow, David Storey and John Wain, were identified as representing a retrieval of an English realist tradition that had been diverted by modernist experimentation. This is a reductive view of the complexity of these writers, however, and many others continued to experiment with narrative form such as Samuel Beckett, Christine Brooke-Rose, William Golding, B. S. Johnson, Muriel Spark and Doris Lessing.[1]

In an oft-cited essay of 1971, David Lodge argued that the contemporary novelist stood at a crossroads in terms of form; in one direction lay realism, whilst in the other was a continued modernist and experimental approach to fiction.[2] This binary opposition owes something to the structuralist thinking of Lodge, and in practice the contemporary novel has seen a mixture of both these styles, along with the increasing popularity in the 1970s, 1980s and 1990s in Britain of a third category: postmodernism, which, stylistically differentiates itself from both realism and modernism. Postmodernism is a tricky concept, but many of the writers covered in this book have at some time or another used narrative and stylistic techniques associated with this mode. Such writers include Martin Amis, Julian Barnes, A.S. Byatt, Angela Carter, Alasdair Gray, Ian McEwan, Salman Rushdie, Iain Sinclair, Graham Swift and Jeanette Winterson. As we shall see, two of the novels discussed in this chapter, Martin Amis's *London Fields* (1989) and Alasdair Gray's *Poor Things* (1992), use a variety of techniques that can be identified as postmodern. Before looking in detail at these novels, then, it is worth taking some time investigating the term further.

Postmodernism loves paradoxes, and the term itself is something of a paradox. If the term modern refers to current or of the present, then how can a form of contemporary writing be 'post' present unless it is referring to the future? This paradox relates to the history of the term itself and how its suffix and prefix have developed from different sources. The root of the word is clearly modern, and as we have suggested relates to the now and carries the connotations of the current and being up-to-date. It thus stands in opposition to the sense of the traditional, the established and in some senses the ordinary and the out of fashion. The kind of experimental writing many British authors were practicing in the 1970s and 1980s clearly saw itself as new and more attuned with contemporary concerns and ideas. However, in literature 'modernism' as a term had already found its definition as relating to the kind of writing that emerged amongst an influential range of writers in the early part of the twentieth century such as Joseph Conrad, James Joyce, Virginia Woolf, Katherine Mansfield, Dorothy Richardson and to some extent Henry James, D.H. Lawrence and E.M. Forster. The 'post' of postmodernism, in literary terms, therefore, served to establish a link with this experimental attitude towards writing, whilst at the same time signalling that the experiment itself had shifted due to the changed historical situation in which writers of the late twentieth century found themselves.

There is, however, a further complexity to the term that needs to be taken into account. Although modern*ism* related to aesthetic and cultural practices roughly from the last decade of the nineteenth century to the early 1930s, modern*ity* has a very different historical etymology. Modernity in Western definitions of the term usually refers to that period after the middle ages in Europe and taking hold in Britain from the mid-fifteenth century. The high point of modernity is often associated with the Enlightenment of the seventeenth and eighteenth centuries and can be seen as establishing modernity in a range of social, political and philosophical contexts. Jean-François Lyotard has been an important theorist in this context of postmodernism. Lyotard suggests that modernity relates to 'any science that legitimates itself with reference to a metadiscourse [that makes] an explicit appeal to some grand narrative, such as the dialectics of Spirit, the hermeneutics of meaning, the emancipation of the rational or working subject, or the creation of wealth'.[3] For Lyotard the postmodern represents an 'incredulity towards meta-narratives' of this kind, which is often understood to mean a scepticism towards the grand narratives of rationalism, science, the Cartesian self, and the prevailing economic theories in the eighteenth, nineteenth and twentieth centuries, including most controversially, Marxism. This scepticism towards grand narratives has provided a fruitful area for novelists who are keen to explore the nature of fictional narratives generally.

The *post*modern, then, operates at (at least) two distinct and interconnected levels in historical terms. It signals a style of writing that supersedes, or at least marks itself as different from the modernist literature of the early twentieth century whilst at the same time employing a philosophical outlook that rejects many of the tenets of modernity as established during the Enlightenment. Philosophers that have been influential to postmodern thinking such as Lyotard, Friedrich Nietzsche, Sigmund Freud, Jacques Lacan, Jacques Derrida, Jean Baudrillard, Michel Foucault, Gilles Deleuze and Felix Guattari all tend to position their respective ideas as in some sense alternative to or critical of the enlightenment thinking of modernity.[4]

This explains to some extent differences in the suffix of the terms postmodernism and postmodernity but more needs to be said about the prefix. The 'post' is complex and can relate to different approaches for different practitioners of postmodern technique. The post can be understood simply as a periodizing term as we have been using it so far. Fredric Jameson, for example, sees postmodernism as a phase in cultural history associated with what he calls late capitalism.[5] As well as being used as a periodizing term, it can also be used to signal an extension of the experimental techniques developed in modernist writing; in the sense that postmodernism extends the boundaries of modernist experimentation. Or it can refer to a term of differentiation from some of the tenets of modernism. For example, postmodernism tends to reject modernism's suspicions of popular culture and mass art and often reworks it through a self-reflexive celebration of the everyday and the kitsch as can be seen in the Pop Art works of Andy Warhol and Peter Blake. One caveat to add to this brief account of postmodernism, however, is that there are many different versions of the postmodern, and each writer studied in this book has their own understanding of how their work relates to, engages with, or rejects its positions. In keeping with its embrace of multiplicity it is more accurate to talk in terms of postmodernisms rather than a clearly defined theoretical discourse. It is important to note therefore that the term postmodernism does not relate to a fixed set of characteristics or criteria, but is a rather fluid term that takes on different aspects when used by different critics and different social commentators.

An area of critical thought that has been influential to the development of postmodern techniques in fiction is poststructuralism. This tends to argue that language, far from being a transparent tool that allows people to describe the world in an accurate way, is in fact more like a gauze or filter through which the world is textually reconstructed. This emphasis on the constructedness of language has challenged the assumption in much realist fiction that the way in which an author used language was as an aid to expressing emotions faithfully or describing aspects of the real world accurately. Poststructuralism, on the contrary, argues that the attempt to record realistic experience through the medium of language is fraught with problems and that when someone attempts to write about some aspect of the world, they are not simply describing what is already there, but constructing it anew, and creating it in a textual form.

Postmodernism, then, has two opposites: modernism and realism. The traditional understanding of formal realism is based on its ability to represent some aspect of the world accurately in a narrative form. Ian Watt, for example, describes formal realism with a series of characteristics including the use of identifiable locations and periods of history, characters that are representative of people you might meet in real life, a plot structure based on cause and effect, and an assumption that language is referential and denotational.[6] Poststructuralist criticism has moved away from this formal definition of realism and argued that its relationship with reality is more problematic than the approach suggested by Watt. Roland Barthes, for example, sees realism, not as a reflection of reality, but as a textual convention that employs a series of narrative codes that attempt to construct the idea of *vraisemblable*, or 'trueseemingness'. According to Barthes, what we understand as realism is thus a series of narrative techniques that produce the lie that what we are reading relates directly to reality.

Realist fiction, then, is really just a structural arrangement of language and: 'Claims concerning the "realism" of a text are therefore to be discounted [. . .] "what happens" is language alone, the adventure of language'.[7] Catherine Belsey, a critic influenced by poststructuralist theory, also identifies realism as a set of novelistic conventions, such as the use of a 'hierarchy of discourses' whereby the opinions provided by certain characters or ideas in a novel have priority over other ideas and opinions. As she explains: 'Realism is plausible not because it reflects the world, but because it is constructed out of what is (discursively) familiar'.[8] Realism, therefore, persuades us to believe that the fiction we are reading is verifiable in terms of its closeness to a believable world. Much postmodernist fiction is interested in interrogating this claim of realist fiction and many of the narrative techniques associated with postmodernism function to pursue this aim. These techniques include metafiction; the disruption of the linear flow of narratives and the relationship between cause and effect; challenging the authority of the author; the use of events and characters drawn from fantasy; self-reflexively drawing attention to the language that is being used to construct the fiction; the use of parody and pastiche, and more generally a scepticism towards fixed ideologies and philosophies. All these techniques can be identified in particular novels covered in this book. In this chapter, Martin Amis's *London Fields* and Alasdair Gray's *Poor Things* employ many of the postmodern characteristics. Zadie Smith's *White Teeth* (2000), on the other hand, although it includes some postmodern techniques, tends, on the whole, to use a realist mode.

MARTIN AMIS, *LONDON FIELDS* (1989)

London Fields is, in many ways, a novel about writing novels and about playing around with fiction's relationship to reality. It is also about the way in which fiction, in its broadest sense, affects the formation of identity: how people create narratives in order to understand their place in the world. In doing so, it seeks to undermine some of the grand narratives by which we have come to understand and interpret the late-twentieth and early twenty-first-century world.

The playful approach to fiction is introduced to us on the first page of the novel, which opens with an unknown voice, later revealed to be a novelist called Samson Young, who is commenting upon the real life situation in which he finds himself providing the ideal material for a novel:

> This is a true story but I can't believe it is happening.
> It's a murder story, too. I can't believe my luck.
> And a love story (I think), of all strange things, so late in the century, so late in the goddamned day.
> This is the story of a murder. It hasn't happened yet. But it will. (It had better.) I know the murderer, I know the murderee. I know the time, I know the place. I know the motive (*her* motive) and I know the means. I know who will be the foil, the fool, the poor foal, also utterly destroyed. And I couldn't stop them, I don't think, even if I wanted to. The girl will die. It's what she's always wanted. You can't stop people, once they *start creating*.
> What a gift. This page is briefly stained by my tears of gratitude. Novelists don't usually have it so good, do they, when

something real happens (something unified, dramatic and pretty saleable), and they just write it down?[9]

In this opening, Amis fixes on the paradox inherent in the phrase a 'true story': if what the narrator is about to present is an accurate reflection of real life, then in what sense can it be seen as a 'story' – something that suggests artifice and an authorial, controlling hand? This paradox is taken further in the suggestion that real life is being represented as part of an established literary genre: the 'murder story' or 'love story'. There is also a reference to the idea that real life might be following a pre-arranged plot ('It hasn't happened yet but it will'), and to the imposing of character types (the murderer, the murderee, the foil) on individual people. Amis is also keen to explore the power relationships suggested in this combination of characters. In one sense the power of the narrator/author figure is diminished in that the events are seen to be playing themselves out without the work and manipulation of the author as suggested by the fact that he is not inventing this story, but just recording it from real life. This is extended by the fact that the characters are outside the control of the author: 'you can't stop people, once they start creating'. The passage ends by alluding to the moral responsibility the author has to the people he is to exploit as characters in that it will eventually be a product that will earn the author money as a saleable commodity. This suggests that the author will only have a dramatic interest in the people he is going to become close to, rather like a journalist's relationship to the people he might use to produce a news 'story'.

The metafictional context of the opening is continued in the structure of the novel. It is organized in alternating sections; the chapters, with headings are supposed to represent the novel that Samson Young will eventually create. Interspersed between them are the reflections he has on his encounters with each of the three main characters: Keith Talent, Nicola Six and Guy Clinch. This format maintains a fairly rigid structure for the first twelve of the twenty-four chapters as they are arranged in blocks of three each one being concerned primarily with Keith, Nicola and Guy respectively. From chapter thirteen onwards, however, the interaction between these three characters becomes more convoluted, and the pattern begins to break down, suggesting that Samson is losing control of the direction the narrative is taking. This formal device is also suggestive of one of the thematic concerns of the novel: that the late-twentieth-century world is beginning to spiral out of control, and where the structuring grand narratives of religion and ethics are beginning to unravel. This suggestion of a world on the brink is set against the Cold War context. Published in 1989, *London Fields* marks Amis's continuing interest in a future in which nuclear weapons have the potential to end humanity and the world on which it survives.[10] Various references are made to the sense of the coming millennium, as the novel is set ten years after it was published, in 1999.

As part of the novel's metafiction, *London Fields* provides us with a series of narrative levels that contribute to the questioning of who has narrative authority in the text. Alongside Samson Young, there is the mysterious figure of Mark Asprey, another novelist in whose flat Sam is living during the course of the novel and who represents a more successful alter ego. The letter at the end of the novel addressed to Asprey shows that Sam has died by the time the novel ends and that he has bequeathed the novel to him. It is never clear, therefore, how much of what we are reading is an account of the events that is faithful to Sam's experiences, or whether Asprey has added his own alterations. Power over the narrative is, then, removed at least one level from the narrator. It is also significant that Mark Asprey's initials are the same as Martin Amis. This produces another narrative level to the novel. The 'Note' that precedes page one of the novel is signed by an 'M. A.', and given the conventions of the novel form, it is assumed on first reading that this refers to the real author, Martin Amis. However, this is hardly a conventional novel and the reader is persuaded to ask whether these are perhaps Mark Asprey's initials. Later in the novel, Sam notes that Nicola refers to an 'MA' in her diaries, which forces him to speculate: 'Nicola and MA? Nicola and Mark Asprey? (p. 205).[11] 'MA' thus becomes a fluid signifier in the text referring simultaneously to Asprey and to Amis, two levels of external author 'above' Sam's narrative. This would also mean that the fiction does not start on page one, as conventionally assumed, but begins as soon as we open the front cover. (This is a technique also used in Alasdair

Gray's *Poor Things*.) In effect, the fictional world is extending beyond the bounds in which it is usually contained and this works at a thematic as well as formal level. Amis seems to be persuading us to think about where fiction begins and, consequently, where it ends.

This questioning of the ontological status of fictional worlds extends to the characters in the text. The novel presents a series of stereotypes: Keith Talent, a white, working-class Londoner; Guy, an English upper-middle-class gentleman; and Nicola Six, who appears as if she has stepped off the pages of a hard-boiled detective novel. It becomes obvious fairly quickly that these characters are so overplayed that they are parodies of the stereotypes. To use a phrase by the French critical theorist Jean Baudrillard, they appear as examples of the hyperreal: they are characters based in recognized interpretations of the world but exaggerated to such an extent as to make them appear strange.[12] Sam effectively misreads the characters because he accepts the stereotypes unquestioningly. However, the reader is also implicated in this misreading, an effect produced by the desire to believe the positions taken by a first-person narrator. This ambivalent form of presenting character draws the reader in, but the unfolding of events signals the dangers of too easily accepting stereotypes.

This can be seen, for example, in the provocative characterization of Keith Talent. Keith is of limited intelligence and his cultural pursuits revolve around darts, football, pornography and TV. He is a violent petty criminal who preys on the weak and vulnerable, mainly because he has 'failed' to be ruthless enough to get into serious violent crime. He is a racist and he abuses women. This is a provocative representation of working-class masculinity and leaves Amis open to the charge of negative stereotyping. As Philip Tew has argued: 'One ought to wonder whether such parodies of the working-class or proletarian male [. . .] can be sufficiently ironic to be reduced to generic, textual, or postmodern matters, especially when articulated from positions of cultural authority'.[13] As Tew goes on to speculate, however, the stereotyping is complicated by the self-reflexive nature of the novel: 'By his perverse attacks is Amis reminding us about the vulnerability of humanity to typological reduction, to the archetypal movement of myth and history?'[14]

All of Keith's negative attributes can be identified in society (and more significantly within what is constructed as working-class culture by certain sections of the middle classes), however, Amis is again alerting the reader to the implications of uncritically accepting these stereotypes. The text is keen to blur the distinction between reality and fiction, but is, by implication, signalling the dangers involved in applying cultural stereotypes to the real world. Keith, like Guy (and, indeed, Sam), is an individual who is unaware of the cultural and ideological forces acting upon him. He is an example of the kind of individual that is produced by Western capitalism, an individual who the post-Marxist critic Louis Althusser would see as subject to the effects of what he calls Ideological State Apparatuses.[15] Althusser argues that under capitalism, people are not only politically exploited, but that their psychological frameworks are such that they are unaware of their exploited condition. For Althusser, ideology works to mask their subject position to themselves. This can be seen in Keith's understanding of class (and his position as a working-class male) as a factor in the creation of his identity:

> Keith acted in the name of masculinity. He acted also, of course, in the name of *class*. Class! Yes, it's still here [. . .] Class never bothered Keith; he never thought about it 'as such'; part of a bygone era, whatever that was, class never worried him. It would surprise Keith a lot if you told him it was *class* that poisoned his every waking moment. (p. 24)

In this passage, class is the determining factor in Keith's behaviour and his social relations with the people he encounters, but he remains oblivious to its controlling effects. This is an exact model of the way in which Althusser suggests class operates in society. Keith perceives himself to be acting freely in his relationships with Nicola and Guy, but in fact the unperceived effects of ideology condition him. This is emphasized in Keith's consumption of TV, an example of one of the Ideological State Apparatuses that control him:

> He watched a very great deal of TV, always had done, years and years of it, aeons of TV. Boy, did Keith burn that tube.

> And that tube burnt him, nuked him, its cathodes crackling
> like cancer. 'TV,' he thought, or 'Modern reality' or 'The
> world'. It was the world of TV that told him what the world
> was. How does all the TV time work on a modern person, a
> person like Keith? [. . . TV] came at Keith like it came at
> everybody else; he had nothing whatever to keep it out. He
> couldn't grade or filter it. So he thought TV was real. (p. 55)

For Keith, TV *is* reality: there is no distance between the way in
which TV represents the world and how it 'really' is. This corresponds to Althusser's understanding of the way in which culture
works to enforce the dominant ideologies of a society, and this,
significantly, affects the way in which he relates to other people: 'In
the days after their first meeting, the image of Nicola Six began to
work on Keith's mind. It worked like television' (p. 55). Note here
the conflation of real and fictional for Keith: it is the 'image' of
Nicola that works 'like television' on him: that is, works in a way
that convinces him of the reality of the constructed fiction Nicola
has tailored for Keith.

However, the Althusserian model only helps so far as a way of
dealing with the way in which identity is constructed in *London
Fields*. The identification of Keith as duped by class and TV only
works as long as there is some sense of the actual conditions of
Keith's life behind his own false perception of it. This is what
Althusser would call 'science' as opposed to ideology: the study of
the real conditions of existence behind the false consciousness.
In the passages quoted above, this works because, through Sam
Young's narrative, we are able to see the ironic distance between
Keith's own perception and the 'truth' of the situation. The basis
of this ironic distance, however, becomes increasingly unstable as
the novel proceeds, and especially as it is revealed that Sam, himself,
has been living under a false understanding of Nicola: that she has
in fact been manipulating him (and, by extension, the reader) in a
similar way to her control of Keith and Guy.

Sam gradually becomes aware of his position within the novel,
not as the impartial recorder of the events being played out in front
of him, as suggested at the beginning of the novel, but as intricately
bound up in the plot. As he finally recognizes, rather than Nicola

being one of the players in *his* narrative, he has been part of *hers*: 'She outwrote me. Her story worked. And mine didn't [. . .] always me: from the first moment in the Black Cross [. . .] I should have understood that a cross has four points. Not three' (p. 466). Here, Sam realizes he is the fourth point on the cross alongside Nicola, Keith and Guy and, therefore, is not above the plot but part of it. In one sense this is another parodic reference to the hard-boiled detective novel in which the detective-narrator increasingly becomes bound up in the criminal world he is investigating. However, this situation raises deeper ontological and ethical issues. If Sam has not recognized his place within the narrative then it forces questions about how far his judgement is to be trusted generally. Up until this moment, the reader has been led to trust in Sam's interpretation of the events and the world in which they have taken place, but his epiphany serves to show how both he, and by implication the reader, have in fact been in a position of false consciousness with respect to what has gone before. This is a postmodern move that undermines the reliability of narratives that one has previously been led to believe.

A similar situation is established in the figure of Nicola Six although Amis develops a more complex characterization than with Keith (or Guy). Nicola essentially performs a series of roles adapted to reflect the fantasy image each of the male characters project on to her, and she ensnares both of them because of her ability to adapt her performance to the recognized type that each desires.[16] For Keith she plays the role of the high-class porn star, whilst for Guy she is the demure virgin. Because of Keith's love of pornography, Nicola produces a porn movie for him with herself as the star. This form of mediated sex also reflects Keith's love of the debased and his inability to engage in meaningful human intimacy. Guy is drawn in by his own fantasy of Nicola's innocence: 'He had long guessed it, he now felt, the pinkness and purity of Nicola Six [. . .] It made sense – it rang true' (p. 146). Guy believes Nicola because he transforms her character into a stereotype and thereby convinces himself of her plausibility. This is because the character she performs is one that is recognizable culturally and, therefore, Guy accepts it uncritically. Nicola, then, uses two of the conventional female stereotypes of patriarchy – the whore and the virgin – against Keith and Guy, who are thereby fooled because of their own prejudices and fantasies.

As suggested earlier, it appears initially that Samson remains outside of Nicola's entrapment but in fact she dupes him as convincingly as Keith and Guy. For Samson, she is the embodiment of the *femme fatale*, a figure that is no less artificial than the ones she performs for Keith and Guy. In reply to Samson's challenge 'But you're not in a story', she replies 'It's always felt like a story' (p. 118). Nicola fools Sam by playing a role with which he is familiar and, therefore, more easily taken in. At one point she rejects the role Samson has imposed on her, replacing it with a far more unsettling type: 'I'm not a Femme Fatale. Listen, mister: Femmes Fatales are ten a penny compared to what I am [. . .] I'm a murderee' (p. 260). Nicola presents herself as a vulnerable female that seems to invite violence against her. This is, of course, another stereotype – a way that culture has designated one of the traditional ways of constructing femininity, especially in the type of detective novel that *London Fields* parodies. As suggested earlier, because of the effects of first-person narration to empathize with the voice telling us the story, then the reader is also implicated in this reading of Nicola.

Nicola's representation has been the subject of much controversy. When the book was published it came under criticism for its apparent sexism, with the novel's portrayal of its main female character as evidence of Amis's misogyny and reproduction of stereotypical images of women.[17] Sara Mills, for example, has taken Amis to task for his sexism in his portrayal of Nicola.[18] There is certainly a case to be made that Nicola constitutes a form of female identity imposed within a patriarchal society. However, this is part of Amis's method of characterization in the novel. The issue turns on how far the book supports these constructions or is critical of the way in which culture and society reproduces them, and this in turn relates to the implications of Amis's use of metafiction. It is important to remember that Amis has taken great pains to establish the fictional context within which all the characters are produced and consequently, the way in which reality is affected by artificial narratives of identity. To suggest that the characterization of Nicola represents a misogynist view of women is, therefore, obvious. What is more complicated is the attitude the reader is supposed to have to that characterization. The slippery nature of postmodern fiction means that the charges of sexism are as valid as the argument that Amis is foregrounding those stereotypes in order to satirize them, as he does with Keith and Guy with respect to class.

In one sense, however, the novel questions the morally ambiguous nature of postmodern representation. Nicola Six is presented as a character that is made up of a series of masks with nothing behind them. Stuart Hall, for one, has identified the postmodern subject as 'having no fixed, essential or permanent identity', and Nicola is a symbol of this kind of identity.[19] She is an empty signifier with nothing at the core; or perhaps more accurately she is a hyper-real character, because she presents constructed identities or masks to the characters she encounters (and the reader) behind which there is a vacuum. As Susan Brook puts it, 'Nicola is the form of the postmodern text, deconstructing the distinction between the real and the fictional to produce the hyperreal'.[20] She is wholly constructed, in a fictional sense, but also in a cultural sense. She adheres to certain images of femininity, but there is no human identity behind these masks. She is a kind of black hole – a motif to which the text keeps returning. As the designated murderee, her only function is to die and yet she is the enigma round which the plot is organized. This represents a paradox in terms of power: the most powerful figure in the novel is also the most obvious victim. *London Fields*, then, is concerned with engaging in a kind of postmodern ethics: a form of critique without necessarily having a fixed moral stance against which to launch that critique. In a filmed interview with Ian McEwan, Amis suggests that when an author creates a character, there is an ethical responsibility to the humanity of that fictional entity.[21] When authors, therefore, cause things to happen to fictional characters they are, in part, entering into an ethical relationship with humanity generally. In *London Fields*, this is related to the enjoyment the reader gets by seeing characters in desperate situations. As noted, however, Amis reverses the power relationship by having certain characters rebel against the controlling narrator. More broadly, then, Amis's novel persuades us to consider the responsibility people have to those over whom they have power. What makes it a difficult text is that it uses postmodern techniques to reflect this postmodern ethical dilemma, whereby the suspicion of all grand narratives results in the difficulty in claiming any fixed moral, ethical or ideological position.

ALASDAIR GRAY, *POOR THINGS* (1992)

As with Amis's *London Fields*, *Poor Things* opens with a deliberate confusion regarding where the fiction begins. To begin with, the title page is unreliable in that it presents 'Poor Things' as an autobiographical work produced by one Archibald McCandless M.D. who is in fact a fictional character within the novel. In the 2002 paperback edition this is followed by a page of quotations from fictional reviews such as the one from the *Skiberreen Eagle*.[22] Pasted across this page is a fake erratum slip referring to one of the etchings included in the novel. The following page continues this playful blurring of fact and fiction by providing a fake biography of Archibald McCandless, and a real, if unusual one of Alisdair Gray, who is referred to as the editor, rather than the author of the book, and is described as a 'fat, balding, asthmatic, married pedestrian who lives by writing and designing things'. This may be true, but it comically disrupts the conventional way of presenting the author to the reading public. Before the main narrative even begins then, Gray introduces us to a textual world in which fact and fiction are intertwined, where the reliability of narratives is constantly under question and where it is up to the reader to ascertain where the truth lies.

This indeterminacy in the veracity of stories is worked into the structure of the novel, where a series of narrative frames are presented in which the accounts of the lives of the main characters, Godwin Baxter, Bella Baxter and Archie McCandless often contradict each other. The main narrative is the account in the 'Episodes From the Early Life' of Archie McCandless, which describes the history of Bella Baxter as a fantastic scientific and biological experiment undertaken by Godwin Baxter. According to McCandless, Bella has been artificially put together using her resuscitated dead body with the brain of the baby she was carrying implanted in her skull. In a characteristically playful way, the 'Introduction' written by Alasdair Gray supports Archie's version of the events while presenting an alternative view by one Michael

Donnelly (a real life historian): 'He thinks it a blackly humorous fiction into which some real experiences and historical facts have been cunningly woven [. . .] I think it [. . .] a loving portrait of an astonishingly good, stout, intelligent, eccentric man recorded by a friend with a memory for dialogue'.[23] The author goes on to try and establish his authority over the text:

> I print the letter by the lady who calls herself 'Victoria McCandless' as an epilogue to the book. Michael would prefer it as an introduction, but if read before the main text it will prejudice readers against that. If read afterward we easily see it is the letter of a disturbed woman who wants to hide the truth about her start in life. Furthermore, no book needs two introductions and I am writing this one. (p. xiii)

Of course, the opinion of this 'Alasdair Gray, editor' is false, as the real author knows the book is a fiction of his own making. Yet in undermining the reliability of the voice that normally carries the greatest authority in a book – the author – Gray alerts us of the slipperiness of all claims to truth. In fact, Donnelly's description of McCandless's book as a 'blackly humorous fiction into which some real experiences and historical facts have been woven' would act as an accurate description of Gray's novel overall.

The novel's concerns with textual complexity is shown in its use of multiple kinds of writing – letters, journal entries, poetry, historical and critical notes, an introduction – each of which add layers of meaning. In addition, Gray's anatomical drawings – which allude to another Gray, *Gray's Anatomy* (1858)[24] – contribute to this web of meaning. One example is the passage where Archie challenges Godwin on his motivations for creating Bella: 'I will preserve her honour to the last drop of blood in my veins as sure as there is a God in Heaven' (p. 37). Archie displays a romantic sensibility, fortified, as he is at this point, by the port that Godwin has been feeding him. This passage is accompanied by a diagram of the heart, which combines the universal signifier of love, but also, in showing it as dissected scientific drawing undercuts these romantic associations and places the organ in a coldly anatomical setting. This is paralleled in the text when Archie assesses his own reactions after the event: 'It still seems weird to recall that after unexpectedly meeting my only friend, future wife and my first decanter of port I raved in the language of novels I knew to be trash' (p. 37). Another example is the diagram of the dissected and inverted penis that forms the introduction to Douglas Wedderburn's letter. This is again ironic because the letter goes on to detail the way in which this predatory male is ultimately emasculated by Bella's excessive sexual appetite.

Gray's use of multiple textual forms and his disruption of the conventional role of the author is reminiscent of Roland Barthes's essay 'Death of the Author' (1967). Barthes argues that our attitudes to authors have changed over the last three hundred years or so and that texts that pre-date modernity tend to see the author of a text, not as its sole creator, but more of a mediator of ideas that already exist in cultural circulation. Rather than a monologic voice, a text provides us with: 'a multi-dimensional space in which a variety of writings, none of them original, blend and clash. The text is a tissue of quotations drawn from the innumerable centres of culture'.[25] According to Barthes, the author is not the sole origin and authority of a work's meaning and, therefore, its meaning should not be found in the author's intention but in the text itself, and in the individual moment of interaction between text and reader in the act of reading. This produces a radical notion of a text as a multi-dimensional space made up of quotations from and allusions to other writings and cultural discourses.

Poor Things dramatizes this idea through its use of allusions to a series of intertexts. The most obvious is *Frankenstein* (1818), another text that includes the creation of a human being by an experimental scientist and in which the creature eventually escapes the restraints placed on it by its creator. The allusions to Mary Shelley's novel are inscribed in the name of Godwin Bysshe Baxter, Godwin being an allusion to Mary's father William Godwin, and Bysshe to the middle name of her husband Percy Bysshe Shelley. Just as *Frankenstein* tells of the consequences of man trying to override the 'natural' role of women as the producers of life, *Poor Things* develops a feminist reading of Bella's empowerment and evasion of patriarchal power, and it is relevant in this context that Mary Shelley's mother, Mary Wollstonecraft, was an early feminist writer. There are a series of other textual allusions that the novel uses, such as the Pygmalion myth, and the series of works Victoria refers to in describing Archie's book. As she says: '*What morbid Victorian fantasy has he not filched from?*' (pp. 272–3).

The fantastic figure of Bella Baxter is part of the novel's charm as a gothic tale, but it also allows Gray to engage in a political commentary on both Victorian and contemporary society. In the figure of Bella, Gray, through Godwin, provides us with a character who has an adult body, with all its attendant adult characteristics, but with the *tabula rasa* of the child's open and enquiring mind. Much of the novel is concerned with Bella's acculturation, her becoming aware of the politics and relationships between people in her society, and which allows Gray to defamiliarize the ideological relationships between people in Victorian capitalist society. Bella travels around the world reflecting on the injustices and absurdities of the dominant capitalist-imperialist system she encounters, as well as the organization of human relationships into patriarchal units. Bella's education represents, therefore, a move from a position of ideological innocence to one of knowing experience and the inevitable sadness that experience brings as she discovers the unfairness, inequalities and injustices of capitalist society.

One fruitful way to approach Gray's novel is by considering the way in which it provides us with a series of ideological systems, which are communicated through different characters. This fits in nicely with theories on the socio-political function of fiction produced by the early twentieth-century Russian critic Mikhail Bakhtin.[26] He argued that in fiction we are presented not with the singular or monoglossic voice of the author, but with multiple language styles and registers from different walks of life, and different socio-economic levels and cultures, each with its own ways of speaking and semantic fields. A novel thereby is able to manipulate, through the expression of characters and narrators, what he calls the 'heteroglossic' nature of the language of society at any particular moment in time. It rejects the idea of a nation's language as a single uniform system but as a series of competing discourses, which put together reveal the ideological debates and contests within society.

Poor Things, in particular, is keen to explore the way in which modes of expression represent different ideological outlooks and its main method of achieving this is through characterization. Many of the characters Bella encounters stand not only as individual subject personalities, but as ideological ways of looking at the world. Godwin Baxter, for example, represents the morally blind rationalism associated with a form of scientific investigation that operates without consideration for human emotions and feelings. He also represents an ideology of power over women, and in spite of his atypical appearance and lifestyle serves to support mainstream Victorian patriarchal attitudes. Archie represents the less intelligent sidekick to Godwin – the Watson to Godwin's Holmes – who, although also a scientist, is tempered with a humanity that rejects the excesses of scientific experimentation. It is Archie that recognizes the dubious intent behind Godwin's creation of Bella Baxter: 'You think you are about to possess what men have hopelessly yearned for throughout the ages: the soul of an innocent, trusting, dependent child inside the opulent body of a radiantly lovely woman' (p. 36). And yet Archie also desires to control and contain Bella, although his approach to her is fashioned by what he sees as a romantic love, which leads to his conventional proposal of marriage to her. His desired relationship with Bella, however, is as containing as Godwin's and is shown in his complicity to restrict Bella from meeting with Duncan Wedderburn. Wedderburn is a predatory misogynist that is driven by an exaggerated male libido. He preys on vulnerable women and disregards their emotional feelings and the consequences of the sexual relationships he enters into with them. Bella, however, is attracted to Wedderburn and, to Archie's dismay, eventually elopes with him.

Bella's narrative, then, is the story of a strong woman's evasion of a variety of male characters who try to impose their power over her. She escapes from the 'parental' confinement of Godwin and Archie by eloping with Wedderburn. The latter is eventually driven to madness by Bella's excessive sexual appetite, which ironically reverses his initial aim to use her. His descent into hysteria also ironically reverses the fate of the traditional female heroine of many Victorian novels, so much so that Wedderburn, in failing to contain Bella, is forced to resort to a series of female stereotypes in order to explain his symbolic emasculation: '*So I know who your niece is now, Mr. Baxter. The Jews called her Eve and Delilah; the Greeks, Helen of*

Troy; the Romans, Cleopatra; the Christians, Salome. She is the White Daemon who destroys the honour and manhood of the noblest and most virile men in every age' (p. 94 – italics in original). That Wedderburn is hardly the most honourable or noble of men increases the irony of his rant here.

Bella's narrative of empowerment over men is, then, part of the text's aim to show the flaws in patriarchy when faced with a strong intelligent woman who enjoys her sexuality, and who in many cases is physically and emotionally stronger than the men she encounters. That this appears as unnatural to the Victorian gender ideology explains, to a certain extent, why Archie has decided to represent her as a 'monstrous' figure, one that transcends the natural order of things in both her creation and her subsequent dealings with men. Textually, Bella also succeeds in evading the representation that Archie attempts to place on her. The letter that follows Archie's book, signed Victoria McCandless, puts forward a contrasting account of her life which undermines the representation of her in the main text. Names, of course, are significant here: 'Bella', the beautiful female that is contained by the male gaze, is replaced by 'Victoria', the strong woman who has escaped each of the claims the men have over her. It is discovered in Victoria's letter that she has become a practising doctor who supports her husband financially, a situation that has clearly affected Archie's masculine Victorian ego, and hints at the real reason for the fantasy he has woven around her 'unnatural' creation.

Alongside the support of Bella/Victoria's feminist empowerment, the novel suggests an alternative socialist ideology to the excesses of Victorian capitalism. This is achieved again through using characters as the mouthpieces for political and ideological systems. The central section of Archie's book is taken over by Bella's account of her journey to Cairo with Wedderburn and her conversations with Dr Hooker, an American evangelist, and Harry Astley, an intelligent upper-class cynic. Hooker represents a form of white supremacist thinking that combines religious Protestant fervour with an unshaken belief in the correctness of his moral positions. Harry is more complex, and a whole chapter is given over to 'Astley's Bitter Wisdom' in which he summarizes a range of political issues and positions and why he regards each of them as flawed. Astley's ideas are presented in a logical and convincing way, however, his cynicism is ultimately undermined by Bella (and by the text as a whole): '*I felt for the first time who he really is – a tortured little boy who hates cruelty as much as I do but thinks himself a strong man because he can pretend to like it*' (p. 164 – italics in original). After considering the political options Astley presents to her, Bella concludes, '*Everyone should have a cosy shell around them, a good coat with money in their pockets. I must be a Socialist*' (p. 164). Through the text's technique of defamiliarizing human society, this conclusion by Bella is powerful and seems to carry the political message of the text as a whole. It is further supported by Bella's experiences in Cairo. A striking central section of her narrative is taken over by five pages of barely legible scrawl (pp. 145–50). It is later explained that this represents her emotional response to an experience she has observed in which the realities of the capitalist-colonial framework as it impacts on exploited human beings is dramatically brought home. The scrawls represent Bella's inability to express the horror she feels at encountering a group of beggars in Cairo, one of which is a partially blind girl carrying a wholly blind baby. The rich Europeans are on a veranda above them and are throwing pennies and scraps to the crowd and laughing at their scrabbling and fighting for their paltry offerings. It is only later that Bella can rationalize this experience and record it in writing:

> I had just seen a working model of nearly every civilized nation. The people on the veranda were the owners and rulers – their inherited intelligence and wealth set them above everyone else. The crowd of beggars represented the jealous and incompetent majority, who were kept in their place by the whips of those on the ground between: the latter represented policemen and functionaries who keep society as it is. (p. 176)

This critique of Western capitalism is powerful in the context of the Victorian setting in which it is placed, however, it is also meant to resonate with the contemporary world and acts as a commentary on the international political and economic situation in the late twentieth century.

The Victorian setting allows Gray to examine the ideological framework of nineteenth-century British imperialism and *laissez faire* capitalism whereby the market is the determining factor in the way in which society is organized. Much of the novel is concerned with highlighting the injustices and absurdities of the pursuance of such an economic system. One of the tenets of Victorian ideology is a belief in progress and accumulation: both the accumulation of knowledge and wealth. Godwin Baxter represents the scientific aspect of Victorian progress – the desire to push forward scientific knowledge at the expense of traditional forms of human morality and ethics. In his experiment with Bella and her unborn child, Godwin disregards the ethical issues involved and thereby justifies to himself the emotional and psychological harm he does to his creation. The discourse of imperialism is shared by a couple of characters, one English and one American: General Sir Aubrey de la Pole Blessington Bart who claims to be Bella's husband, and Dr Hooker, both of whom represent the belief in colonial expansion as a legitimate form of progress. Hooker, in particular, attaches a belief in the superiority of the white race and Protestant Christianity as legitimising factors in colonial expansion. The events of the novel show, however, the hypocrisy of their position in terms of the poverty and human suffering that imperialism causes despite their certainty in the moral rectitude of their position.

Although the novel is set in the late Victorian period, it has one eye focused on its contemporary social and political context. The novel was first published in 1992 after a decade of Thatcherism. Margaret Thatcher was a great advocate of returning to what she called Victorian values, by which she meant a belief in the work ethic, support of the traditional family unit and the need for individuals to take responsibility for their own economic and social well being. Gray, however, is interested in delving behind these commendable characteristics to show the practical injustices that such an ideology produces – an exploited working class, who are not protected by the state from avaricious capitalists, the reinforcement of inequalities in the sexes through the continuation of the patriarchal family unit, and the exportation of that system of exploitation into a colonial context. By a shift of historical perspective, Gray, who has described himself as an anarchic socialist, uses the Victorian context of *Poor Things* to challenge the aspects of Thatcherism that would advocate a return to such a system of social organization. *Poor Things*, then, is a novel that aims to challenge certain ideologies that were becoming common currency in Britain in the 1980s and early 1990s. It does this formally by highlighting the inconsistencies in all narratives that claim authority over the subjects they represent. The intricacies of the structure of the novel lends itself to the disruption of discourses that claim authority and this encourages scepticism towards the ideological and political bases on which those discourses are based. That Gray produces a novel that is postmodernist in its undermining of fixed points of reference, and yet attempts to offer a critique of Victorian values makes it somewhat of an oddity in terms of its relationship between form and content. In many ways it is represents a kind of socialist postmodernism – a form of writing that challenges grand narratives of authority, but nevertheless achieves the partial advocacy of a certain way of looking socially and politically at the contemporary world.

ZADIE SMITH, *WHITE TEETH* (2000)

White Teeth is Zadie Smith's first novel, and was published when she was just twenty-three. It includes an ambitious range of characters and narratives that represent the multicultural nature of contemporary Britain and shows how historical factors affect the ways in which people in the present relate to each other. Like *London Fields*, it is a novel interested in analyzing the Zeitgeist of contemporary Britain, but, unlike Amis, she approaches this through issues of multiculturalism, ethnic diversity and colonial legacies. At one level the novel embraces ideas of pluralism and the coming together of different cultures, ethnicities and races, but it also shows the problems for individuals caught up within a postcolonial world.

Formally, *White Teeth* differs from both *London Fields* and *Poor Things* in that its main mode is realism. Smith uses an omniscient narrator that is able to float between the consciousnesses of a series of characters thus allowing her to present the personal stories of characters with a variety of ethnic cultures and backgrounds: the three interconnected families of the Joneses, the Iqbals and the Chalfens. Archie Jones, who describes himself as from good old English stock (although his Welsh surname ironically qualifies this fixed national identity) is married to Clara Bowden, a black

Carribean/British woman who has a secret white-colonial grand-father.[27] Samad and Alsana Iqbal are originally from Bangladesh, Samad having settled in London after fighting alongside Archie in the latter stages of the Second World War. This represents a variety of ethnicities that included English, Asian and Caribbean, and the introduction of Joyce and Marcus Chalfen in the second half of the novel extends this multiethnic framework to a middle-class family that combines a white English (Joyce) and East European Jewish (Marcus) background. The novel moves through three generations identifying these characters' parents, and in the second half of the novel, their children, the twins Magid and Millat Iqbal, Irie Jones and Joshua Chalfen. This nexus of family relationships, therefore, offers a microscopic image of multicultural Britain at the end of the millennium. Smith is also keen to regard these not as combinations of discrete ethnicities but as an indication that the old categories of race are an inaccurate way of describing the ethnic diversity of con-temporary England:

> This has been the century of strangers, brown, yellow and white. This has been the century of the great immigrant experiment. It is only this late in the day that you can walk into a playground and find Isaac Leung by the fish pond, Danny Rahman in the football cage, Quang O'Rourke bouncing a bas-ketball, and Irie Jones humming a tune. Children with first and last names on a direct collision course. (p. 326)

In this way, she echoes Stuart Hall's thinking on ethnicity discussed in the Introduction. Hall suggests that the politics of race should move beyond the idea of 'black' as a useful indicator of racial difference, and like Hall, Smith's novel emphasizes that multicul-turalism should accept a mixing of ethnicity identified at the level of the individual rather than the nation. This suggests a model of race in which each individual is multicultural due to the cultural influences (and biological heritages) that are at play in contempo-rary Britain. This is distinctly and radically different from the model of multiculturalism that represents a series of monoethnic individuals who combine to produce a multicultural nation. It also moves beyond the idea of 'hybrid' identities, which again suggests a 'mix' of discrete races or ethnicities. Irie Jones, with her complex 'racial' background (and even more so her unborn child) becomes, therefore, symbolic of this new kind of ethnicity, one that the text presents as the emerging model for the contemporary nation.

The novel is set mainly in Willesden, North London, a location at once part of the old colonial centre but at the same time retaining elements of the ordinary and everyday. It is this mix of the provincial and the cosmopolitan that reflects the way in which most people live their lives in multicultural Britain, that is engaged in day-to-day experiences of the places they inhabit but with historical and cultural links with areas around the world. *White Teeth* also has a broad historical canvas which in essence covers the whole of the twentieth century (with one episode going back to the Indian Mutiny of 1857) as the narrative moves backwards and forwards across the century from 1903 and ends more or less on New Year's Eve 1999: the end of the millennium. It describes the experiences not only of a generation of immigrants who came to Britain in the 1950s and 60s but also 'second generation' immigrants – those people whose parents had moved to Britain in the 1950s, 60s and 70s, but who were born, and have been brought up wholly in Britain

Smith explores the issues of multiculturalism through a negotiation of sameness and difference. Much of its comedy lies in the recognition of the foibles of its characters and the universal human themes of growing up and crises that they experience. For example, the mid-life crises that both Archie Jones and Samad Iqbal go through in the first half of the novel are equated, which suggests universal human concerns shared across cultural and racial divisions. Alongside this recognition of sameness, however, cultural difference determines the path by which the mid-life crises are played out. For Archie, his attempted suicide at the opening of the book is precipitated by his divorce from his Italian wife of twenty-eight years, which sees him scrabbling around for possessions that results in his searching for a broken vacuum cleaner. This symbol of failed domesticity is the crisis point for Archie's decision to kill himself. He is saved by a restaurant owner and this fortuitous event leads to the opening up of his new life with Clara Bowden, a black Caribbean woman thirty years his junior. For Samad, the crisis revolves around a renewed interest in his religion and the Bangladeshi culture he has gradually abandoned during his time in Britain. For Samad, the crisis manifests itself firstly in guilt over masturbation, and eventually in an affair with the white, English art teacher, Poppy Burt-Jones. These personal stories show that, for Smith, multiculturalism is about accommodating sameness and difference and by balancing shared values, customs and meanings across a series of discrete cultural groups co-existing side-by-side in the same nation.

This play of sameness and difference is also registered in the title of the novel. Teeth are a universal human characteristic, and yet everyone's teeth are different and thus a marker of individuality. *White* teeth are a mark of sameness; Smith, however, draws attention to the way in which they have been culturally constructed to mark out racial difference. At one point in the text, Irie, Magid and Millat visit a racist old widower who informs them: 'When I was in the Congo, the only way I could identify the nigger was by the whiteness of his teeth' (p. 171). This way of distinguishing individuals by the very aspect that marks out their similarity is challenged by the text as part of a cultural construction. Teeth act as an extended metaphor in the novel and several of the chapter titles refer to them: 'Teething Trouble', 'The Root Canals of Alfred Archibald Jones and Samad Miah Iqbal', 'Molars', 'Canines: the Ripping Teeth' amongst others. Teeth are, therefore, also markers of history and genealogy. The teeth individuals are provided with connects them to their biological heritage, however, what happens to them in the journey through life is part of individual experience. This can be seen in the fate of Clara Bowden's two front teeth. Clara has inherited the prominent overbite of her mother, however, in the scooter crash she has with her first boyfriend Ryan Topps, she loses them and has them replaced with false ones. This event effectively ends her relationship with Ryan and opens up her new life with Archie, which leads her to reject her mother's religion.

Despite its serious subject matter, comedy and satire are a major element of the novel. It is a gentle social satire that tends to dwell on humanity's unavoidable foibles, hypocrisies and moral expediencies. This style serves to avoid the didacticism of political correctness, whilst maintaining an underlying serious approach to the experiences of first and second-generation immigrants to Britain. One good example is the passage that describes Samad's involvement with the Parent-Teacher Association at his sons' school (pp. 127–31).

> 'The Harvest Festival is part of the school's ongoing commitment to religious diversity, Mr Iqbal'
>
> 'I see. And are there many pagans, Mrs Owens, at Manor School?'
>
> 'Pagan – I'm afraid I don't under –'
>
> 'It is very simple. The Christian calendar has thirty-seven religious events. *Thirty-seven.* The Muslim calendar has *nine.* Only nine [. . .] My motion is very simple. If we removed all the pagan festivals from the Christian calendar, there would be an average of' – Samad paused to look at his clipboard – 'of twenty days freed up in which the children could celebrate Lailat-ul-Qadr in December, Eid-ul-Fitr in January and Eid-ul-Adha in April [. . .]'
>
> 'I'm afraid,' said Mrs Owens, doing her pleasant-but-firm smile and playing her punchline to the crowd, 'removing Christian festivals from the face of the earth is a little beyond my jurisdication [. . .]'
>
> 'But this is my whole point. This Harvest Festival is *not* a Christian festival. Where in the bible does it say, *For thou must steal foodstuffs from thy parents' cupboards and bring them into school assembly, and thou shalt force thy mother to bake a loaf of bread in the shape of a fish?* These are pagan ideals! Tell me where does it say, *Thou shalt take a box of frozen fishfingers to an aged crone who lives in Wembley?*' (pp. 129–30 – italics in the original)

The comedy of this section operates through a gentle mockery of each character: Samad's pedantic scrutiny of the school's policy on religious tolerance and equality, and the somewhat patronizing tone and mistaken logic of Mrs Owens (the headmistress of school) in her support of the school's religious traditions. This section also satirizes the over-enthusiastic attempts by officials to avoid any accusation of unfairness or racism. The narrative voice refuses to take sides in the encounter and leaves the matter open to evaluation, but at the same time alerts the reader to serious issues of race and ethnicity in the educational system. It is part of Smith's subtle control of the narrative that the later visit by Samad's sons to the pensioner as part of the Harvest Festival activities results in them being subject to racist abuse as discussed earlier (pp. 168–74).

Alongside the elements of postcolonial comedy, then, Smith recognizes the very serious contexts in which multiculturalism and postcolonial issues are played out in contemporary Britain. *White Teeth* shows how postcolonial history continues to affect people's actions in the present and the influence it still has in the formation of individual identities. This can be seen particularly in the narrative trajectory of Magid and Millat, Samad's twin sons. The two characters are clearly doubled in their appearance, but both are subject to very different cultural experiences. Magid is sent off to Bangladesh by Samad in an attempt to stop him from being contaminated by Western ideas; Millat meanwhile stays in Britain. However, an ironic cultural inversion takes place that frustrates Samad's ambitions for his sons. Magid returns from Bangladesh not, as Samad wished, reconnected with his Eastern roots, but imbued with the ideologies of nineteenth-century British imperialism indicated by his liberalism, scientific rationalism, and sensitivity to attitudes to art and culture based on Western values. This is because the education he receives has been appropriated, through the processes of colonization, by educational and ideological frameworks established by the British. In effect, Magid returns a reflected Englishman: a late product of the British colonization of the Asian sub-continent. Millat, on the other hand, is influenced first by American gangster movies and later by Islamic fundamentalism: both of which are 'foreign' to his North London location, and are responses to differing forms of colonialism. The contemporary British culture in which Millat is brought up is subject to the neo-colonialization of American culture; whilst the form of Islamic fundamentalism that begins to attract him represents a form of resistance to the increasing influence of American culture. That Millat becomes more devout is no comfort to Samad as the form of Islamic fundamentalism he engages in is barely recognizable to Samad as legitimate Muslim practice. This difference between first and second-generation immigrants is pursued in a telling passage towards the end of the novel. On a demonstration in London, Millat searches out, in Trafalgar Square – a public space devoted to Britain's colonial history – a bench where his father had written his surname in blood when he first came to Britain. The name is still there, but Millat re-reads the situation as representing colonial power as Samad's scrawled piece of furtive graffiti is nothing in comparison to the statue of the British colonial General Havelock that towers above the bench. Havelock, significantly, was the general who had ordered the death of their ancestor Mangal Pande in the Indian Mutiny. Millat sees this symbol as his father's weakness and vows to seek revenge: 'If Marcus Chalfen was going to write his name all over the world, Millat was going to write it BIGGER [. . .] "Ding, ding" said Millat out loud, tapping Havelock's foot, before turning on his heel to make his hazy way to Chandos Street. "Round two" ' (pp. 506–7).

That the legacies of colonial history are driving actions in the present is often shown to be debilitating for those individuals in the present, and often in ways that they do not recognize. The Glenard Oak School, for example, that is attended by Irie, Magid, Millat and Joshua Chalfen has its own colonial history. It was founded by an owner of a tobacco plantation in the Caribbean, who in a misguided social experiment imported several of his slaves over to North London at the end of the nineteenth century. Once the experiment failed, he abandoned them to fend for themselves in London's urban underclass. The legacies of the colonial encounter are ironically reproduced in the present:

Everyone at Glenard Oak was at work; they were Babelians of every conceivable class and colour speaking in tongues, each in their own industrious corner, their busy censor mouths sending the votive offering of tobacco smoke to the many gods above them (Brent School Report 1990: 67 different faiths, 123 different languages)

Laborare est Orare. [. . .]

And everybody, everybody smoking fags, fags, fags, working hard at the begging of them, the lighting of them and the inhaling of them, celebrating their power to bring people together across cultures and faiths, but mostly smoking them – *gis a fag, spare us a fag* – chuffing on them like little chimneys till the smoke grows so thick that those who had stoked the chimneys here back in 1886, back in the days of the workhouse, would not have felt out of place. (pp. 192–3)

This passage brings together many of the colonial contexts in a way in which the meaning of the various actions of the individuals described are unknown to them. The school motto, established with reference to Glenard, *Labore est Orare* (Work is Prayer) is ironically transformed into the work of consuming tobacco, the very product on which the colonial exploitation of the Caribbean slaves built up the capital to build the workhouse, that later became the school. Fags are, ironically, the currency on which economic exchange in the schoolyard operates. The use of religious lexis increases the irony (censor mouths, votive offering, celebration) as any actual religious feeling is transferred to the cigarettes. The link back to the Victorian context shows that very little has changed in terms of the frameworks of power and exploitation, the children represent modern versions of the workhouse children, both of which are subject to the legacies of colonialism

White Teeth, then, alongside its celebration of certain aspects of multiculturalism, shows how the entanglement of personal and colonial history can act as a negative force. The difficulty of escaping this force can be seen clearly in the encounter between Magid and Millat towards the end of the novel:

Because we often imagine that immigrants are constantly on the move [. . .] weaving their way through Happy Multicultural Land. Well, good for them. But Magid and Millat couldn't manage it. They left that neutral room as they entered it: weighed down, burdened [. . .] They seem to make no progress. The cynical might say they don't even move at all – that Magid and Millat are two of Zeno's headfuck arrows, occupying a space equal to Mangal Pande's, equal to Samad Iqbal's. The two brothers trapped in the temporal instant. [. . .] In fact, nothing moves [. . .] Because this other thing about immigrants ('fugees, émigrés, travellers): they cannot escape their history any more than you yourself can lose your shadow.' (pp. 465–6)

Here, Smith shows how a utopian multiculturalism is not applicable for every immigrant narrative. Magid and Millat are locked in interminable conflict due to the colonial histories that are weighing them down. Smith describes the twins with reference to Zeno's paradox: a classical philosophical conundrum. This paradox relates to the situation in which an arrow in flight is seen to be in motion over a period of time, and yet at any single instant of time it can be said to be motionless. This paradox is used metaphorically to represent the stand-off between Magid and Millat, both of whom appear to be moving forward individually on their own trajectories but are locked into stasis by their immovable antagonism towards each other. Multiculturalism emerges here, not as a panacea for the problems of Britain's relationship with its own colonial past, but as a displacement of the legacies of colonialism that continue to impact on individuals in the present. Smith achieves this by halting the temporal trajectory at this point – by placing all events in the immediate present. This serves to tie together in this one encounter the legacies of colonialism and the perpetual encounter between two subjects – one resisting, the other being appropriated by colonialism – both of whom are forced to communicate through a metalanguage that continues to be controlled by colonial discourse. The end of history is seen here as the inability of individuals to recognize the validity of the opposing position: any sense of progress beyond the present is thereby impossible.[28]

Magid and Millat's entrenched positions represent an impasse, but this is not the only position on multiculturalism that the text makes available. One of the ways around this impasse is in the figure of Irie's unborn child, which emerges at the end of the novel as the hope for a positive, forward-looking model of multiculturalism. Irie has slept with both Magid and Millat and which of them is the father of the child she is carrying can never be identified (p. 515). This represents a significant (although not total) evasion of the weight of the past, and symbolizes an escape from the ideological determinism of colonial genealogy: 'Irie's child can never be mapped exactly nor spoken of with any certainty. Some secrets are permanent. In a vision, Irie has seen a time. A time not far from now, when roots won't matter any more [. . .] She looks forward to it' (p. 527). A parallel can be made be made here between Irie's unborn child and the genetically engineered FutureMouse©, the product of Marcus Chalfen's genetic experiments. The genetically engineered mouse is, of course, pre-programmed in its moment of artificial creation, and its genesis and confinement in laboratory surroundings emphasizes the predetermined nature of its existence. That it is a 'Future' mouse works on two levels: the adjective suggests the enabling future possibilities of science and technology, but at the same time its future is already encoded in its creation – a predeterminism that evokes much older forms of containment and authority. However, it ultimately manages to evade its predetermined narrative by escaping from the genetic scientists that have created it. This does not mean that it can evade its genetic codes (or by extrapolation) its genealogical heritage, however, in claiming its stake for freedom it defies those who wish to contain it: 'He [Archie] watched it [FutureMouse©] dash along the table, and through the hands of those who wished to pin it down' (p. 540). The link between Irie's unborn child and the escaped mouse emphasizes the possibility of a limited freedom from the narratives that are imposed upon individuals.

SUMMARY OF KEY POINTS

- Postmodernism has been an important feature of much contemporary British fiction, both in terms of formal techniques and as a form of social and cultural critique.
- Many contemporary novelists have continued to work in a realist mode.
- In *London Fields*, Martin Amis uses several metafictional devices to question the relationship between fiction and society. He questions the role of the author and the way in which identities are formed through writing and other cultural sources.
- Alasdair Gray uses a variety of postmodern techniques in order to interrogate ideas of reliability and authority in written sources. *Poor Things* is interested in producing a critique of a series of ideologies of power including patriarchy, imperialism and capitalism.

- *White Teeth* uses a predominantly realist form in order to explore the multicultural make-up of contemporary Britain. Zadie Smith is interested in the way identities formed in the present are influenced by inherited discourses such as Empire and colonialism.

NOTES

1. For a discussion of this debate see Rubin Rabinovitz, *The Reaction Against Experiment in the English Novel 1950–1960* (New York and London: Columbia Universtiy Press, 1967); and Andrzej Gasiorek, *Post-War British Fiction: Realism and After* (London: Arnold, 1995). See also David Lodge, *The Modes of Modern Writing: Metaphor, Metonymy and the Typology of Modern Literature* (London: Edward Arnold, 1979); and Richard Bradford, *The Novel Now: Contemporary British Fiction* (Malden, MA: Blackwell, 2007).
2. David Lodge, 'The Novelist at the Crossroads', in *The Novel Today: Contemporary Writers on Modern Fiction*, ed. Malcolm Bradbury (London: Fontana/Collins, 1977), pp. 84–110.
3. Jean-François Lyotard, *The Postmodern Condition: A Report on Knowledge*, trans. Geoff Bennington and Brian Massumi (Manchester: Manchester University Press, [1979] 1984), p. xxiii.
4. For an excellent account of the history and meaning of postmodernism see Stuart Sim, *Irony and Crisis: A Critical History of Postmodern Culture* (New York: Totem, 2002).
5. Fredric Jameson, *Postmodernism, or, The Cultural Logic of Late Capitalism* (London: Verso, 1991).
6. Ian Watt, *The Rise of the Novel* (London: Hogarth Press, [1957] 1987). See also Terry Lovell, 'Capitalism and the Novel', in *Consuming Fiction* (London: Verso, 1987), pp. 19–45.
7. Roland Barthes, 'Introduction to the Structural Analysis of Language', in *A Roland Barthes Reader*, ed. Susan Sontag (London: Vintage, 1993), pp. 251–95, pp. 294–5.
8. Catherine Belsey, *Critical Practice* (London: Routledge, 1980), p. 47.

9. Martin Amis, *London Fields* (Harmondsworth: Penguin, 1989), p. 1. All subsequent references in the text are to this edition.

10. Amis had already pursued the theme of the nuclear threat in a series of short stories he published two years before *London Fields*, called *Einstein's Monsters* (London: Jonathan Cape, 1987).

11. Amis intensifies the metafictional conundrum here by having Mark Asprey introduce the work of another 'M. A.' novelist to Sam, *Crossbone Waters* by Marius Appleby. Given this vertiginous network of narrative levels, is it too far to read 'Sam' as an inversion of 'MAs'?

12. Jean Baudrillard, *Simulacra and Simulation*, trans. Sheila Faria Glaser (Ann Arbor, MI: University of Michigan Press, 1995).

13. Philip Tew, 'Martin Amis and Late-twentieth-century Working-class Masculinity: *Money* and *London Fields*', in *Martin Amis: Postmodernism and Beyond*, ed. Gavin Keulks (Basingstoke: Palgrave, 2006), pp. 71–86, p. 81.

14. Ibid., p. 84.

15. Louis Althusser, 'Ideology and Ideological State Apparatuses', in *Lenin and Philosophy and Other Essays*, trans. Ben Brewster (London: New Left Books, 1971), pp. 122–73.

16. In many ways she exemplifies what Judith Butler has described as the way in which gender is performed, although in Nicola's case the performances are exaggerated and reflected. See the discussion of Butler's theories, with respect to Angela Carter, in Chapter 3.

17. See the discussion of this debate in 'Pity the Planet: *London Fields*', in *The Fiction of Martin Amis: the Essential Criticism*, ed. Nicolas Tredell (Cambridge: Icon Books, 2000), pp. 97–125.

18. Sara Mills, 'Working With Feminism: What Can Feminist Text Analysis Do?', in *Twentieth-Century Fiction: From Text to Context*, ed. Peter Verdonk and Jean Jacques Weber (London: Routledge, 1995), pp. 206–9.

19. Stuart Hall, 'The Question of Cultural Identity', in *Modernity and Its Futures*, ed. Stuart Hall, David Held and Tony McGrew (Cambridge: Polity, 1992), pp. 274–316, p. 277.

20. Susan Brook, 'The Female Form, Sublimation, and Nicola Six', in *Martin Amis: Postmodernism and Beyond*, ed. Gavin Keulks (Basingstoke: Palgrave, 2006), pp. 87–100, p. 81.

21. Ian McEwan, 'Interview with Martin Amis', Guardian Conversations (London: ICA Video/Trilion, 1988).

22. The *Skibbereen Eagle* (spelt differently to Gray's version) was an Irish newspaper in the nineteenth century, but ceased publication in 1889.

23. Alasdair Gray, *Poor Things* (London: Bloomsbury, 2002), p. xiii. All subsequent references in the text are to this edition.

24. Henry Gray's *Anatomy of the Human Body* is a classic nineteenth century medical textbook which includes illustrations of parts of the human body similar to those presented in *Poor Things*.

25. Roland Barthes, 'The Death of the Author', in *Image, Music, Text*, ed. and trans. Stephen Heath (London: Fontana, 1977), pp. 142–8, p. 146.

26. M. M. Bakhtin, 'Discourse in the Novel', in *The Dialogic Imagination: Four Essays by M. M. Bakhtin*, ed. and trans. Carl Emerson and Michael Holquist (Austin, TX: University of Texas Press, 1981), pp. 259–422.

27. Zadie Smith, *White Teeth* (Harmondsworth: Penguin, [2000] 2001), p. 99. All subsequent references in the text are to this edition.

28. Chapter 18 in the novel alludes to Francis Fukuyama's book *The End of History and the Last Man* published after the fall of communism in a series of Eastern European states. Fukuyama's book provocatively suggests that once the Cold War was over, the dialectical opposition of communism and capitalism that had driven prevailing ideas of history over most of the period of modernity was at an end. For Fukuyama this represented the victory of liberal democracy and a global capitalism that signaled the end of history. See Francis Fukuyama, *The End of History and the Last Man* (London: Hamish Hamilton, 1992).

CHAPTER 2

Writing Contemporary Ethnicities

As discussed in the Introduction, one of the most important contexts for contemporary British fiction is postcolonialism, a term
that encompasses a range of discourses and issues that relate to the
construction of national identity, race, immigration and multiculturalism. This range of topics has provided a rich source for the contemporary British novel. One of the legacies of Empire is that the
English language and English literature were exported to many parts
of the world resulting in a generation of writers emerging in the
1950s, 60s and 70s from South-East Asia, Africa and the Caribbean
who were producing work in fiction that opened up a dialogue with
traditional forms of British fiction. Writers such as Buchi Emecheta,
V. S. Naipaul and Sam Selvon have been interested in the way their
experiences of colonialism and postcolonialism can be expressed in
fiction.[1] In addition, the processes of decolonization and immigration to Britain from these areas throughout the post-Second World
War period has produced a multicultural context for writers working
in Britain whose cultural heritage might have allegiances to a range
of locations and ethnicities. This multicultural influence has seen
the cultural enrichment of the contemporary British novel manifest
in a range of styles and subject matter.

As with all the chapter topics in this book, it was difficult to
decide which texts to include and many of the novels covered in

other chapters could easily have been included in this chapter, especially Hanif Kureishi's *The Buddha of Suburbia* (1990) and Zadie Smith's *White Teeth* (2000). The three texts finally chosen were selected because they give a reasonably broad range in terms of style, setting and ethnic background. Salman Rushdie's *Shame* (1983) is mostly set in a fictional version of Pakistan and uses postmodern narrative techniques. Both Courttia Newland's *Society Within* (1999) and Monica Ali's *Brick Lane* (2003) are more realistic in style and are both set in London. They differ, though, in the ethnic group represented in each: *Society Within* is set on a housing estate made up of mostly first and second generation immigrants from the Caribbean; *Brick Lane* focuses on the Bangladeshi community in East London.

SALMAN RUSHDIE, *SHAME* (1983)

Shame is Salman Rushdie's third published novel and continues the distinctive style he had established with *Midnight's Children* two years earlier. It is set in the fictional country of Peccavistan, an invented state that is clearly meant to relate to Pakistan in the period after decolonisation. It approaches this topic through the interrelated narratives of a series of families, some of the members of which represent the main power brokers in the political framework of the country. In this way it presents the politics of postcolonial Peccavistan (Pakistan) as an intricate family saga, one that affects the nation as a whole. It also raises questions about how cultural, national and personal identities are formed, and maintained, through particular ways of writing and speaking. In addition, it explores the idea of individuals crossing cultural boundaries encapsulated in the metaphor of translation in the sense of moving from one culture or ideology to another. It is interested, therefore, in the idea of borders between cultures, and what happens when they are crossed.

Rushdie is keen on analyzing the way in which writing and language are intricately bound up in power relationships, both in terms of postcolonial politics and the continuing influence of the colonial legacy on issues in the present. Like *London Fields* (1989) and *Poor*

Things (1992) discussed in Chapter 1, *Shame* is an example of post-modern fiction in that it plays around with the mode of representation in which fiction (and history and politics) are represented. It self-consciously alludes to the way in which fictions are produced though the deployment of a playful and idiosyncratic narrative voice. Rushdie has often been associated with magic realism, a novelistic genre established mainly by Latin American writers such as Carlos Fuentes, Alejo Carpentier and Gabriel Marcia Marquez. This form of writing often merges classic European realism with magical stories (drawn in Rushdie's case from Asian and Middle-Eastern legends) which deconstruct the notions of rationality and order normally associated with the Western Enlightenment. It is, then, a hybrid form that combines two modes of fiction that are most usually separate. In *Shame*, this formal hybridity is incorporated into the narrative style. This can be seen, for example, in the opening paragraphs:

> In the remote border town of Q., which when seen from the air resembles nothing so much as an ill-proportioned dumbbell, there once lived three lovely, and loving, sisters. Their names . . . but their real names were never used, like the best household china, which was locked away after the night of their joint tragedy in a cupboard whose location was eventually forgotten, so that the great thousand-piece service from the Gardner potteries in Tsarist Russia became a family myth in whose factuality they almost ceased to believe . . . the three sisters, I should state without further delay, bore the family name of Shakil, and were universally known (in descending order of age) as Chhunni, Munnee and Bunny.
> And one day their father died.[2] (p. 11)

This passage sets the stylistic framework for the novel. There are two separate modes of discourse here, the first of which appears to belong to the traditional fairy story, as shown in the use of phrases like 'there once lived' and 'And one day'. This can also be seen in the situation of the three sisters with unlikely sounding names, and the fact that they are orphaned. Within this fantasy framework, however, another voice intrudes, that of a more playful and worldly-wise narrator who offers factual and reflective statements about the situation of the three sisters. This other voice digresses to provide details about the 'joint tragedy' and the 'great thousand-piece service' and is of a register not normally found in traditional fairy tales. This stylistic feature of Rushdie's writing also tells us something of his approach to fiction generally. The novel, like the passage, is keen to disrupt, reflect on and question received stories that attempt to provide instructional guides to behaviour. Rushdie alludes to those kinds of stories, but he also wants to interrogate and disrupt them and thereby to encourage a questioning attitude to the ideologies on which they are based. This adoption of magical realism is well suited for Rushdie in his aim to explore the political narratives of Peccavistan (and by extension Pakistan) a country that he is keen to show has been victim to mollifying, yet false narratives that mask the political corruption and infighting of its ruling class.

This suspicion towards the value and accuracy of received stories extends to his discussion of history. As the narrator explains:

> History is natural selection. Mutant versions of the past struggle for dominance; new species of fact arise, and old saurian truths go to the wall, blindfolded and smoking last cigarettes. Only mutations of the strong survive [. . .] History loves only those who dominate her: it is a relationship of mutual enslavement. (p. 124)

In this passage, the idea of history as a faithful account of the events of the past has been replaced by the political function of history as a means to maintain prevailing power frameworks. The analogy between history and the theory of evolution shows that multiple interpretations of past events are determined not by veracity, but by power. It is the strongest accounts that survive not the most accurate, and again this relates to the novel's account of the political history of Pakistan.

The magic realist context that serves to question the status of stories extends to the characters, some of which operate as realistic figures, some with grotesque features and fantastic abilities. The first section of the novel details the early years of Omar Khyamm Shakil who shows characteristics of both the real and the fantastic.

His mother is one of the three sisters, although it is never revealed which as the sympathetic pregnancies of two of the sisters means that the actual parentage of Omar remains a secret. Again this unlikely situation is the stuff of fantasy, even though Omar develops into an adult who takes part in a realistic social setting as first a doctor and then son-in-law to General Raza Hyder. Omar's father similarly remains unknown, but is one of the British sahibs who visit the palace on the one night that its gates are open to the colonizers. Symbolically, Omar represents a physical consequence of the colonial encounter, the product of the British 'invasion' of an Eastern citadel. His hybrid identity is a symbolic legacy of imperial involvement in South East Asia, and the fact that he turns out to be weak, slothful and corrupt is a comment on the impact of colonialism in the region.

This hybrid identity is also registered in Omar's name, which, of course, alludes to Omar Khayyam, the author of the *Rubaiyat*, an Eastern work that was translated by British writer Edward Fitzgerald in the nineteenth century and became a bestseller in Britain.[3] An Eastern genre – the exotic story – was thereby reconfigured and marketed for a Western audience. Fitzgerald's translation of Omar Khayyam is an example of Edward Said's definition of orientalism (as discussed in the Introduction to this book) in that it produces a discourse that serves to represent the East as romantic and exotic, but in doing so, implies a positional superiority for Western rationalism and science.[4] Part of the appeal of *Shame* is that it encourages an inversion of this kind of orientalism in its playing around with the point of observation, and the way things are viewed is bound up with the interplay of reality and fantasy discussed earlier. Omar, for example, sees the world inverted: 'Hell above, Paradise below; I have lingered on this account of Omar Khayyam's original, unstable wilderness to underline the propositions that he grew up between twin eternities, whose conventional order was, in his experience, precisely inverted' (p. 23). The 'twin eternities' relate to a variety of oppositions the novel serves to invert: the orient and the occident, the colonizer and the colonized, reality and fiction, realism and fantasy, shame and shamelessness. Omar is an outsider; he stands on the borders of these oppositions and is thus able to see both of them. Like the narrator, he has something of the translated man about him and in certain passages this presents the colonial encounter as a negative experience. The narrator also suggests, however, that a positive result can be gained from the interaction of two cultures: 'It is generally believed that something is always lost in translation; I cling to the notion – and use in evidence the success of Fitzgerald-Khayyam – that something can also be gained' (p. 29). This relates to the benefit of being able to move between cultures, to fly beyond the boundaries of the monolithic identities that serve to maintain established power relationships and ways of viewing the world.

The other main figure in the novel who combines realistic and fantastic characteristics is Sufiya Zinobia, the daughter of General Raza Hyder and Bilquis, and eventually Omar's wife. In what appears to be a second beginning to the book at the start of Part II, the narrator explains that: 'This is a novel about Sufiya Zinobia [. . .] Or perhaps it would be more accurate, if also more opaque to say that Sufiya Zinobia is about this novel' (p. 59). This reversal of 'abouts' again signals that the way to read the novel demands a certain amount of changing of perspective. That the novel is about Sufiya is, in fact, inaccurate in that not many of its pages deal with the experiences and events surrounding this grotesque, magic realist character. Nevertheless, what she stands for is central to all the events of the novel and connects with the title. Sufiya embodies shame: the shame of individuals, the debilitating shame imposed by families, and the shame of a nation's political corruptions. The complexity of shame as a concept is identified in the word itself:

> This word: shame. No, I must write it in its original form, not in this peculiar language tainted by wrong concepts and the accumulated detritus of its owners' unrepented past, this Angrezi in which I am forced to write, and so for ever alter what is written.
> *Sharam*, that's the word. For which this paltry 'shame' is a wholly inadequate translation [. . .] A short word, but one containing encyclopaedias of nuance [. . .] embarrassment, discomfiture, modesty, shyness, the sense of having an ordained place in the world, and other dialects of emotion for

which the English has no counterparts [. . .] What's the opposite of shame? What's left when *sharam* is subtracted? That's obvious: shamelessness. (pp. 38–9)

In this passage, Rushdie suggests the legacies of colonialism in the imposition of the language in which his narrator is 'forced to write', although his translation of the term into 'Angrezi' simultaneously offers resistance to that imposition. It also shows the way in which a language, when imposed on a colonized country, fails to understand the nuances of that culture. It is ironic, of course, that the English are shown to have only one word for 'shame', suggesting that it is not an emotion of which it has much experience (but perhaps should). *Sharam*, on the other hand, has so many intricate nuances that it appears to overly inhibit Eastern cultures. Both shame and its opposite are seen in negative terms here, both the Eastern focus on shame as a debilitating ideology of restriction and repression, and Western shamelessness over colonial oppression, which reveals a resistance to accept responsibility for legacies of Empire. If the Western idea of shamelessness is associated with Omar, then the consequences of repressing shame is explored in the figure of Sufiya. She represents the return of the repressed in an alternative and violent form shown in her magical transformation into an inhuman force. She is presented as a symbol of a monstrousness that cannot be contained: 'Overandover in her empty room, she feels something coming, roaring, feels it take her, the thing, the flood or perhaps the thing in the flood, the Beast bursting forth to wreak its havoc on the world [. . .] The monster rises from the bed, shame's avatar' (p. 219).

Sufiya, then, is transformed into an embodiment of shame, and her presence in this symbolic form stalks the pages of the novel. The shame she represents is caused by both the colonial legacy and the subsequent history of Peccavistan after independence. Peccavistan, Rushdie's invented country, is alluded to as a representation of Pakistan but is 'at a slight angle to reality': 'The country in this story is not Pakistan, or not quite. There are two countries, real and fictional, occupying the same space, or almost the same space' (p. 29). The national setting parallels the blurring of reality and fantasy that works throughout the novel. Peccavistan is a fiction, but so too, the novel suggests, is Pakistan, itself based on an artificial construction invented in the West:

> It is well known that the term 'Pakistan', an acronym, was originally thought up in England by a group of Muslim intellectuals. P for the Punjabis, A for the Afghans, K for the Kashmiris, S for Sind and the 'tan', they say, for Baluchistan [. . .] So it was a word born in exile which then went East, was borne-across or trans-lated, and imposed itself on history; a returning migrant, settling down on partitioned land, forming a palimpsest on the past. (p. 87)

The colonial legacy continues in the irresponsible context in which the nation of Pakistan was moulded before and during independence, and the novel refers to the fact that Pakistan was an artificially constructed nation imposed on an area without regard for its broader cultural and historical divisions. Pakistan, thereby, is a kind of political and cartographical palimpsest – one narrative laid over another. The problems arise in the fact that with a palimpsest, despite its attempt to 'obscure what lies beneath [. . .] the obscured world forces its way back through what-has-been-imposed' (p. 87).[5] Rushdie's Peccavistan is similarly invented from a colonial context:

> There's an apocryphal story that Napier, after a successful campaign in what is now the south of Pakistan, sent back to England the guilty, one-word message, 'Peccavi'. *I have Sind.* I'm tempted to name my looking-glass Pakistan in honour of this bilingual (and fictional, because never really uttered) pun. Let it be *Peccavistan*. (p. 88)

The fictional Peccavistan is produced by a colonial pun in the translation of two languages, and yet the analogy to the real history of Pakistan is made clear. According to Rushdie, Pakistan is an invented nation, but one that was '*insufficiently imagined*' (p. 87), suggesting that the original demarcation of territory in the creation of the area now known as Pakistan did not pay enough attention to the long historical and social contexts of the area.

The relationship Rushdie establishes between the fictional and real countries enables a political critique of Pakistan in the post-independence period, but one that is angled through the commentary on Peccavistan. This allows the power of his metaphors to operate at an aesthetic level, whilst adding to the satirical power of the novel. The political contest between Iskander Harappa and Raza Hyder in the novel is analogous to the real life conflict between Ali Bhutto, president of Pakistan from 1972 until 1977, and General Zia Ul-Haq, whose military led coup ousted Bhutto. The 'virgin Ironpants', Arjumand Harappa, is thus a fictional representation of Benazir Bhutto, the ousted president's daughter (and later president of Pakistan after Zia Ul-Haq's removal). That this period of Pakistani political history is also part of a family feud lends itself to a fictional context, and thus the power of Rushdie's decision to interweave and overlay the real and fictional to the extent that the boundaries between the two are difficult to discern.

The infighting of this enclosed political world is one of the series of containments that the narrator, for one, is able to escape. The narrator occupies a space in the novel that is liminal. He exists, like Omar Khayyam, 'between twin eternities' (p. 23), in what Homi Bhabha might refer to as the 'third space', a location that signals a hybrid combination of two or more cultural identities.[6] This advantageous position allows the narrator to escape the ties that bind most of the characters in the novel to one particular culture, just as the magic realist context of the novel allows him to move freely between realism and fantasy. The migrant, both in cultural and physical terms, is presented as a positive figure and the narrator stresses the freedom that occupying this third space brings: 'We have performed the act of which all men dream, the thing for which they envy the birds; that is to say we have flown' (p. 85). This inverts the typically negative images associated with the migrant (or immigrant). As the narrator goes on to say:

We know the force of gravity, but not its origins; and to explain why we become attached to our birthplaces we pretend that we are trees and speak of roots. Look under your feet. You will not find gnarled roots sprouting through the soles. Roots, I sometimes think, are a conservative myth, designed to keep us in our places. (p. 86)

Roots are a powerful metaphor when speaking of cultural heritage and identity, but here, the discourse around belonging and place is inverted. Roots are not something that connect you to a place, but contain and restrict movement. That Rushdie connects this to a 'conservative' ideology shows the way in which strict demarcations of cultural identity, and of people staying where they 'belong', have been used politically to maintain order and prevailing power relationships.

The idea of flight, however, is not presented as wholly positive. Something is always lost in the move between cultures despite the benefits that the ability of flying between them suggests:

All migrants leave their pasts behind, although some try to pack it into bundles and boxes – but on the journey something seeps out of the treasured mementoes and old photographs, until even their owners fail to recognize them, because it is the fate of all migrants to be stripped of history, to stand naked amidst the scorn of strangers upon whom they see the rich clothing, the brocades of continuity and the eyebrows of belonging. (pp. 63–4)

The free but exiled position of the narrator, therefore, contains an ambivalence towards the process of migrating between cultures, although on the whole, the novel appears to come down on the side of the liberated migrant. The migrant is able to escape the cycle of shame that, according to the novel, is the dominating feature of Pakistani politics in the post-Second World War period, a situation for which the colonial legacy of the British Empire is partly held accountable. The novel's position on some of these ideas, like its narrator, is ambivalent. The novel is clearly a satire on postcolonial politics, but it is a kind of postmodern satire, where there is a refusal to suggest an alternative situation that would act as a positive position. The satire is cynical without necessarily offering an alternative worldview. Nevertheless, Rushdie's control of metaphor and narrative technique make it a powerful example of the combination of a postcolonial subject matter in a postmodern form.

COURTTIA NEWLAND, *SOCIETY WITHIN* (1999)

Courttia Newland's second novel, *Society Within*, is similar to *Shame* in its postcolonial context, but very different in form and location. The predominant literary mode adopted by Newland is realism presented in a series of interconnecting stories that reveal the experiences, attitudes and ambitions of a series of individuals, both black and white, on a housing estate in West London. It differs from *Shame* (and is similar to *White Teeth* and *Brick Lane*) in that it is the old colonial centre that is the location for the exploration of the interactions of a multicultural community that carries with it legacies of Britain's colonial history.

Each of the book's interlinked short stories focuses on one of the inhabitants of the Greenside Estate. Four of the stories, including the first and the last are focalized through Elisha, a nineteen-year-old woman who has just moved to Greenside from the neighbouring estate of Winton. Elisha provides a frame for describing the community from the outside, although she is very quickly accepted into her new community. Time moves forward through the novel with a series of overlapping incidents and flashbacks that give a background to the setting and the characters. The device of collecting stories from people in the same area allows Newland to develop the sense of a full community made up of individual voices. Each of the characters has their own concerns, but the accumulation of stories suggests the communal sense of shared experiences: some harrowing, some life-embracing. Together, the individual narratives build to show a discrete subcultural community that has its own lifestyles, concerns and ethical and moral frameworks. There is very little direct discussion of the impact of colonial history on the individuals presented in the novel, but this context lies behind the situation of the re-colonized space within the heart of the old colonial centre of London. The impact of colonialism in the present in Newland's writing shows the way in which a group of individuals see themselves as culturally separate from, and yet intricately bound up with the dominant codes of behaviour and culture of the nation in which they find themselves.

The theorists Gilles Deleuze and Félix Guattari have discussed the role of what they call a 'minor literature' in the articulation of a marginalized culture within a nation, and their theories fit well with one of Newland's aims in *Society Within*. Deleuze and Guattari introduce the concept of deterritorialization as a way of challenging dominant cultural discourses and opening up a space to express the concerns and experiences of a marginalized community. In referring to the writing of Franz Kafka, a Jewish writer working in Czechoslovakia, they identify that one feature of a minor literature is that:

> everything takes on a collective value [. . .] what each other says individually already constitutes a common action, and what he or she says or does is necessarily political [. . .] literature finds itself positively charged with the role and function of collective, and even revolutionary, enunciation. It is literature that produces an active solidarity in spite of skepticism; and if the writer is in the margins or completely outside of his fragile community, this situation allows the writer all the more the possibility to express another possible community and to forge the means for another consciousness and another sensibility.[7]

In *Society Within*, the individual voices build to produce a 'collective enunciation' of cultural difference. As a character says at one point in the novel: 'Dis come like society within society, y'get me. A world inside another world, operatin' with its own rules and regulations, its own terms and understandin's' (pp. 131–2).[8] These sentiments – a society within – echo the way in which Newland presents the subcultural context of the characters in the novel.

The subcultural nature of the society presented in the book is made up of a series of factors including the economic situation and exchanges between those within the community; cultural signifiers such as music, fashion, literature and other cultural practices such as food and drugs; and the social spaces in which people encounter each other: some public, some private. In terms of economics, most of the characters are either unemployed or have low paid jobs. Elisha, at the beginning of the novel, tries, unsuccessfully at first, to get a job in Smallie's, the local West Indian fish and chip shop. One of Elisha's new friends, Valerie, 'despite her qualifications, intelligence and stunning good looks, the only work she seemed able to find was in retail – usually in places like Argos, Sainsbury's or Tesco' (p. 95). Although it is not explicitly stated, the novel intimates that the employment frameworks in Britain serve to disadvantage black and Asian teenagers. Despite the lack of employment opportunities, however, most of the characters harbour ambitions for alternative careers and some achieve them. Valerie's narrative ends with her about to enrol on a course in desktop publishing, which offers an outlet for her artistic talents.

As a consequence of the lack of fulfilling employment an alternative economics of semi-criminal behaviour is described in the novel, which is implied to be a reaction to the lack of opportunities for legitimate advancement. Most of this revolves around an established drug culture. Far from moralizing about the use of drugs, however, the novel is keen to show it as an alternative system of cultural practice that has its own ethical framework. Smoking cannabis, for example, is accepted by most of the characters in the book and the operation of dealing in 'ash' is seen as a viable, and on the whole accepted way to earn a living. Orin, for example, in the story 'The Yout' Man and the Ki' is fortunate to find a kilo of marijuana resin which he then, after an encounter with the original white owners of the stuff, sells on: 'Hashish. Cannabis. Ash. Rocky. Pox. Call it what you like, he'd found it, and he was already making plans as to how this little package could make him a small fortune' (p. 27). In 'A Little Bump and Grind' Orin reappears, and to cement relations between him and Little Stacey, the son of the man Orin's mother is now seeing, he gives him 'a small block of ash' to sell (p. 183). This represents younger Stacey being accepted into the older Orin's circle. There is, of course, an issue here in the way in which West Indian culture is being represented, and although Newland is clearly attempting to celebrate this culture, there is the danger of stereotyping black individuals on inner city estates as inevitably involved in drugs. He tries to avoid this by showing the way in which recreational cannabis use is regarded as a harmless cultural pastime rather than a criminal activity, suggesting the fault lies with current drug legislation. The apology for illegal drug use does not extend to harder drugs such as crack cocaine. The characters who indulge in this darker subculture within the community, referred to as 'Cats', are presented in a negative light. As Elisha says of them: '*Cats*. Elisha mentally kissed her teeth. Young men like these turned some girls on, but she'd had enough dealings with them on Winton to know she didn't need any more' (p. 91). In the harrowing chapter, 'Valerie's Stolen Soul', for example, the perpetrators of Valerie's rape are the crackheads Ray Miles and Johnny Winsome who are presented as thoroughly nasty characters. Within this stratification of ethical response to the use of different kinds of drug is the chapter 'The Art of Long Games with Short Sharp Knives' which details Arthur Lyne (Art) weaning himself from addiction to crack and is one of the empowering narratives the book provides, although to succeed, Art has to leave his community and at the end is about to fly off to a new life in America.

One of the main ways in which the subcultural status of the group is presented in the novel is through the use of language. Although the main narrative voice in all the stories uses predominantly Standard English, the dialogue given to the characters marks itself as different. This is partly due to the West Indian heritage of most of the characters, and partly to do with the youth culture to which most of them belong. It is useful here to return to a theoretical perspective that was discussed in Chapter 1 with respect to Alasdair Gray's *Poor Things*: that of Mikhail Bakhtin's ideas on the socio-economic place of language in fiction.[9] Bakhtin identifies that a nation's language in any age has two mutually antagonistic forces working on it. One of these is what he calls the 'centripetal' forces of a nation's official language, which attempts to enforce a unified and authorized way of speaking, for example, 'Received Pronunciation' or 'BBC English'. At the same time, though, an oppositional or 'centrifugal' force serves to challenge that official way of speaking with 'unlicensed' language. This is the language of the street, and particularly that used by subcultural groups within, but at the same time offset from, the dominant culture. The use of 'unlicensed language' can be seen clearly in the way Newland records the speech patterns of his characters.

Virtually all of the dialogue is written in some form of deviation
from Standard English. To take an example from 'The Yout Man
and the Ki': 'Innit. Lissen anyway – we got a change ah plans star.
Maverick wants dat ki now, he's got the wong together' (p. 45).
Here, words such as 'lissen' for listen, and 'ah' for our, are changed
to represent the dialect of the speaker, whilst other words such as
'ki' for kilogram (of cannabis resin) and 'wong' for money are col-
loquial abbreviations or substitutions. The language used on the
street is laced with coded ways of speaking that is understandable
within the subcultural group, but marks out its difference from
'official' ways of speaking. The drug culture referred to earlier, also
carries several examples of an alternative vocabulary. The illegality
of the drugs that some of the character deal in necessitates the
development of a coded language in an attempt to keep such illicit
practices secret from the authorities. The novel uses this coded
vocabulary generously throughout the book assuming knowledge of
most of the words with the readership.

Music is also an area that helps to define subcultural identity in
the novel. An important theorist on the role of music in the construction of subcultures in society is Dick Hebdige. His book,
Subcultures: The Meaning of Style first came out in 1979 and
focussed especially on the importance of music and fashion as a
semiotic indicator of subcultural identity. Hebdige was particularly
interested in the semiotic function of fashion in punk identity, but
he also provided a broad historical account of the different kinds of
subcultures that had developed around musical styles from the
1950s onwards in Britain. For Hebdige, a subculture serves to self-
consciously project itself as an alternative to dominant culture, and
it represents, 'a visible construction, a loaded choice. It directs
attention to itself; it gives itself to be read'.[10] This function of music
and fashion can be seen quite clearly in *Society Within*. There are
numerous references to R 'n' B and Hip Hop as the main forms of
music the characters listen to, and there are several references to
specific songs and artists. The subcultural music styles and fashions
contribute to the sense in which the youth of this community stands
out as a society 'within' mainstream society. Music serves to bind
the community together, but also has specific emotional effects for
individual characters. Valerie, for example, feels the soothing effects

of listening to Kelly Price, which helps her to escape, momentarily, from her traumatic memories (pp. 98–9); while Sissy likes to 'make out' while listening to Roy Ayres' 'Searching' (p. 165). The fact that Elisha's new R 'n' B tape has been stood on by her sister Tawanda at the beginning of the novel is one of the casualties of her moving house, and suggests the emotional (and economical) weight she attaches to music (pp. 2–3).[11]

In this context, the setting up of the pirate radio station in 'Midnight on Greenside' is more than just an entrepreneurial project undertaken by the two main characters in this story, Nathan and Garvey. It represents an alternative subcultural space that helps to gel the community. It is significant that at the beginning of this story Nathan walks through the park and passes the demolished Youth Club (that formed the subject of a previous story): 'Nathan shook his head but kept moving; there was no time to dwell on ghosts of the past, when the future held so much in store' (p. 253). 'Midnight FM', the radio station Nathan and Garvey form replaces the Youth Club as an alternative location for binding together the youth of the area. The fact that the station is pirate underlines the idea of a do-it-yourself cultural space (rather than the government funded Youth Club) suggesting that the community is empowering itself. The underground nature of the station also parallels the use of underground language in the novel as the unlicensed radio station serves to mark out a deterritorialized cultural space.

Location also plays a vital role in the expression of subcultural identity, and the sense of belonging to a particular estate comes out strongly in the novel. Elisha, for example, although only having moved from a neighbouring area, has a clear sense of trepidation when she first moves to Greenside: 'Zipping up her puffer jacket, she shot quick glances left and right, checking out her surroundings while attempting to look as much like a local girl as possible [Her best friend Sheri . . .] had seemed to know every spooky story Greenside had to offer' (p. 7). Here, an element of danger is associated with walking around the estate, especially if you are not one of the known faces of that community. The estate represents the closed environment that marks out the physical territory of the society within. Visibility is crucial to this understanding of belonging, and the novel balances the sense of the public environment with the closed private spaces of the individual houses and apartments. The incident in which Orin and his young friends expel the white drug dealers from the estate by bombarding them with stones is an example of the public spectacle of a community looking after its own by warding off potentially dangerous outsiders. The park is also one of these public spaces and where many of the drug deals take place (p. 23). The open areas of the estate are also the meeting ground for sexual flirtation and the beginning of relationships amongst some of the teenagers. Dangerous locations are not only related to public spaces and one chilling example is the room in the crack den occupied by Spider, one of the few white characters in the book. The room has already gained a reputation and it is where Valerie's rape takes place. 'Valerie's Stolen Soul' describes her traumatic experience but is in part a narrative of revenge, empowerment and ultimately closure. Significantly, Val's revenge also takes place in one of the estate's underground private spaces, Ray's hideout. Newland's handling of these cultural geographies is one of the strengths of the book and shows the intimate relationship between location and cultural identity signalled by the socio-geographical context of the title of the book.

One of the other significant spaces on the estate is the Youth Club, but tellingly this is referred to in the past tense as it is revealed in 'The Club' that it is already in the process of being demolished because the council have judged it to be no longer viable. Trisha, the only main white character in the novel to whose internal thoughts we are given access, emphasizes the political context of this short-sightedness with respect to the social problems on the estate. Her commitment to the youth of the area is undercut by the bureaucratic decision to close the club, and the anger she feels is fully justified by the sympathetic narrative. Although *Society Within* is not a novel with an overt political agenda, situations such as the fate of the Youth Club serve to suggest a political commentary on the lack of public money and commitment to cater for the youth population on inner-city estates such as the one presented in the novel. It is not difficult to see that the lack of alternative pursuits for the youth is bound up with the alternative entertainments found in drug culture and petty crime. In addition, it is apparent that the youth worker, Lacey, who because he is no longer employed at the

Youth Club, gets involved in the attempt to rob the crackhouse run by Spider, resulting in the death of Lacey's brother Richard.

Newland is also keen to stress the importance of writing itself. The novel is certainly not self-reflexive in the way that some of the other novels discussed in this book are, but it does attempt to create a literary context for the stories we are presented with. In 'Bump and Grind', Sissy gives Little Stacey a novel by the Afro-American writer Chester Himes.[12] She recognizes that Himes's subject matter, detective fiction that engages with underground and criminal culture that is critical of the black experience in New York City, along with an expression of masculinity, is a form of writing that will appeal to Little Stacey and counters his initial reaction that 'I don't really read books' (p. 144). Another novel, *Iced* by Ray Shell, is referred to in 'The Art of Long Games with Short Sharp Knives', and mirrors the subject matter of the debilitating effects of hard drugs.[13] Newland, in referring to these novels, is showing the effects of fiction on the actions of characters but is also attempting to place his novel within an alternative canon of black writing; one that it is suggested has more affinities with African-American writing than it does with the traditional British canon, despite the national context in which Newland sets his fiction. One main difference, however, between Newland and Himes and Shell is the emphasis the former places on female experience and how far he is critical of the way in which certain cultures of masculinity work to harm not only the women who are victims of it, such as Valerie, but also the men themselves.

The role of writing for the characters is also significant in a couple of the stories. In 'The Art of Long Games with Short Sharp Knives' Art's setting down in writing his emotional response to using drugs is shown to be therapeutic and helps in his difficult struggle to kick the habit. In 'Rejection', Michael, a struggling writer, has already had a number of his stories rejected by publishers. The stories he has written are similar to the kind presented in *Society Within*. After one such rejection letter, Michael considers giving up his aspirations to become a writer and to turn to crime as a more immediate way out of his difficult economic situation. However, after witnessing a gun battle from his high-rise window (a situation in which he was nearly involved) he returns to his computer:

Lynette led Michael to his computer table and m
down [. . .] 'Now do you see?' she told him [. . .] 1
gazing at the monitor for a long time, finally noddir
and starting to type. Lynette watched him for ࣛ ᴍoment
longer – then slowly headed for the front door to greet the
police. (p. 251)

Michael's role emerges in this story as a duty to record the marginalized experiences he witnesses on the estate. The placing of this
story is significant in the structure of the novel. It comes before the
longest, penultimate chapter which serves to bring together many
of the characters encountered in the rest of the book. (The final
chapter is a short concluding piece that rounds off Elisha's framing
narrative.) The placing of Michael's story acts, then, as an indication of what the rest of the novel contains – an expression of
authentic working-class, black experience in contemporary Britian.

To record the experiences of a marginalized minority culture is
also one of the aims behind Monica Ali's *Brick Lane*, a novel like
Society Within, that is also set in contemporary London, but in Ali's
case dealing with a different ethnic community.

MONICA ALI, *BRICK LANE* (2003)

When Monica Ali published *Brick Lane* in 2003, it came under
a certain amount of hostile criticism from members of the
Bangladeshi community living in the area in which it is set. Brick
Lane is the main thoroughfare in an area of East London that has
become famous for its South-East Asian (and particularly Sylheti)
community.[14] A group called the The Greater Sylhet Welfare and
Development Council charged Ali with misrepresenting that
community in her novel claiming that, 'most of the content of this
book [. . .] is a despicable insult to Bangladeshis at home and
abroad'.[15] In response to these objections a Labour Councillor commented, 'I am certainly aware of the public concern about Brick
Lane the book among people who actually live in Brick Lane'.[16]
This last comment in particular reveals something of the fraught
relationship between fiction and reality, and it is the tricky issue of

representation in fiction that is one of the most interesting aspects of Ali's debut novel.[17] In one sense, Ali is attempting to represent the experiences, through her main character Nazneen, of a group of Bangladeshi women that have rarely before been represented in British fiction. The criticism she received, however, addressed the question of what right and insider knowledge Ali, as an Oxford-educated woman brought up mostly in the north of England, has to speak for this under-represented minority.[18] This question, of course, is one that is pertinent to fiction generally, especially fiction that has an element of sociological concern. If writers were not allowed to use their imaginations to empathize with characters from a different class, gender or cultural background, then novels would be limited to a series of semi-autobiographical, first-person narratives. Once a novel is published, however, the reading public has the right to challenge the way in which that fiction might impact on the cultural reception of the communities it represents.

A theoretical context that is pertinent here is that of the literary theorist Gayatri Spivak who claims that the lack of representation of marginalized groups serves to maintain their powerlessness in the political arena. Spivak puts these ideas forward in her influential essay, 'Can the Subaltern Speak?' (1988). Subaltern, as Spivak uses it, is a term for anyone who is subordinate in rank, status or importance and refers to any member of a group that because of their class, gender, race or cultural background (or a combination of these) has little access to the mechanisms of representation and power within any given society. She discusses the difficulties for those on the margins to articulate their feelings, experiences and grievances in a public space, because the vehicles of public discourse such as the media, literature and politics necessitate a certain level of status and control over language to allow their voices to be heard. As she writes: 'On the other side of the international division of labor from socialized capital, inside *and* outside the circuit of the epistemic violence of imperialist law and education supplementing an earlier economic text, *can the subaltern speak?*'.[19] Spivak, here, refers to the 'epistemic violence' of imperialism and education by which she means the way in which language and discourse are used ideologically to maintain power and control over subjected peoples both within the colonized country through education and onto colonized subjects through legislation. This control over the ability to voice an opposition to power is what Spivak means when she poses her question on the possibility of the marginalized finding a public voice. Within this subaltern position, Spivak also identifies several categories of marginalization such as class and gender leading her to the conclusion that women from marginalized cultures are doubly subjugated: 'If, in the context of colonial production, the subaltern has no history and cannot speak, the subaltern as female is even more deeply in shadow' (p. 28).

One of the aims of Monica Ali's novel is to provide a textual space in which the subaltern can speak. If marginalized subjects find it difficult to articulate their grievances, then there needs to be an alternative form and medium through which that voice might be heard. Fiction is one good place to produce this, although it has to be remembered that fiction, like any discourse, is subject to the power structures in place at any one moment. Fiction, despite this caveat, can produce a representative voice by adopting the marginalized position of the subaltern. This is what Ali attempts in the character of Nazneen in *Brick Lane*. Ali, therefore, is speaking *for*, or *on behalf of* a particular group – working-class, Bangladeshi women settled in Britain – and this entails a certain amount of ventriloquism and artifice.

Like *Society Within*, the dominant mode of *Brick Lane* is realism. There is a third-person narrator, who describes the characters' emotions and the events in which they are involved in a fairly unobtrusive way. There is no complicated framework of narrative levels, or self-reflexive concern about the position of authors and narrators. The narrator's job in the novel is to describe the events and characters without drawing attention to itself. There is a broadly linear narrative in terms of plot, although there is some jumping around of the temporal relationship between Nazneen and Hasina's stories, and a significant gap in Nazneen's narrative of about sixteen years after her son's death. On the whole, though, the chronology moves forward based on a realist framework of cause and effect.

The realist mode is also adopted in the use of language in the novel. The main narrator's voice uses a Standard English that does not foreground itself stylistically and language is used unselfconsciously to express Nazneen's experiences. There are, however, issues related to the use of language in a postcolonial context in the decision to articulate Hasina's letters in a non-standard, grammatically incorrect language. This seems primarily to emphasize her cultural as well as geographic distance from the main setting for the text, but also to show her emotionally charged narrative and her desire to articulate feelings without caring too much about how accurate is her writing style. The use of non-Standard English represents this desire to convey her experiences quickly and it is presumed that the letters are in a grammatically incorrect Bengali, although Ali, because of her desire not to foreground issues of language, does not refer to issues of translation as, for example, Rushdie does in *Shame*. Although the narration could be described as omniscient, in that it has the power to enter the minds of characters, this, as often is the case when used in describing third-person narrative, is a misleading term. The narrator might have the power to provide access to the private thoughts of all the characters, but in practice, focalization is limited to Nazneen, and most of the other characters' inner thoughts are filtered through her interpretation of them. On the whole, then, the narration emphasizes Nazneen's perspective on events, sometimes treating her with an ironic distance, but always with an empathetic approach.

Ali chooses to work in a realist tradition, then, despite dealing with characters that come from a culture where, on the whole, classic realism is a foreign form. Spivak's theories are useful here: if Ali's aim is to allow a textual space for the articulation of a marginalized voice, then the mode of communication chosen needs to be one that is accessible to a mainstream audience. *Brick Lane*, then, adopts the conventions of a traditional Western form because her novel is intended, primarily, for a white, middle-class readership. Ali has decided to overlook the political issues involved in the mechanics of representation because politically, she wants to encourage the dominant readership to think about issues related to marginalized cultures. This is a problematic move in the context of postcolonialism, as Alistair Cormack has pointed out.[20] If Ali is to use a narrative mode that corresponds with the novelistic traditions of a colonizing nation, then there is the threat that any radical expression of postcolonial difference might be compromised. As Cormack argues: 'Realism may not be synonymous with cultural conservatism, but it does seem to bar a more radical conception of subjectivity – a conception that is crucial for post-colonial critiques of epistemology'.[21]

To emphasize Nazneen's cultural distance from this dominant readership, Ali establishes a narrative relationship with her main character that mixes ironic distance with defamiliarization. As referred to in the Introduction, defamiliarization is a narrative technique identified in literary texts by the Russian school of formalist criticism, and in particular by Viktor Shklovsky. In an essay called, 'Art as Technique' (1917), Shklovsky defines this technique in the following terms:

> The purpose of art is to impart the sensation of things as they are perceived and not as they are known. The technique of art is to make objects 'unfamiliar', to make forms difficult, to increase the difficulty and length of perception because the process of perception is an aesthetic end in itself and must be prolonged.[22]

The technique of making the everyday appear unfamiliar is one that Ali often uses in *Brick Lane* in order to convey Nazneen's sense of alienation within her new environment. Consider, for example, the following passage, where she decides, in response to a particularly worrying letter she has received from her sister, to lose herself in the City:

> She looked up at a building as she passed. It was constructed almost entirely of glass, with a few thin rivets of steel holding it together. The entrance was like a glass fan, rotating slowly, sucking people in, wafting others out. Inside, on a raised dais, a woman behind a glass desk crossed and uncrossed her thin legs [. . .] The building was without end. Above, somewhere, it crushed the clouds. The next building and the one opposite were white stone palaces. There were steps up to the entrances and colonnades across the street. Men in dark suits trotted briskly up and down the steps in pairs or in threes. They barked to each other and nodded sombrely [. . .] Every person who brushed past her on the pavement, every back she saw,

was on a private, urgent mission to execute a precise and demanding plan [. . .] Nazneen, hobbling and halting, began to be aware of herself. Without a coat, without a suit, without a white face, without a destination.[23]

The location for this passage is Bishopsgate in the financial district of London, very close geographically to Brick Lane in East London, but culturally very different. The juxtaposition of these two areas provides a microcosmic view of contemporary globalized economies as rich and poor neighbourhoods are shown in close proximity. Defamiliarization is used well here in the description of the immense office blocks that make up the newer buildings in Bishopsgate: they appear to Nazneen as buildings drawn from fantasy, for example, the building of glass with its 'glass fan' entrance, and the 'white stone palaces'. Most of these buildings would be reasonably familiar to people brought up in Britain. However, the passage serves to show how alien they appear to Nazneen, who has been raised in a very different culture. The technique of defamiliarization, therefore, is useful here for describing the experience of the newly arrived immigrant. Ali, through Nazneen's perception, encourages the reader to look at Western capitalist culture afresh. The behaviour of the people in these locations is described in terms that separate them from Nazneen, in terms of clothing, racial characteristics, the way they communicate with each other and gender. Her marginalized position is made clear at the end of the passage where her difference marks her out as separate from this strange environment that exists less than a mile from where she lives in the run-down area of Tower Hamlets.

This passage emphasizes Nazneen's feelings of alienation and powerlessness, however, the novel as a whole follows her gradual empowerment as she begins to come to terms with the alien environment in which she is placed at the beginning of the novel. This empowerment is set against various cultural discourses that initially serve to contain her. One of these is the belief in fate that she inherits from her mother: 'As Nazneen grew she heard many times this story of How You Were Left To Your Fate [. . .] fighting against one's Fate can weaken the blood. Sometimes, it can be fatal' (p. 15). This deterministic view of the world stresses that

Nazneen's future is already mapped out, restricting her power to change her situation, and it is this belief in fate that forces her to accept the arranged marriage with Chanu resulting in her being bundled off from her loving home in Bangladesh to the alien environment of the East End of London.

Despite her powerless position in the marriage with Chanu there are glimpses of an alternative freedom to which she is attracted. One emblem of this is the figure of the ice skater that first draws her attention on TV:

> Nazneen held a pile of the last dirty dishes to take to the kitchen but the screen held her. A man in a very tight suit (so tight that it made his private parts stand out on display) and a woman in a skirt that barely covered her bottom gripped each other as an invisible force hurtled them across an oval arena [. . .] The woman raised one leg and rested her boot (Nazneen saw the thin blade for the first time) on the other thigh, making a triangular flag of her legs, and spun around until she would surely fall but didn't. She did not slow down. She stopped dead and flung her arms above her head with a look so triumphant that you knew she had conquered everything: her body, the laws of nature, and the heart of the tight-suited man who slid over on his knees, vowing to lay down his life for her. (p. 36)

This is another scene in which Ali uses defamiliarization to great effect, in this case the common television images of ice-skating. The romantic image of the woman freed from the constraints of dress, subordination to the male and seemingly gravity itself, present an alternative world to Nazneen who is weighed down with domestic duties, and the figure of the ice skater becomes a symbol of freedom in the novel.

As in this scene, Ali often uses clothing as a symbolic indicator of cultural identity. Razia, for example, Nazneen's close friend, is less concerned with retaining traditional Bangladeshi clothing and in one scene is described as wearing a Union Jack sweatshirt to represent her easy acceptance of British culture (p. 189). Another passage that emphasizes a connection between clothing and identity occurs when Nazneen is alone and is trying to imitate the dance of a jatra girl. She slips and suddenly gets tangled up in one of her saris nearly choking herself. This experience produces an epiphany:

> Suddenly she was gripped by the idea that if she changed her clothes her entire life would change as well. If she wore a skirt and a jacket and a pair of high heels then what else would she do but walk around the glass palaces of Bishopsgate [. . .] And if she had a tiny tiny skirt with knickers to match and a tight bright top then she would – how could she not? – skate through life with a sparkling smile and a handsome man who took her hand and made her spin, spin, spin.
>
> For a glorious moment it was clear that clothes, not fate, made her life. (pp. 277–8)

She soon dismisses this thought and returns to her sewing, but the moment represents a challenge to her previous reliance on fate as the primary controlling factor in her life. At this moment she gets an intimation that it might be possible to control identity by simply gaining control over what you wear. It is significant, in this context, that through Nazneen's work as a seamstress she eventfully meets and has an affair with Karim, the Bangladeshi who visits her house to pick up the saris that she makes thus connecting her to the outside world of business. It is through her sewing skills that she is able to develop her own economic independence from Chanu. The end of the novel confirms this sense of empowerment in the ability to choose clothing as a way of taking control of personal identity and thus evading the determinism of fate. The last scene shows Nazneen skating in a sari representing a hybrid confluence of the two cultures that have made up her identity. Razia's assertion that, 'This is England [. . .] You can do whatever you like' (p. 492) in response to the incongruity of the Bangladshi dress and the Western footwear, represents the affirmation of a cultural freedom for Nazneen marking her sense of liberation.

Parallel to Nazneen's empowerment is Chanu's gradual disillusionment with British society. Chanu is presented for most of the first six chapters as a domineering and uncaring patriarch. It is only after his emotional response to the death of their first child that he emerges as a more sympathetic character. Initially Chanu has an encouraging, if naïve, view of Britain as a land of humanism, fairness and opportunity. He ambitiously undertakes a programme of education, taking an Open University degree, because his degree from Dhaka University is not valued in Britain (pp. 38–9). He also praises the British social security system that will not allow people to starve when they are unemployed (p. 73). It is only through bitter experience that he comes to realize the embedded, yet often hidden racism in British society. At work, his expectations of promotion are repeatedly frustrated, while his intellectually inferior, white colleague Wilkie is promoted ahead of him. Later in the novel, Chanu works as a taxi driver and his disillusionment increases: 'You see, when the English went to our country, they did not go to stay. They went to make money, and the money they made, they took it all out of the country. They never left home. Mentally. Just taking money out. And that is what I am doing now' (p. 214). Chanu's narrative is another example of the legacy of colonialism on individuals in the present. His initial celebration of English culture and learning show him at first to be an appropriated colonial subject. His later position, however, represents colonization in reverse as he is now satisfied by taking money from the nation that had exploited his people in the days of Empire. This bitter, yet more realistic position shows Chanu coming to terms with the economic realities of postcolonialism. He eventually decides to return to Bangladesh, a reversal of his plans that parallels Nazneen's decision to stay in Britain, despite her wanting to return to her childhood home for most of the novel.

One of the grievances Chanu has in his later life is his daughters' rejection of Bangaldeshi culture and their Westernization. The novel as a whole, however, rejects Chanu's criticisms of the effects of British culture on his daughters and his political comments are often undercut by his lack of recognition of the way his relationship with Nazneen is itself political. In a telling scene at Dr Azad's house, Chanu is firmly put in his place by Azad's wife, who embraces her position as a Westernized Muslim woman. After Chanu has given a tirade against the younger generation, Mrs Azad replies: 'Let me tell you a few simple facts. Fact: we live in a Western society. Fact: our children will act more and more like Westerners. Fact: that's no bad thing. My daughter is free to come and go. Do I wish I had enjoyed myself like her when I was young? Yes!' (p. 113).

This reveals levels of cultural difference in terms of gender, and Chanu's resistance to the Westernization of his daughters is partly because of the weakening of his patriarchal power. Implicit in Mrs Azad's celebration of her daughter's freedom is recognition of what she sees as the empowerment of women in contemporary Western society. Throughout the novel, it tends to be the women who gain most by accepting British culture.

Karim, although he represents a better prospect physically than Chanu, is just as much caught up in the complexities of postcolonial identity. Nazneen notices that although his English is good, he stutters when speaking Bengali, showing the difficulty he has in coming to terms with one of the influences on his cultural identity. Karim has been brought up in Britain despite his Bangledshi heritage, and his involvement in underground local politics is part of his working out of his cultural identity. His experiences are used by Ali to comment on the relationship between local and global politics. At the local level, this is identified in the leaflet war between the Lion Hearts, a right-wing gang in Tower Hamlets, and the Bengal Tigers, a Muslim group that is set up to resist them. The Bengal Tigers is a predominantly male group, the members of which seem to spend as much time positioning themselves within the group as they do in working out a clear response to racism. In the global context, *Brick Lane* is one of the first novels to include description of the events of 11 September in New York, but it focuses attention on the local response to this international event: 'A pinch of New York dust blew across the ocean and settled on the Dogwood Estate. Sorupa's daughter was the first, but not the only one. Walking in the street, on her way to college, she had her hijab pulled off. Razi wore her Union Jack sweatshirt and it was spat on' (p. 368). The global impact of the New York attacks is played out in the local arena with small-scale attacks on individuals.

Brick Lane represents an individual's narrative of empowerment set against contemporary and historical contexts that inform the way in which ethnicities and cultural identities are formed, maintained and negotiated. It places emphasis on the need for an accommodation and blending of Western and Eastern cultures if an individual with a cross-cultural background is to live a fruitful life in a Western environment. Although examining and expressing the experience of individuals in marginalized communities in Britain, it does so on Western terms and this is perhaps bound up with the realist form the novel uses. The ideologies supported by the novel tend towards the moderate and the liberal and these lie with certain female characters: Nazneen, Razia and Mrs Azad in particular. The criticism of the male characters is an attack on both the cultural separatism expressed by Chanu in the later parts of the novel, and Karim's dalliance with the oppositional politics of a militant Islam. This ultimately, however, represents a critique of the politics of difference and multiculturalism and this can be a provocative message, especially to a culture that feels itself to be under threat. The politics of *Brick Lane* make it palatable to a Western liberal tradition, and maybe it is this that fuelled the criticisms it drew from parts of the Bangladeshi community in East London.

SUMMARY OF KEY POINTS

- The legacies of Empire and the postcolonial situation have provided subject matter for a large amount of contemporary British fiction.
- Postcolonialism refers to the situation in countries and parts of the world that were formerly part of the British Empire but are now politically independent.
- Although similarities can be identified between different postcolonial countries, there are a variety of individual contexts that make each situation unique.
- Writers such as Salman Rushdie are keen to identify the way in which colonial legacies and postcolonial politics affect the way in which people's identities are constructed.
- Several writers, such as Courttia Newland and Monica Ali, have attempted to speak on behalf of marginalized voices and communities that otherwise have only limited access to public platforms.

NOTES

1. See, for example, Buchi Emecheta, *Kehinde* (London: Heinemann, 1994); V. S. Naipaul, *The Enigma of Arrival*

(London: André Deutsch, 1987); and Sam Selvon, *Moses Ascending* (Oxford: Heinemann, 1975).

2. Salman Rushdie, *Shame* (London: Picador, [1983] 1984), p. 11. All subsequent references in the text are to this edition.

3. Edward Fitzgerald, *Rubaiyat of Omar Khayyam* (London: Collins, [1859] 1965).

4. Edward Said, *Orientalism: Western Conceptions of the Orient* (Harmondsworth: Penguin, [1978] 1991).

5. The palimpsest metaphor is also written into the form of the novel as it overlays several discourses and narratives – some based on fact and history, some on myth and legend, some on fiction.

6. Homi Bhabha, *The Location of Culture* (London: Routledge, 1984). See the discussion of Bhabha's concept of the 'third space' in the Introduction.

7. Gilles Deleuze and Felix Guattari, *Kafka: Toward a Minor Literature*, trans. Dana Polan (Minneapolis, MN: University of Minnesota Press, 1986), pp. 16–27, p. 17.

8. Courttia Newland, *Society Within* (London: Abacus, 2000), pp. 31–2. All subsequent references in the text are to this edition.

9. M. M. Bakhtin, 'Discourse in the Novel', in *The Dialogic Imagination: Four Essays by M. M. Bakhtin*, ed. and trans. Carl Emerson and Michael Holquist (Austin: University of Texas Press, 1981), pp. 259–422.

10. Dick Hebdige, *Subculture: The Meaning of Style* (London: Routledge, [1979] 1988), p. 101.

11. It is significant in this context that later editions of the paperback version of Newland's novel came with a free CD that included a number of R'n'B and Hip Hop tracks presented as if part of a broadcast from Midnight FM, the pirate radio station set up in the story 'Midnight on Greenside'.

12. See, for example, Chester Himes's novel, *The Real Cool Killers* (London: Vintage, [1959] 1988).

13. Ray Shell, *Iced* (London: Flamingo, 1993).

14. Sylhet is a city and region in the north-east of Bangladesh.

15. Matthew Taylor, 'Brickbats Fly as Community Brands Novel "Despicable"', *The Guardian* 3 December 2003, p. 5.

16. Ibid.

17. A similar outcry occurred when the film adaptation of *Brick Lane* attempted to use the street in East London for filming. See Paul Lewis, 'Brick Lane Film Protests Force Film Company to Beat Retreat', *The Guardian* 27 July 2006.

18. Monica Ali was born in Bangladesh but moved with her parents to Bolton, Lancashire when she was three. She was educated at Oxford and lived near to Brick Lane in East London for a few years prior to the publication of the novel.

19. Gayatri Chakravorty Spivak, 'Can the Subultern Speak?', in Ashcroft, Giffiths and Tiffin (eds), *The Post-Colonial Studies Reader* (London: Routledge, 1995), pp. 24–8, p. 25.

20. Alastair Cormack, 'Migration and the Politics of Narrative Form: Realism and the Postcolonial Subject in *Brick Lane*', *Contemporary Literature* 47(4) (2006), 695–721.

21. Ibid., p. 697.

22. Viktor Shklovsky, 'Art as Technique', in *Literary Theory: An Anthology*, ed. Julie Rivkin and Michael Ryan (Malden, MA: Blackwell, 1998), pp. 17–23, p. 18.

23. Monica Ali, *Brick Lane* (London: Black Swan, [2003] 2004), p. 56. All subsequent references in the text are to this edition.

CHAPTER 3

Gender and Sexuality

The period since the Second World War has seen a paradigm shift in attitudes to gender and sexuality. The sexual revolution of the late 1950s and 1960s and the work of the feminist movement during the period covered by this book have profoundly changed the way in which men and women relate to each other socially, economically and culturally. A cultural revolution has also taken place in terms of social attitudes to the make-up of the family, same-sex relationships and our understanding of sexual identity. Any of the fifteen novels covered in this book could have been included in this chapter on gender and sexuality in contemporary fiction. However, I have chosen to focus on Angela Carter's *The Passion of New Eve* (1977), Jeanette Winterson's *Oranges Are Not the Only Fruit* (1985) and Nick Hornby's *Fever Pitch* (1992) because together they offer a range of perspectives and they span the period from the 1970s to the 1990s.

The Passion of New Eve is an innovative and experimental exploration into the way in which gender is constructed in contemporary society. Jeanette Winterson's novel *Oranges Are Not the Only Fruit* interrogates the articulation of sexual identities in British society through the experiences of a character recognizing her lesbian identity within a closed society that rejects same-sex relationships. These two novels are similar in their use of postmodern narrative techniques. Nick Hornby's *Fever Pitch*, on the other hand, uses a broadly realistic mode. It considers the meaning of contemporary masculinities with respect to individual and collective identity and the importance of psychological factors in the development of gender identity. *Fever Pitch* is as an example of a recent interest in the recovery of an individual's past, as evidenced in the diary format, and will signal the move to the next chapter.

ANGELA CARTER, *THE PASSION OF NEW EVE* (1977)

Angela Carter began publishing fiction in the mid-1960s and has produced a number of innovative and challenging works that include *The Magic Toyshop* (1967), *The Infernal Desire Machines of Doctor Hoffman* (1972), *The Bloody Chamber* (1979), *Nights at the Circus* (1984) and her last novel *Wise Children* (1991). She died in 1993 and, therefore, is not strictly speaking contemporary, however, she has become one of the most important literary figures of the latter third of the twentieth century and her work continues to stimulate and influence British fiction. She courted a certain amount of controversy in that she claimed to be both a socialist and a feminist, while her writing tended to use postmodern forms that did not sit easily with political commitment, and her representations of sexuality and the relationship between men and women attracted criticism from some feminists.[1]

The Passion of New Eve was published in 1977 and involves the adventures of a character that begins the book as a man, but ends it, through an enforced sex change, as a woman. Evelyn thus becomes the new Eve of the title. On the way he/she encounters a number of grotesque characters that engage in either sexual or violent (or both) relationships with the main protagonist. These include Leilah, a black prostitute he meets in New York, Mother, the leader of an underground women's group, and Zero, a mad misogynist poet who has a harem of subservient women. Eve/lyn eventually encounters Tristessa, an iconic screen goddess that, in an inversion of Eve/lyn's storyline, turns out to be a man. Although the novel operates in a non-realist tradition of gothic fantasy and science fiction, it engages with a specific set of historical contexts important in 1970s British and American culture. One of those contexts is the rise of second wave feminism during the 1960s and 1970s and the threat that feminism offered to right wing or neo-conservative values on both side of the Atlantic. The novel attaches radical feminism to a series of other marginalized groups in American culture that were engaged in various forms of political resistance including Black, Hispanic and Gay Rights groups. The historical context for this are the culture wars of the last quarter of the twentieth century in which the various cultural changes of the 1960s were beginning to generate a right wing backlash from neo-conservative religious groups, especially in America. The futuristic context of the novel presents this as a final battle between the Civil Rights Movement and the reactionary forces of religion. Towards the end of the novel a religious children's army appears: 'beyond the ridge, the Colonel told me, lay California and the Holy War against Blacks, Mexis, Reds, Militant Lesbians, Rampant Gays etc etc etc' (*sic.*).[2] In interview, Carter has commented on some of the historical contexts informing *The Passion of New Eve*:

> The novel was sparked off by a visit to the USA in 1969. It was the height of the Vietnam War, with violent public demos and piles of garbage in New York streets. If you remember, it was the year of the gay riots in Greenwich village, when they even chucked rocks; so my scenario of uprisings isn't all that far-fetched.[3]

The novel is mixed in terms of genre. There is clearly a science-fiction aspect to the fantastic and futuristic events of the novel, and although no specific date is provided, it appears to represent a society on the verge of collapse at some point in the near future. It also has elements of the gothic in its use of grotesque characters in a series of environments that generate fear. Its attitude to both these genres, however, is partly parodic and the novel as a whole is a good example of what Linda Hutcheon has described as 'complicitous critique'.[4] This is a form of writing that presents itself in a particular genre, but simultaneously criticizes some of the ideological positions traditionally associated with that genre. *The Passion of New Eve* complies with some of the situations, atmosphere and structuring devices of science fiction and the gothic, but at the same time implies a critique of the representations of masculinity and femininity those forms have traditionally supported. It is also a parody of the traditional coming-of-age story as although the central character learns from his/her experiences it is not a conventional example of the form in that the protagonist is not reintegrated back into society at the end.

As already suggested, part of the novel's engagement with the genres of science fiction and gothic is its use of grotesque characters both in the sense that they function in a non-realistic way, and often are exaggerations and crystallizations of particular abstract ideas or concepts. Evelyn's transformation into a woman, for example, is presented as a fantastic event (despite the realities of sex change operations) and the process he goes through have nothing to do with conventional medical procedures. Eve/lyn's *Bildungsroman* involves crossing genders as he moves from male to female biologically and masculine to feminine culturally, although arguably, at the end of the novel, these gender distinctions slip away. The process he goes through teaches him that gender is not fixed as a tangible series of properties in the natural world, but is located inside the mind. When he goes through his enforced sex change at the hands of Mother he finds himself approaching the other within himself – the feminine aspects of his unconscious identity: 'She, this darkest one, this fleshy existence beyond time, beyond imagination, always just beyond, a little way beyond the finger tips of the spirit, the eternally elusive quietus who will free me from being, transform my I into the other and, in doing so, annihilate it' (p. 59). What is annihilated is the cultural construction of Evelyn's gendered identity, which involves transforming 'the linear geography of inwardness, a tracing of the mazes of the brain itself' (p. 56). The conversion Evelyn goes through in becoming Eve dramatizes the idea that gender identity is not fixed in nature but is fluid and relies on culturally constructed signification. This is also shown in the interstices between the two gendered states in which Eve/lyn finds him/herself in the central sections of the book. At one point s/he feels this as a dislocation between the body and the mind: 'I was literally in two minds; my transformation was both perfect and imperfect. All of New Eve's experience came through two channels of sensation, her own fleshy ones and his mental ones' (pp. 77–8). The time lag suggested here between the female body and the male mind shows that biological and cultural gender is detachable, and not dependent on each other. Evelyn's narration significantly moves to the third person in this passage, as s/he does not yet recognize this 'New Eve', and the duality of the self is felt in 'two channels of sensation'. Later, Eve/lyn explains 'I have not yet become a woman' echoing Simone de Beauvoir's famous quotation referred to in the Introduction.[5] Eve/lyn's coming of age serves, then, to emphasize that gender is something that is attached onto the body through socialization, and not something that is fixed at birth. This idea of gender as detached from the body is the basis of the metaphoric character framework that Carter develops in the novel.

Included in Eve/lyn's *Bildungsroman* is the encounter with a series of characters that embody traditional aspects of femininity. One of these is Leilah, who represents an object of male sexual desire manifest through her external characteristics, both in terms of her body and her clothing. Leilah is able to draw Evelyn in by performing pornographic images that appeal to his masculine desire. This relationship represents a complex understanding of the place of power in such a heterosexual relationship. Leilah, in one sense is the perfect gothic victim, one who fully satiates Evelyn's lust through her performance of the subjugated female. However, the power that she has over Evelyn complicates the situation as her image is a constructed reflection of masculine desire:

> Her beauty was an accession. She arrived at it by a conscious effort. She became absorbed in the contemplation of the figure in the mirror as, in any degree, herself. The reflected Leilah had a concrete form, and although this form was perfectly tangible, we all knew, all three of us in the room, it was another Leilah. Leilah invoked this formal other with a gravity and ritual that recalled witchcraft; she brought into being a Leilah who lived only in the not-world of the mirror and then became her own reflection. (p. 28)

This reflected Leilah is a culturally created image of femininity imposing itself on both Evelyn's consciousness and on Leilah's manipulation of that image: '[She] seemed to abandon her self in the mirror, to abandon her self to the mirror, and allowed herself to function only as a fiction of the erotic dream into which the mirror cast me' (p. 30). The image of femininity Leilah projects controls Evelyn, and what he sees in the mirror is a constructed image that is determined by the conventional codification of femininity and, in reflection, masculinity. What Carter suggests, here, is that the powerful images of femininity that circulate in the Western world are as manipulative of men as they are of women, although with different consequences in terms of power. This scene is paralleled later when Evelyn sees his newly constructed female self: 'But when I looked in the mirror, I saw Eve; I did not see myself [. . .] for this was only a lyrical abstraction of femininity to me' (p. 74). This 'lyrical abstraction of femininity' is similar to the image Leilah has projected onto the mirror earlier. Leilah, then, is the abstract projection of Evelyn's masculine desires. Sex within this unequal power relationship, however pleasurable, is not ultimately seen as fulfilling for Evelyn, so much so that he soon tires of her, and she begins to generate feelings of guilt: 'But I soon grew bored with her. I had enough of her, then more than enough. She became only an irritation of the flesh, an itch that must be scratched; a response, not a pleasure. The sickness ran its course and I was left only with the habit of her sensuality, an addiction of which I was half ashamed' (p. 31).

It is later discovered that 'Leilah' is, in fact, a created persona, a performance by Lilith, one of the women attached to a radical women's group and a trap set to lure Evelyn towards his gender transformation. This all-women group is led by another grotesque character called Mother, and they inhabit an underground complex in the middle of the desert called Beulah, 'the place where contraries exist together' (p. 48).[6] Mother represents an abstract image of maternal power; the 'abstraction of a natural principle' (p. 49). As with Leilah, however, her exaggerated and grotesque characterization allows Carter to deconstruct this received image of femininity. In many ways Mother provides grist to the mill of those critics like Robert Clark who are dubious of Carter's feminist credentials, as she appears to be an ironic manifestation of some elements within radical feminism as it was developing in the 1970s.[7] Radical feminism argued that the only way to overturn centuries of patriarchal power was to attack the grounds upon which masculinity had been based and to reject all aspects of male culture. There are elements of this in Mother's violent transformation of Evelyn as revenge for his treatment of Leilah. This can also be seen in Mother's attempt 'to reactivate the parthenogenesis archetype', and thereby circumvent the role of men in reproduction (p. 68).

The collective of women pursue an attack on phallocentrism, represented by one of Mother's pseudonyms, 'the Great Emasculator' (p. 49), and visually by the broken phallus badge worn by the women: the symbol that looks 'like a broken arrow or truncated column' (p. 45). This deconstruction of phallocentrism is dramatized in the castration of Evelyn and his re-construction as a woman. But to read Mother as an image of radical feminism is not the whole story. A precedent has already been set in the characterization of Leilah, and Mother is another grotesque that represents a reflected image of femininity constructed in patriarchy. As her name suggests, she is an exaggerated embodiment of the maternal instinct – a kind of grotesque earth goddess. Mother's largeness in comparison with Evelyn suggests that she not only transforms him into a woman, but also returns him to a state of childhood. This inversion of power of the female over the male is part of the process through which Evelyn has to pass in order for him to be reborn as a woman. The psychoanalytic theories of Jacques Lacan are useful, here, in exploring the symbolism Carter gives to this relationship.[8] Lacan argues that the child in its earliest relationship with the mother cannot identify a sense of itself as distinct from the body of the mother. He calls this the 'semiotic' stage. It is only when the child passes through the 'mirror stage', when it recognizes its own reflection, and thereby as having a distinct social identity apart from the mother, that it enters into the 'symbolic' stage. According to Lacan (and following Freud) it is at this stage that the father imposes himself between the mother and child, manifest as the 'Law of the Father'. In *The Passion of New Eve*, Eve/lyn is returned to the semiotic stage when she is reborn as a woman and her experiences after this replicate the transition through the mirror stage, which involves readjusting the way in which her identity will be reformed now that society will view her as a woman.

When Eve (as it is now more accurate to call her) escapes from Mother she encounters what in some ways is Mother's antithesis, Zero, an embodiment of a traditional form of masculinity. In addition, and to pursue the Lacanian model, he represents the law of the father imposing itself between Mother and the now female child. Zero controls a harem of women in which patriarchal power is reflected as a form of love, but a perverted form: a love for the thing that dominates. Zero, like Mother, uses violence ostensibly to teach Eve/lyn a lesson. When Zero rapes Eve, his phallus symbolically imposes the violence inherent in patriarchal power relations, which in turn acts to remind Eve/lyn of his previous treatment of Leilah. 'When he mounted me [. . .] I felt myself to be, not myself but he; and the experience of this crucial lack of self [. . .] forced me to know myself as a former violator at the moment of my own violation' (p. 102). However, Zero's authority, as his name suggests, is based on a false assumption, and his one eye, wooden leg and sterility represent the limitations of the form of extreme masculinity he practices. There is an allusion here to the Oedipus story. Oedipus, who inadvertently slept with his mother and murdered his father, was eventually blinded and was disabled in one foot, symbolic of the physical damage of the result of his actions. Oedipus, similar to Zero, is a king whose power is ultimately undermined by his actions.

Zero's power is negated when he encounters the kind of femininity represented by Tristessa. Tristessa is the third in a series of embodiments of patriarchy's construction of femininity. She represents a form of ideal, untouchable and pure femininity and as such is beyond Zero's libidinal power. It is her celibate status that Zero resents most and he reconfigures this by regarding her as a lesbian. Part of this third image of women is to suffer in silence, without complaint, as the physical embodiment of the power of the masculine over the feminine, recycled as romantic love of the powerless. In this traditional image of femininity, it is only through the suffering and powerlessness of the unattainable female that the male's role to protect, and thereby retain power, is reconfirmed: 'For Tristessa's speciality had been suffering. Suffering was her vocation' (p. 8). The power that her iconic status has over men threatens to disrupt the conventional hierarchies in patriarchy, so the images of her suffering are necessary to accommodate her potentially subversive power.

Tristessa's image of ideal femininity is based on the idea of her as an iconic projection of the male gaze. In this sense, her identity is constructed through external observation and she is a figure based on an illusion: 'And all you signified was false! Your existence was only notional; you were a piece of pure mystification, Tristessa' (p. 6). The film context is important here. Tristessa is, in part, a parody of the iconic Hollywood film actresses of the mid-twentieth century such as Jean Harlow and Mae West and the celluloid construction of Tristessa reflects the impossibility of her real existence. She exists only as a constructed visual image: 'You were your own portrait, tragic and self-contradictory. Tristessa had no function in this world except as an idea of himself; no ontological status, only an iconographic one' (p. 129). In Eve's acculturation as a woman she is made to watch films of Tristessa that show 'every kitsch excess of the mode of femininity' (p. 71). It is when Eve encounters the 'real' Tristessa that her imaginary status is exploded. That she turns out to be a man reinforces the idea that her particular form of femininity is in fact a male construct. As with Leilah, Tristessa performs a role that has, in effect, been constructed by men (and in Tristessa's case literally by a man). Far from indicating any essence of femininity, her identity reveals more of the objectified desires of men in a patriarchal context. Laura Mulvey's theories on the role of women in 1930s Hollywood film are relevant here. In an essay entitled 'Visual Pleasure and Narrative Cinema' (1975), Mulvey argues that the image of woman in film represents two impulses, of voyeurism and narcissism.[9] Voyeurism is represented by the position of the audience in a movie theatre who observe actions without being recognized by the people on screen. She identifies narcissism in this context as the situation whereby the observer associates with the screen figure. Mulvey relates this to Lacanian psychology and the mirror stage: 'The mirror phase occurs at a time when the child's physical ambitions outstrip his motor capacity, with the result that his recognition of himself is joyous in that he imagines his mirror image to be more complete, more perfect than he experiences his own body' (p. 588). The mirror image the child observes is called the 'ideal ego', and represents a projection of the self as a more complete and better functioning other to the real self.

Hollywood film in the 1930s is produced out of a society that adheres to patriarchal codes and, according to Mulvey, this ideology is replicated in the designated roles of male and female both on the screen and in the audience. The ideal ego, therefore, is conventionally projected onto the male hero of a film. As Mulvey argues: 'A male movie star's glamorous characteristics are of the more perfect, more complex, more powerful, ideal ego conceived in the original moment of recognition in front of the mirror' (p. 590). The narcissistic association with the male actor replicates the situation in the mirror stage, when a more confident self is presented to the (male) individual in the 'screen space' of the mirror.

However, Mulvey identifies an unsettling disruption of the voyeuristic/narcissistic framework: 'in psychoanalytic terms the female figure poses a deeper problem. She also connotes something that the look continually circles around but disavows: her lack of a penis, implying a threat of castration' (p. 591). According to Mulvey, the processes of voyeurism and narcissism can get mixed up for the observer, the female figure can begin to generate narcissistic desires in the male observer. If this alternative female figure begins to represent the ideal ego, then it is unsettling because of its lack of a penis. According to Freudian theory, this process reminds the male viewer of another early psychoanalytic anxiety: the fear of castration. This theory is problematic in that it assumes the male child as the norm and females as 'lacking', but it is apposite to the situation of Tristessa in *The Passion of New Eve*, as, in one sense she/he is the living symbol of a castrated male (as, of course, is Eve/yln). For Tristessa to perform the role of femininity, he has to castrate himself symbolically. The anger that Zero has towards Tristessa, therefore, can be explained with reference to this model. Zero is driven to inflict pain on Tristessa (and ultimately to try to kill her) because she serves to remind him psychologically of his castration complex, and consequently of his lack of the symbol into which he has projected his sense of masculine power. Tristessa threatens to disrupt the whole gender framework on which Zero's power rests and therefore his survival relies on him destroying her.

Tristessa's idea of gender as performance relates to another useful critical perspective suggested by Judith Butler's work on gender and performativity. Butler is interested in the way that gender roles are performed in society, and uses the example of the drag queen to make her point.[10] According to Butler, the drag queen embodies the idea of the performative nature of femininity, where the signs of femaleness are taken on in a particular social situation. In the case of the drag queen, the signification of maleness accompanies the performance of femininity because it is made clear that the figure's 'true' gender is male. However, this sense of gender as being essentially a socially constructed performance is relevant to *The Passion of New Eve*; as Eve notes at one point: 'I was now also passing for a woman, but, then, many women born spend their whole lives in just such imitations' (p. 101). In the case of Tristessa, this is slightly different, as the performance of femininity is so convincing that all traces of his biological gender are removed. It is only at the moment that Tristessa's biological sex is revealed that the drag situation comes into play, and this deconstruction of her image is suitably accompanied by the metaphoric breaking of a 'great glass' (pp. 127–8).[11] Significantly, it is Zero, the paradigm of masculinity that shatters this ideal image of femininity. It is her untouchability and sterility that so offend Zero and which, therefore, threaten his masculine power. The text shows, however, that these constructions of masculinity and femininity are interdependent and to remove one serves to destroy the other. Like Zero, Tristessa's identity is based on an illusion: 'You had turned yourself into an object [. . .] and this object was, itself, an idea [. . .] Tristessa had no function in this world except as an idea of himself; no ontological status, only an iconographic one' (p. 129).

The *Bildungsroman* structure of the novel, albeit a deconstruction of the form, culminates in the last sections of the novel as Eve experiences, metaphorically, a second return to the womb. Unlike the experience in Beulah, the return to the mother is this time consciously sought and is represented as a kind of reverse birth:

> I saw there was nothing for it but I must fold myself into the interstice of rock so in I went and my sneakers were thoroughly soaked in a moment by the freezing little stream [. . .] I edged my way forward, flat as a flounder. Every movement necessitated the most extreme exertion; I was soon drenched with sweat. (p. 179)

After moving through a rock crevice, Evelyn finds herself in a 'wide, shallow pool of pleasantly warm water', and this metaphoric return to the womb results in her 'taking great gulps of the fresh, pure air that now blew from an invisible source into my face' (pp. 180–1). This experience is accompanied by the dissolution of time, which again takes on a gendered context as the movement forward of time, or historicity, has already been associated with masculinity (p. 53). Consequently, the return to a state of timelessness relates to a return to the moment of creation, the moment when time begins for the individual, here taking on a geological context: 'The amber was undergoing a process of reversal in which I and the rock itself were involved' (p. 183). At this point Eve virtually merges with the rock itself, replicating the moment in which the mother and the child are of the same body.

However, Eve does not find her mother and the desire to return to the womb is frustrated. This aspect of Carter's narrative relates to a concept in Freudian theory known as the death drive, or Thanatos.[12] In this model, death is welcomed as a resting place and provides an end to desire. Through his/her experiences, Eve/lyn has learnt that the pursuance of objects of desire results in an endless series of frustrations. The desire for the end of desire is thus the logical endpoint of her narrative of self-knowledge. However, this final desire is also thwarted as only in death can desire be terminated, and in that sense leaving the subject finally and wholly fulfilled. The last sections of the novel are ambiguous in this context as although Eve/lyn emerges from the womb-cave, she heads off on the ocean to seek 'the place of birth' (p. 191), which could also be read as the place of death. The main character's journey from Britain over the Atlantic to New York, and westward across America ends in reaching the Pacific. It is at this point that s/he discovers that the 'vengeance of sex is love' (p. 191). This ambiguous phrase suggests that where sex tends towards movement and desire, love is a kind of stasis, a form of negative capability in which desire slips away to leave full contentment. It also seems to suggest that love transcends gender difference and it is in the coming together of the sexes on an equal footing that removes the power differentiation between male and female that is a defining function of patriarchal society. This is anticipated earlier in the novel in the sexual encounter between Eve and Tristessa in which gender binaries are deconstructed in the coming together of the man who has become a woman and the iconic woman who has been revealed as a man. The sexual inversions at play in this situation, and in the text as a whole, serve to question radically the construction of gender and sexuality in contemporary society, although it has to be said that despite the inversions, the prevailing sexual relationships and the frame of reference for the sexual metaphors are heterosexual. In Jeanette Winterson's *Oranges Are Not the Only Fruit* a different kind of deconstruction of sexuality takes place, one that moves beyond the framework of heterosexuality.

JEANETTE WINTERSON, *ORANGES ARE NOT THE ONLY FRUIT* (1985)

Oranges Are Not the Only Fruit was published in 1985 and clearly tapped into the increasing popular interest in the way in which gender and sexual identities were constructed in mainstream British culture. It attempted to do this by breaking down and challenging prescribed attitudes (especially religious ones) to sexuality and to the role of the nuclear family in maintaining established gender roles. The book is fictional, but is presented in a way that suggests a sense of a closeness and authenticity to the experiences of the author. The main character, for example, is called Jeanette and certain sections and chapters, such as 'Deuteronomy' sound like statements of belief that come direct from Winterson. This is a novel, however, that is keen to scrutinize received distinctions between fiction and fact. Winterson comments on it: 'Is Oranges an autobiographical novel? No not at all and yes of course'.[13] In terms of structure the novel is consciously experimental, interweaving the main linear and chronological narrative of Jeanette's rite of passage with other stories: fairy tales, dream sequences, Arthurian legend, and structuring references to other texts such as the Bible and *Jane Eyre* (1847). *Jane Eyre*, in particular, is a significant intertext on a number of levels. Like Charlotte Brontë's novel, *Oranges* is a *Bildungsroman*, and the main protagonist in each is an orphan who is placed within a harsh (though at times loving in the case of *Oranges*) environment.[14] In addition, *Jane Eyre* is Jeanette's mother's favourite novel. However, her mother recounts a bowdler-ized version to Jeanette by adapting the ending. In her mother's version, Jane Eyre marries the religious and safe St. John Rivers, avoiding the return to the more passionate and sexually charged Rochester. This reworked narrative relates to Jeanette's mother's own life, in that she chose to marry her safe and, throughout the novel, silent husband. Rochester thus stands for unrepressed desire, and consequently, by one of the many gender reversals that the novel effects, lesbian desire.

Oranges is clearly of its moment. It appeared during a period in the mid-1980s where commentators on the political right were blaming left-wing radicals and the sexual revolution of the 1960s for a series of ailments in contemporary society, such as the break down of family values and the disruption of traditional moral codes as set out in conventional religious discourses. Winterson's novel openly engages in political debates and acts as an iconoclastic challenge to a series of related discourses. As she writes in an introduction to a later edition of the book: '*Oranges* is a threatening novel. It exposes the sanctity of family life as something of a sham; it illustrates by example that what the church calls love is actually psychosis and it dares to suggest that what makes life difficult for homosexuals is not their perversity but other people's' (p. xii).

The traditional nuclear family structure is challenged in a number of ways. Firstly, the father in Jeanette's household is a weak figure and does not play a great part in family decisions or in the narrative as a whole. As Jeanette says of him: 'Poor Dad, he was never quite good enough' (p. 11). Jeanette's mother is the dominant figure in the relationship and controls her father either through ignoring him completely or making sure he adheres to the codes of behaviour set down within her religion. Her mother also takes on the household roles conventionally attached to the male; she is, for example, building a bathroom for the family (p. 16). The marriage appears to be one of convenience. It is explained on the first page, for example, that Jeanette's mother 'had a mysterious attitude towards the begetting of children; it wasn't that she couldn't do it, more that she didn't want to do it. She was very bitter about the Virgin Mary getting there first. So she did the next best thing and arranged for a foundling' (pp. 3–4). Later Jeanette tells us: 'As long as I have known them, my mother has gone to bed at four, and my father has got up at five' (p. 15) and this appears to have always been the case. The lack of a sexual relationship between her parents also suggests the reason why Jeanette was adopted. Another clue to her mother's sexuality is given when the pair of them are looking through the 'Old Flames' section of her mother's photograph album. There are a few men there – Mad Percy, Eddy and Pierre with whom Jeanette's mother has had sex with because she has confused the 'fizzing and buzzing and a certain giddiness' to be love but turns out to be a stomach ulcer (p. 85). Her conclusion is that, 'What you think is the heart might well be another organ'. More significant is the picture of 'Eddy's sister', which is initially in the old flames section, but is removed after Jeanette asks her mother about her. It is only a hint, but the suggestion is that Jeanette's mother has had uncomfortable (for her) desires towards this woman, desires that she has presumably repressed and continues to do so – the photograph is never mentioned again. Later in the text, Miss Jewsbury, herself a lesbian, tells Jeanette that her mother is 'a woman of the world, even though she'd never admit it to me. She knows about feelings, especially women's feelings' (p. 104). This also explains to a certain extent the marriage of convenience that she has made with Jeanette's father.

Although Jeanette's family is not conventional, one of the alternative social units in the novel is the church group to which Jeanette and her mother belong. Women predominantly people this group and it is, in one sense, a kind of matriarchy, at least in its everyday organization, although the authority of the male pastors at crucial times in the text, show that this is a contingent and localized form of female power. That Jeanette has loving relationships within the church is an indicator of an alternative matriarchal family structure. The social relationships Jeanette experiences in both her family and the church serve to disrupt conventional roles of masculinity and femininity and this extends to Jeanette's perceptions of gender codes around her. From an early age, she resists the prevailing codes of femininity that society tries to impose on her, for example, when the man in the Post Office gives her 'Sweethearts' she reacts with rage:

Sweet I was not. But I was a little girl, *ergo*, I was sweet, and here were the sweets to prove it. I looked in the bag. Yellow and pink and sky blue and orange, and all of them heart-shaped and all of them said things like,

Maureen 4 Ken

Jack'n'Jill, True

On the way home I crunched at the *Maureen 4 Ken's*. (p. 70 – italics in original)

This passage represents the way in which seemingly innocent cultural products such as sweets help to reinforce dominant heterosexual codes of sexuality, but also reveals Jeanette's inherent dislike of having those codes imposed upon her. This extends to her dreams about marriage, one of which sees her walking up the aisle to meet a husband but, 'sometimes he was blind, sometimes a pig, sometimes my mother [. . .] and once just a suit of clothes with nothing inside' (p. 69). This reveals Jeanette's awakening sexuality and her anxieties about becoming part of a traditional heterosexual relationship.

Jeanette's sexuality offers another challenge to the traditional codes of masculinity and femininity. When Pastor Finch tries to account for the relationship Jeanette has with Melanie he argues that it is due to Jeanette subverting the established roles between men and women. Finch defines lesbianism in terms of Jeanette unnaturally taking the role of the man in her relationship with Melanie. This of course serves to posit desire as a masculine trait, which Jeanette's narrative firmly denies:

The real problem, it seemed, was going against the teachings of St Paul, and allowing women power in the church. Our branch of the church had never thought about it, we'd always had strong women, and the women organized everything [. . .] There was uproar, then a curious thing happened. My mother stood up and said she believed this was right: that women had specific circumstances for their ministry [. . .] but the message belonged to the men [. . .] She ended by saying that having taken on a man's world in other ways I had flouted God's law by trying to do it sexually. (p. 131)

The sentiment here is clearly coming from Pastor Finch, even though Jeanette's mother is the messenger. Jeanette feels particularly betrayed by the fact that her mother agrees with the Pastor reimposing a patriarchal narrative onto Jeanette's behaviour, especially as this goes against the strong female image that Jeanette has come to expect of her mother.

The novel, then, sets out to challenge the connection between religion and conventional discourses of gender and sexuality that, in the Protestant Christian church (both High Church and non-Conformist variations), traditionally upholds the heterosexual nuclear family as the ideal social unit. The direct target is the form of Old Testament, non-Conformist Evangelism that Jeanette's mother practices. This leads the novel, however, to question some of the bases on which Christian doctrines rest generally. Part of this critique is seen in the parodic attitude to the Bible suggested by the chapter titles and structure of the novel. As Susana Onega has argued, a parodic equivalent is established between 'the stages in Jeanette's quest for maturation and [. . .] the biblical narration'.[15] Each of these chapters is loosely based on the first eight chapters of the Bible and has a connection with the experiences Jeanette goes through: for example, 'Genesis' recounts Jeanette's earliest memories and the details of how her mother has 'got' Jeanette (p. 10). 'Exodus' details Jeanette's journey from the home environment to the unfamiliar social world of school, described by her mother as the 'Breeding Ground' (p. 17). The Pentateuch (the first five books of the bible) represents the laying down of the law, and in Winterson's novel the first five chapters detail the establishment of the ideology against which Jeanette eventually places herself. The last three chapters of the novel, 'Joshua', 'Judges' and 'Ruth', find Jeanette establishing her own alternative world view and correspond to those books in the Old Testament that offer stories of individuals who either adhere to or set themselves against the word of God. Unlike the corresponding books in the Bible, the last three chapters of *Oranges* seem to support Jeanette's attempt to escape religious laws, and are part of her challenge to the patriarchal framework of the Old Testament.

Despite its iconoclasm, however, the novel is more ambivalent about the place of God within her narrative of empowerment. At one point towards the end of the text, Jeanette reflects nostalgically on the ideology she has rejected:

> But where was God now, with heaven full of astronauts, and the Lord overthrown? I miss God, I miss the company of someone utterly loyal. I still don't think of God as my betrayer. The servants of God, yes, but servants by their very nature betray. I miss God who was my friend. (p. 165)

As Jeanette becomes more at ease with her sexual identity, the Old Testament, patriarchal God to which her mother, perhaps somewhat grudgingly, concedes is replaced by an alternative discourse that is closer to a New Testament, Christian doctrine that celebrates love over obedience, and tolerance and forgiveness over discipline and punishment. As Peter Childs has argued: 'Against the Old Testament logic of her mother, there is however a New Testament counter-narrative running from Jeanette's miraculous birth to the story's conclusion on Christmas Day'.[16] Jeanette's arguments for her love of Melanie are significantly taken from the New Testament, encapsulated in the quotation she cites from St. Paul 'To the pure all things are pure' (p. 103). However, it is also St Paul's teaching that is used by the Pastor and her mother to challenge Jeanette's taking on the traditional role of the male in pursuing relationships with women. Despite this, Jeanette stresses her belief in a pure love that is reconfigured as a love between women:

> Romantic love has been diluted into paperback form and has sold thousands and millions of copies. Somewhere it is still in the original, written on tablets of stone. I would cross seas and suffer sunstroke and give away all I have, but not for a man, because they want to be the destroyer and never be destroyed. (p. 165)

In this sense, Jeanette's *Bildungsroman*, like many a modernist text, models the trials of the central character on Christ.[17] The parallels with Christ are many, although often parodic: Jeanette is the product of a kind of Virgin birth (as Childs points out) who faces a time in the wilderness, and who eventually rejects established codes of a religion that are shown to be too draconian. She preaches a doctrine of love and is ultimately betrayed by those closest to her. In a telling passage that suggests Jeanette as a prophet Christ-figure, she argues:

> I could have been a priest instead of a prophet. The priest has a book with the words set out. Old words, known words, words of power [. . .] The prophet has no book. The prophet is a voice that cries in the wilderness, full of sounds that do not always set into meaning. (p. 156)

Where the priest preaches the established doctrine, the prophet's message is unsettling and threatening to the prevailing power relationships in society. The prophet's meaning, however, is not necessarily anti-spiritual, it is a different understanding of the religious nature of man. *Oranges*, then, does not reject outright a spiritual outlook on life. Religion becomes one of a series of valuable narratives that go towards the building of an individual's identity. In this sense *Oranges* is not an atheistic book, nor is it an example of the nihilistic variety of postmodernism despite its engagement with ideas of pluralism, its suspicion of the grand narratives of history and patriarchy, and its formal experimentation. It is, in fact, closer to what Patricia Waugh has called 'weak postmodernism' as opposed to the more Nietzschean-influenced 'strong' version:

> Unlike strong postmodernism, the weak version may accept the human need to invest in grand narratives, though its proponents would reject monocausal varieties and insist that all knowledge is embedded or situated in particular cultures or cultural traditions. According to weak postmodernism, understanding arises through the practices, customs, traditions and textures of a particular culture and we may arrive at a shared structure of values, a sense of personal significance, and the possibility of belief in historical progress through collective engagements which do not require foundations of truth or value.[18]

This type of postmodernism, according to Waugh, is more open to the liberatory struggle of the feminist movement, which wants to question certain grand narratives, but rejects an outright relativism, because it needs to have some ethical basis on which to construct an alternative politics. This form of tempered postmodernism fits well with Winterson's approach in *Oranges*.

This can also be seen in the form of the narrative. Although Winterson makes a bold claim for the experimental nature of the novel, in comparison with other texts covered in this book its experimentalism is far from radical. In fact, it tends to use a traditional linear realism, which is then disrupted by the non-realistic sections. Much of the novel reads like a traditional tragi-comedy, a dominant feature of British fiction from the 1950s onwards; the description of Northern working-class life make its setting similar to novels such as *Saturday Night and Sunday Morning* (1958), *Billy Liar* (1959) and *A Kestrel for a Knave* (1968).[19] However, Winterson disrupts this essentially male, working-class tradition with the incorporation of the non-realistic narratives of fairy tales and dream sequences. In her 1991 introduction she emphasizes that the novel has 'a spiral' form and 'I really don't see the point of reading in straight lines' (p. xiii). Formally, the novel's disruption of a linear narrative corresponds to its aim to challenge patriarchy. As Susana Onega has argued, the use of the spiral has become established in lesbian film iconography in particular, and the use in *Oranges* of this alternative formal structuring disrupts a patriarchal grand narrative, which is represented by 'reading in straight lines' as Winterson puts it.[20]

Within the linear frame there are a number of other narratives that obliquely comment upon Jeanette's experiences: the fairy tales, passages influenced by Arthurian legend, dream sequences and statements of opinion. These other forms of writing disrupt the linear time frame and problematize the notion of time in writing as a continuum and this disruption can be related to the novel's suspicion towards the grand narratives of religion, the family and the heterosexual norm. In the important short chapter 'Deuteronomy: The last book of the law' the narrative voice of the novel sets out a philosophical approach to the function of stories and storytelling in which traditional history is seen to be a reductive form of linear narrative: 'this reducing of stories called history' (p. 91).

This attitude to linear story-telling is similar to the kind of reduction that Jeanette observes in her mother's explanation of the world through her religion. For her mother, religion orders the world (and how to behave in it) in a fixed way with clear demarcations between right and wrong: a discourse that resembles the organizing principles of a linear narrative. What Jeanette learns is that the world is far more complicated than this and the interaction of the differing stories expresses this in a formal way: 'that is the way with stories; we make of them what we will. It's a way of explaining the universe while leaving the universe unexplained, it's a way of keeping it all alive, not boxing it into time' (p. 91). History, for Jeanette, can be used to impose strict ideologies on people as in the way Jeanette's mother and the Pastor interpret the bible as a means to control what they see as Jeanette's unnatural behaviour. Stories, on the other hand, supply a more complicated way of interpreting the world:

> Everyone who tells a story tells it differently, just to remind us that everybody sees it differently. Some people say there are true things to be found, some people say all kinds of things can be proved. I don't believe them. The only thing for certain is how complicated it all is, like string full of knots. It's all there but hard to find the beginning and impossible to find the end.
> (p. 91)

This suggests a way for the reader to approach the relationship between the main narrative and the various fairy tales and legends in the novel. For example, the story about the woman in the forest and the prince's search for perfection follows the Pastor's sermon on perfection, and links with Jeanette's mother's attempt to live life in perfect adherence to a set of religious codes (p. 58). The story shows that this search for perfection is inevitably flawed. This is not to say that the story is a direct analogy of Jeanette's relationship with her mother, rather that the stories feed off each other, and this is what Winterson means when she explains that the novel can be 'read in spirals' (p. xiii). The different narratives often share motifs that help to form the connections. For example, the significance of the rough brown pebble Jeanette finds in her pocket after she has finished her affair with Katy, is only explained with reference to the raven in the Winnet story for whom a 'brown pebble' represents his heart because he has chosen to stay in the restricting village (p. 144); and the invisible thread that the sorcerer ties round the Winnet's button (p. 144) reappears as a metaphor for Jeanette's strong connection with her mother despite their differences (p. 171).

Both Winterson and Carter are interested in the way that dominant and prevailing codes of behaviour and ideologies have served to fix traditional gender roles and sexual conventions, and they are particularly interested in the way these codes have restricted women's behaviour. The next novel we will consider, Nick Hornby's *Fever Pitch*, is also interested in gender roles, but takes codes of masculinity as one of its main subjects.

NICK HORNBY, *FEVER PITCH* (1992)

One of Nick Hornby's concerns in *Fever Pitch* is to represent the way in which the 'new men' of the 1980s and 1990s have to struggle with reconfigured constructions of masculinity. This reconstruction is in part a retrieval of older forms of masculinity with a negotiation of the newly 'feminized' masculine identities that were emerging. In addition, the early 1990s saw the beginning of the 'new lad', a retrieval of older forms of masculinity that was seen as a backlash to the success of feminism. Hornby was associated, perhaps unfairly, with this 'new lad' phenomenon and particularly in the way that middle-class, university-educated men found themselves having to negotiate a range of conflicting discourses of contemporary masculinity. Through association with a new lad culture, it was felt that middle-class anxiety over the loss of masculine power could be regained (culturally, if not economically) by attaching itself to those aspects of society in which masculinity was still perceived to be flourishing particularly in working-class society. The middle-class appropriation of football (and to a certain extent popular musical forms such as rock, punk, reggae etc.) can be read in Hornby's book as a response to a more general middle-class crisis of masculinity during the period.[21]

The subject matter of the book is centred on Hornby's obsession with football and, in particular, Arsenal Football Club. This main focus, however, provides a way of addressing other concerns, personal, psychological, cultural and social. It is autobiographical but uses several fictional techniques to develop its themes and characterizations. In one sense, the whole book is an extended metaphor on the ways in which football provides analogies to other aspects of life, coupled with the invention of various ingenious images for describing the experience of being an obsessive football supporter. The book is organized as a series of short reflections given a chronological order by subtitling them with football matches that Nick has attended, for example, the first chapter is titled 'HOME DEBUT' followed by the subheading 'ARSENAL v STOKE CITY, 14.9.68'.[22] Each subheading generates a discussion of an experience related to the listed match or of the period in which it took place, or sometimes a reflection on some past event evoked by some aspect of that particular game. Although operating in the realist mode, this is an experimental form: a kind of journal that uses football fixtures as its organizing principle. This form fits neatly with the subject matter as the fixture list provides a pattern that he cannot find in other aspects of his life whilst at the same time reflecting his obsession. As he writes at one point: 'I have measured out my life in Arsenal fixtures' (p. 81). This measuring out suggests that the place football has in his life is far more than simply an interest and is intricately connected with his psychological make-up.

Similarly to *The Passion of New Eve* and *Oranges, Fever Pitch* is a kind of coming-of-age narrative, although as with those other novels, it has an ironic take on the genre. As we have seen, the coming-of-age narrative, or *Bildungsroman*, traditionally follows the protagonist's journey from childhood into adulthood and eventual reintegration in the social world from which they had initially felt distanced. The difference with *Fever Pitch* is that in many ways Nick fails to advance out of his childhood because he fails to escape his teenage obsession. By the end of the book he has matured to a certain extent, but this involves accommodating rather than rejecting the obsession. The book repeatedly returns to the idea that football represents his inability to grow up.[23] The first part of the book suggests that it completes a rite of passage, in that it seems to offer a moment when he has achieved maturity, however, as the second part shows ('My Second Childhood') this is a false end and he is soon plunged back into his adolescent obsession with football.

There are various scenes that suggest moments of transition, for example, when he watches Arsenal from the North Bank of Highbury for the first time (as opposed to in the stands), but these tend to be underplayed: 'My only rite of passage then, involved standing on one piece of concrete as opposed to another' (p. 75).[24] Later in the text, there are several references to the way in which being a football fan keeps Nick in a state of permanent adolescence and that football acts as a 'retardant' because 'for the duration of the games I am an eleven year old boy' (p. 106). The end shows that his coming-of-age involves a shift in his relationship with Arsenal and football but not a rejection of it as a childish obsession. The obsession continues, but his move to buying a season ticket shows a more mature attitude to the club (p. 232).

This unwillingness to mature is, therefore, tied up with the way Nick has become an obsessive about football and indeed the book is as interested in the nature of obsession as it is about football. For the most part, the older Hornby acknowledges his condition, although there is often an unrepentant attitude towards the effects it has on his friends and family, often similar to the way that addicts do not care about the way their addiction affects those around them. When he acknowledges that, 'sometimes hurting someone is avoidable' (p. 214), we feel that this is self-deceptive pandering to his obsession. He is, however, aware that he has to temper his behaviour in order to lead a relatively normal life. At the opening of the book, for example, when asked what he is thinking about by his partner he replies: 'At this point I lie [. . .] obsessives have no choice [. . .] If we told the truth every time, then we would be unable to maintain relationships with anyone from the real world' (p. 10). By the end of the novel, the obsession has not gone away, but he has become able to cope with it, although on his own terms. The author information before the title page details that 'Nick Hornby lives within walking distance of the Arsenal ground with his wife and son'. This is an early indication of the central theme of the book and in the way it is phrased suggests an anticipated balancing of the obsession with his personal relationships.

Football and personal relationships are intimately connected for Nick and this is shown in the frequency of metaphors connecting the two, including several that suggest a sexual relationship. The opening of the first main chapter, for example, indicates: 'I fell in love with football as I was later to fall in love with women: suddenly, inexplicably, uncritically, giving no thought to the pain or disruption it would bring with it' (p. 15). This link between sexuality and football sets the scene for the psychological contexts in which the novel operates. This is grounded in his feelings of anxiety around his parents' divorce and it is in 1968, during the period when his father leaves his mother that he first develops his obsession with Arsenal: 'I would have to be extraordinarily literal to believe that the Arsenal fever about to grip me had nothing to do with all this mess' (p. 17). Arsenal supplies an external and surrogate family to replace the sense of loss he feels at the break-up of the family home and it is in the visits he makes to the ground with his father that initially reconnects them: 'The Arsenal pitch was to be our lawn [. . .] the Gunners' Fish Bar on Blackstock Road our kitchen; and the West Stand our Home' (p. 18). The wholeness that the Arsenal ground supplies lies at the heart of the obsession, and it is the certainties of the fixture list that offer an organized pattern that simplifies the complexities of life beyond football. As he later writes, with respect to his psychological problems: 'I wish I could draw one of those big knock-out trophy diagrams to show how I'd ended up playing on the unfamiliar turf of a Hampstead psychiatrist's carpet' (p. 176).

The psychological context of Nick's obsession can be understood with reference to the Oedipus complex, as defined by Freud.[25] According to this theory, the male child goes through a series of quasi-sexual relationships with both his mother and father whereby the initial physical contact with the mother in the early stages of a child's life has to be restricted as the child moves into a social world. According to Freud, this restriction placed on the child can be seen in sexual terms as a desire for a return to the body of the mother. The father figure, however, steps in to restrict access to the mother's body and in psychological terms, the child enters into conflict with the father in response to this prohibition and a struggle over the right to the mother's affections ensues. Eventually, the child should be able to overcome this conflict by passing through adolescence and becoming fully adult, and thereby recognizing the role of the father in the social world and going on to enter into a 'healthy' psychological relationship with another woman. According to Freud, however, individuals can get caught up in any of these stages and therefore remain, psychologically speaking, in one of the phases of childhood or early adolescence, and this is what seems to be the root cause in Nick's case.

It has to be stressed, however, that the attitude the book takes towards this Freudian model is often ironic and it is presented as if this is another way of developing a useful metaphor for his obsession with football rather than the text taking on, wholesale, agreement with this aspect of Freudian theory. There are many problems with the Freudian model, not least that it presupposes that the only way of achieving a healthy psychosexual make-up in adult life is to follow a heterosexual relationship in a traditional nuclear (and paternalistic) family framework. It is the break down of this framework in Nick's case, however, that allows the Freudian reading of his experience to be apposite. One example is in the way that the Oedipal conflict with the father is represented in terms of a difference over the kind of football team they each wanted to support. For his father, Chelsea, with their sheen of celebrity and money, is more attractive, whilst Nick is intrigued by the '*otherness*' and '*real* exoticism' of Arsenal with its roots in working–class north London (p. 47). There is another section where this Oedipal conflict results in Nick supplanting the place of the father in relation to his mother: 'On Saturdays, it seems to me now, we enacted a weird little parody of a sitcom married couple'. Again, however, the tone of this passage treats the Oedipus theory with a certain amount of comic distance: 'There is, I know, an argument which says that acting out the role of one's father with one's mother isn't necessarily the best way of ensuring psychic health in later years. But then, we all do it at some time or another, chaps, don't we?' (p. 53).

One of the clearest suggestions that the book signals this Oedipal relationship with his father is the section that details his adopting of the then Arsenal manager George Graham as a surrogate, fantasy father.[26] In a telling passage Nick writes:

> George is my dad, less complicated but much more frighten-ing than the real one [. . .] I dream about George quite

regularly, perhaps as often as I dream about my own father. In dreams, as in life, he is hard, driven, determined, indecipherable; usually he is expressing disappointment in me for some perceived lapse, quite often of a sexual nature, and I feel guilty as all hell. Sometimes, however, it is the other way round, and I catch him stealing or beating someone up, and I wake up feeling diminished. (p. 169)

It is interesting, here, that the connection with Graham as an alternative father centres on anxieties of masculinity. Graham is described in terms that appear to be the epitome of a traditional form of maleness: 'hard, driven, determined'. But he is also 'indecipherable', suggesting that he is beyond the understanding of the adolescent male who is trying to work out his masculinity. That the dream is reversed and he is caught beating someone up suggests that Nick's psyche is recognizing that the older form of masculinity is at odds with the modern liberal versions that he is also encountering. That the dreams are vaguely sexual again suggests something of the role of the father in the Oedipus conflict. The need for a surrogate father figure suggests, then, a break in the relationship with his real father and relates to the break down in his family. Because of this, Nick cannot complete the conventional Oedipus narrative of adopting the role of the father, and therefore attaches his desires to an alternative form of masculine association, not only with the figure of George Graham, but more symbolically with the football culture of Arsenal generally. This explains to a certain extent why Nick's obsession with football represents a continued attachment to childhood: 'I appeared to have got stuck somewhere around my fourteenth birthday' (p. 140). The age of fourteen, of course, is right in the middle of male puberty and the repeated metaphors that present the love of Arsenal as a sexual relationship reveals something of the deeper anxieties to which Nick often refers. Part of the allure of football, then, is the connection with a form of masculinity that Nick is drawn to but feels unable to achieve. The attraction is registered in his first visit to a match, which showed the 'overwhelming *maleness* of it all' (p. 19). Later, he reflects on the way in which the individual male has to negotiate already constructed forms of masculinity as 'a shared set of assumptions and values that men can either accept or reject' (p. 80).

For Nick, masculinity is tied up with issues of class. As we have seen, part of the attraction of Arsenal is that it offered an exotic taste of working-class culture that appears to be so much more masculine. This explains the way in which he tries to take on the appearance of being part of that working-class culture by, for example, altering his nondescript accent to fit with a form of North London dialect, and in one scene his attempt to pass himself off as an inner city North Londoner (pp. 49–50). He describes this process as 'mock-belonging, whereby pasts and backgrounds are manufactured and massaged in order to provide some kind of acceptable cultural identity' (p. 48). The identity he chooses reveals his desire to attach himself to a recognized, if stereotypical form of masculinity. This stereotype is especially attractive amongst middle-class men, as Ben Knights has argued: 'A set of inverse snobberies and widespread ignorance leads to a belief that working-class men [. . .] expresses masculinity in a purer form. They thus become the objects of social horror [. . .] and simultaneously a kind of awed admiration'.[27] Attachment to a working-class group is a way of resuscitating the loss of power that the individual might feel and there are plenty of examples of the sense of aggrandizement Nick gets when he is part of the football crowd: 'I was as yet nowhere near as big as I should have been, and wore black-framed Brains-style National Health glasses, although these I hid away for the duration of the route marches, presumably to make myself just that little bit more terrifying' (p. 54). This can often show an unsettling attachment to more dubious, and yet attractive elements of football. Being 'an organ in the hooligan body' (p. 54) may have unpleasant associations, yet on an individual level it supplies the sense of living up to older codes of masculinity that the middle-class boy from Maidenhead cannot manage on his own. Part of this is the desire for wholeness where being at Arsenal represents occupying, 'the one spot where I feel I belong absolutely and unquestionably' (p. 215).

Attached to this sense of wholeness is a nostalgic narrative he weaves around the group identity of Arsenal. This is shown in the section where he details moving to North London, as close as he can to Highbury. His expectations of being incorporated as a 'much-loved and valued member of a happy, working-class Arsenal community' (p. 211) are misplaced. What he discovers is that the demographics of North London mean that most of the people living in the area in the late 1980s are neither working class nor Arsenal fans suggesting that the community spirit he was looking for has long gone: 'I suspect that I moved here a good twenty years too late' (p. 212).

Alongside the personal narrative, then, the book comments obliquely on the major social changes that have taken place in Britain from the late 1960s to the early 1990s – the period of Thatcherism. Given the nature of the book, this social commentary is filtered through football and the sections that discuss the politics of changing attitudes to the consumption of football are related to deeper social and cultural changes. The upheavals that football fans went through in the 1980s in particular, such as the changes in the way the grounds were organized and the consequent exclusion of some of the poorer fans because of increased ticket prices, can be seen as an effect of a dismantling of working-class identity generally in the 1980s (p. 76).

Hornby is far from an apologist for the violence and racism he describes observing at football matches (and disasters such as at Heysel and Hillsborough) but he tries to suggest deeper social and cultural causes that have a part to play in the manifestation of violence on the terraces. He is also keen to rescue football from media misrepresentation that sees 'football grounds as a bolt-hole for a festering, vicious underclass' (p. 97). It may appear at certain points in the text that Hornby has an ambivalent attitude towards violence, but this is part of the internal division he experiences in trying to come to terms with changing gender roles overlaid during a period of great social and cultural change in Britain in relation to class. The anxieties he describes relate to a clash of cultures between his desire for both an older masculine identity and middle-class liberal sensibilities, both of which are, to a certain extent, imposed upon him. This is the psychological conflict that is being played out through the obsession with football, and the novel succeeds in interrogating what it means to be a man in an age when gender roles have been significantly reconfigured.

SUMMARY OF KEY POINTS

- The cultural understanding of femininity and masculinity has changed significantly over the forty years or so since the 1960s and contemporary British novelists have explored the implications of these changes.
- Similarly, changed attitudes to sexuality have occasioned many late twentieth-century novelists to examine and express new ways of approaching sexual identity.
- The role of the family has been of significant interest to novelists in their exploration of sexual identity.
- The success of the feminist movement has realigned power relationships between men and women both publically and privately, and given rise to the popular idea that the personal is political.

NOTES

1. For a discussion of Carter's relationship with feminism see Sarah Gamble, 'Introduction', in Sarah Gamble (ed.), *The Fiction of Angela Carter: A Reader's Guide to Essential Criticism* (Basingstoke: Palgrave, 2001), pp. 7–11; and Rebecca Munford, 'Angela Carer and the Politics of Intertextuality' in *Re-Visitng Angela Carter: Texts, Contexts, Intertexts*, ed. Rebecca Munford (London: Palgrave, 2006), pp. 1–20.
2. Angela Carter, *The Passion of New Eve* (London: Virago, [1977] 1985), p. 161. All subsequent references in the text are to this edition.
3. Quoted in Gamble, *The Fiction of Angela Carter*, p. 89.
4. Linda Hutcheon, 'Historiographic Metafiction: "the pastime of past time"', in *A Politics of Postmodernism: History, Theory, Fiction* (London: Routledge, 1988), pp. 105–23.
5. Simone de Beauvoir, *The Second Sex*, ed. and trans. H. M. Parshley (London: Jonathan Cape, [1949] 1953).
6. The place name of Beulah alludes to William Blake's use of the term as a region of the unconscious. In his poem, *Milton*, he writes: 'There is a place where Contrarieties are equally

True / This place is called Beulah, It is a pleasant lovely Shadow / Where no dispute can come', William Blake, 'Milton: A Poem in Two Books', in *Blake: Complete Writings*, ed. Geoffrey Keynes (Oxford: Oxford University Press, 1957), p. 518. For Carter, this place without contraries is an ironic allusion to the breakdown of gender, however, it is clearly not a place without dispute in *The Passion of New Eve*.

7. Robert Clark, 'Angela Carter's Desire Machine', *Women's Studies: An Interdisciplinary Journal* 14(2) (1987), 147–61.

8. Jacques Lacan, 'The Mirror Stage as Formative of the Function of the I', in *Literary Theory: An Anthology*, 2nd edn, ed. Julie Rivkin and Michael Ryan (Malden, MA: Blackwell, 2004), pp. 441–6.

9. Laura Mulvey, 'Visual Pleasure and Narrative Cinema', in *Literary Theory: An Anthology*, ed. Julie Rivkin and Michael Ryan (Malden, MA: Blackwell, 1998), pp. 585–95.

10. Judith Butler, *Gender Trouble: Feminism and the Subversion of Identity* (London: Routledge, 1990).

11. For a good analysis of the way in which Carter's novel engages with Judith Butler's theories see Alison Lee, 'Angela Carter's New Eve(lyn): De/Engendering Narrative', in *Ambiguous Discourse: Feminist Narratology and British Women Writers*, ed. Kathy Mezei (Chapel Hill, NC: University of North Carolina Press, 1996), pp. 238–49.

12. Sigmund Freud, *Beyond the Pleasure Principle*, ed. and trans. James Strachey (New York: W. W. Norton, [1929] 1975).

13. Jeanette Winterson, *Oranges Are Not the Only Fruit* (London: Vintage, [1985] 1991), p. xiv. All subsequent references in the text are to this edition.

14. Following Winterson's lead, I will refer to the novel by its shortened title from this point onwards.

15. Susana Onega, *Jeanette Winterson* (Manchester: Manchester University Press, 2006), p. 21.

16. Peter Childs, 'Jeanette Winterson: Boundaries and Desire', in *Contemporary Novelists: British Fiction since 1970* (Basingstoke: Palgrave, 2005), p. 266.

17. See, for example, D. H. Lawrence, *Sons and Lovers* (Harmondsworth: Penguin, [1913] 2006); and James Joyce, *A*

Portrait of the Artist as a Young Man (Harmondsworth: Penguin, [1916] 2003).

18. Patricia Waugh, 'Postmodernism and Feminism?', in *Contemporary Feminist Theories*, ed. Stevi Jackson and Jackie Jones (New York: New York University Press, 1998), pp. 177–92, p. 88.

19. Alan Sillitoe, *Saturday Night and Sunday Morning* (London: Flamingo, [1958] 1994); Keith Waterhouse, *Billy Liar* (London: Michael Joseph, 1959); Barry Hines, *A Kestrel for a Knave* (Harmondsworth: Penguin, [1968] 1969).

20. Onega, *Jeanette Winterson*, p. 33.

21. See Ben Knights, *Writing Masculinities: Male Narratives in Twentieth-Century Fiction* (London: Macmillan, 1999); and Daniel Lea and Berthold Schone (eds), *Posting the Male: Masculinities in Post-War and Contemporary Literature* (Amsterdam: Rodopi, 2003).

22. Nick Hornby, *Fever Pitch* (London: Indigo, [1992] 1996). All subsequent references in the text are to this edition.

23. *Fever Pitch* is one of a group of novels from the 1990s that extended the *Bildungsroman* narrative into the protagonist's thirties. See, for example, Helen Fielding's *Bridget Jones's Diary* (London: Picador, 1996), and two of Nick Hornby's other novels *High Fidelity* (London: Gollancz, 1995) and *About a Boy* (London: Gollancz, 1998).

24. Highbury was the old Arsenal ground, where they played their home games during the period covered in Hornby's book. The North Stand was the terrace at one end of the ground where the most dedicated Arsenal fans stood. Arsenal have since moved to the Emirates Stadium.

25. Sigmund Freud, *The Interpretation of Dreams*, trans. James Strachey (New York: Avon, [1900] 1965).

26. George Graham was Arsenal's manager from 1986 until 1995 and was therefore still the manager when *Fever Pitch* was published in 1992.

27. Knights, *Writing Masculinities*, p. 181.

CHAPTER 4

History, Memory and Writing

One of the most important trends in contemporary British fiction is the attempt to address and rewrite narratives of the past. This chapter will begin by addressing some of the issues related to the interconnected terms of history and memory and the role fictional narratives play in recuperating and/or constructing the past. The chapter will begin with a discussion of Graham Swift's *Waterland* (1983) in terms of the relationship between personal and national histories and the novel's interest in examining the way that history is articulated in the present. The chapter will move on to discuss A.S. Byatt's *Possession* (1990) and the focus on the relationship between its two fictional narratives, one set in the present and one set in the Victorian period. The third novel discussed here is Ian McEwan's *Atonement* (2001), which deals with ideas of memory, historical truth and the fictionalizing of the past. Each of these novels questions the relationship between identity, history (both official and personal) and fiction and each, therefore, is discussed in relation to some of the formal issues raised in Chapter 1, especially with reference to the way in which they use techniques associated with postmodernism. In addition, the focus on time and history in the novels covered in this chapter connects closely with issues of space and cultural geography in Chapter 5.

As noted in Chapter 1, one of the key features of the condition of postmodernity is a suspicion towards grand narratives, and one of these is the idea of history as a single monolithic account of the past. In recent critical theory, the idea of history has been pluralized to accommodate the sense in which accounts of past events are different according to the position from where they are viewed, especially in terms of the ideological agendas that may lie behind the presentation of what appears to be an impartial view of historic events. Salman Rushdie, as we saw in Chapter 2, provides a striking image of this idea of historical narratives as a set of competing stories, the most powerful of which survive at the expense of the less powerful, remarking that 'History loves only those who dominate her'.[1] The relationship between history and power is an area that has been addressed by Michel Foucault, who replaced a conventional understanding of history and replaced it with what he calls genealogy. For Foucault, genealogy differs from traditional history in that it tries to take account of the submerged narratives that have been discarded by the prevailing accounts of the past. It is also keen to show how history is determined by systems of what he calls 'power/knowledge'. Jago Morrison has summarised this well: 'For Foucault, traditional history systematically works to suppress evidence of discontinuities, disjunctions and struggles between rival regimes of knowledge, because its overriding goal is to portray the present as the product of a clear and traditional development [. . .] Genealogy, by contrast, is actively concerned to uncover evidence of alternative and submerged knowledges'.[2] As can be seen from this description, the Foucauldian approach to history lends itself well to postmodern and poststructuralist ideas whereby a single unified account of the past is replaced by a plurality of contrasting and competing histories.

Some theorists, however, have been suspicious of the role this undermining of traditional history has taken in postmodernity. Fredric Jameson, for example, raises concerns about the 'weakening of historicity, both in our relationship to public History and in the new forms of our private temporality'. He identifies certain practices of postmodernism that have been guilty of this trend, resulting in, 'a society bereft of all historicity, one whose own putative past is little more than a set of dusty spectacles. In faithful conformity to poststructuralist linguistic theory, the past as "referent" finds itself gradually bracketed, and then effaced altogether, leaving us with nothing but texts'.[3]

While Jameson worries that postmodernism tends to flatten out historical thinking in an endless surface of the present, literary critic and theorist Linda Hutcheon identifies a number of postmodern novels that are interested in recounting narratives that engage with the past. She defines a trend in contemporary fiction that she calls 'historiographic metafiction' which actively promotes a sense of historicity, and of thinking through our relationship with the past. This kind of writing is historiographic in that it self-consciously interrogates the way in which history is recorded. In this sense it is as much concerned with the process of writing history as it is in the historical narratives that are produced. She identifies many examples of texts that also show a similar self-consciousness towards the writing of fiction. As she writes, 'The interaction of the historiographic and the metafictional foregrounds the rejection of the claims of both "authentic" representation and "inauthentic" copy alike, and the very meaning of artistic originality is as forcefully challenged as is the transparency of historical referentiality'.[4] Unlike Jameson, she posits this trend as revealing a questioning and critical evaluation of the received stories of history, whilst at the same time emphasizing the problems associated in attempting to uncover the truth of the past when the very concept of truth has been relativized. For Hutcheon, however, postmodern fiction does not 'weaken historicity' but represents an endless desire and imperative to look again at the past, reviewing and reassessing received histories, but without the striving for closure as represented by a grand narrative of history. As she writes, 'The postmodern [. . .] reinstalls historical contexts as significant and even determining, but in so doing, it problematizes the entire notion of historical knowledge'.[5]

Some historians, such as Hayden White have commented on the fact that similar structuring devices and systems of emplotment and characterization are shared between fictional and historic discourses.[6] This idea can be seen in a number of novels in the period that share historical and fictional narratives such as Beryl Bainbridge's *Young Adolf* (1978), which fictionalises a possible visit Adolph Hitler made to Liverpool before the First World War, or Julian Barnes's *Arthur and George* (2005), which weaves a fictional story around the real life involvement by Sir Arthur Conan Doyle in the case of the wrongful imprisonment of George Edalji in the 1890s.[7] Some of these theoretical positions are addressed in the discussion of the three novels in this chapter, each of which engage with ideas of the postmodern, both on a formal and thematic level.

GRAHAM SWIFT, *WATERLAND* (1983)

Graham Swift's *Waterland*, published in 1983, engages with many of the theoretical issues regarding the nature and limitations of history as a textual discourse. This is not to say, however, that it is an example of what Fredric Jameson might describe as a depthless sense of postmodern history that reduces historical perspectives to an ever-present now.[8] *Waterland*, although using many narrative techniques associated with postmodernism, is certainly not dismissive of history as a way of engaging with the past and it encourages a sense of thinking historically. It is closer to the kind of historiographic metafiction that Linda Hutcheon identifies as a trend in postmodern fiction. Swift's novel problematizes and pluralizes the idea of history, and the context for this is established through Tom Crick, the hero and narrator of the novel. Tom is a history teacher in his fifties who is embarking on unusual teaching methods in his attempt to communicate a sense of history to his pupils. This includes personal narratives and stories drawn from his family background mapped against events in political and social history. It becomes apparent, however, that Tom's deviation from the curriculum in his history classes reveals a personal crisis generated by the teacher's recent experiences and how these relate to his past.

There are many kinds of historical narrative employed and referred to in the novel. The school curriculum Tom's class are following has the history of the French Revolution as one of its topics, and this is referred to at various stages throughout the text, usually as a theme against which the personal and family narratives are compared. This topic is part of a wider 'official' history, which acts as a largely chronological backdrop to the other kinds of history in the novel. Included in this official history is the rise and fall of Britain as an industrial and imperial power from the end of the eighteenth century through to the present. In addition, there is the local history of those living on the Norfolk Fens and in the nearby town of Gildsey. This combination of types of historical narrative reflects the debate on the relative importance of political and social history in education in the 1980s, a debate which was ideological as many in the Thatcher government tended to support the history of kings, wars, and political movements, whereas the progressive Left favoured a more social (if not necessarily socialist) form of history teaching.

Alongside the text's engagement with these contemporary political arguments over history curricula, there is the family history of the Cricks and Tom's maternal family, the Atkinsons. The history of these two families is told in such a way that Tom makes parallel references to official history, mapping personal stories on to broader political and social movements and events. This is part of his newly developed and unorthodox way of teaching, but it also presents a wider symbolic narrative of the rise and decline of Britain as an industrial power. This is established primarily in the longest chapter in the book, 'About the Rise of the Atkinsons'. In this chapter, which unlike the rest of the book presents a broadly chronological narrative, we are informed of the rise of Josiah Atkinson, an ambitious and forward-looking farmer born early in the eighteenth century who establishes a barley farm and has ambitions towards diversifying into the brewing industry. His son William, and then his grandson, another William (who comes to prominence during the French revolution and the Napoleonic wars) further pursue the brewing trade. The rise of the Atkinsons is thus emblematic of Britain's emergence as an industrial and commercial power from the mid-seventeenth century onwards. In later chapters, the interweaving of narratives of family history alongside parallel public events moves forward to cover the Victorian period and then on to the gradual decline of Britain in the twentieth century, especially registered in the two World Wars. In contrast to the Atkinsons' entrepreneurial skills, the Cricks are 'water people', organically tied to the Fenland on which they have worked for centuries. They are stolid and unemotional and have a phlegmatic attitude to the world. Contained in this family history, or what might more accurately be called genealogy, there are a number of inherited motifs and symbols handed along the generations that serve to connect the past with the present, including madness, ghosts, secrets and beer.

The novel was published in 1983, and Tom and his class are contemporary. The 1980s was a period in which the Cold War stand-off between the West and the Soviet bloc meant that the threat of a nuclear fuelled Third World War was a constant, if underlying feature of life. As Daniel Lea has noted: 'Swift is not so naïve to suppose that any age was markedly superior to the present, yet *Waterland* nurtures a conviction that the international pressure points of the early 1980s threaten a uniquely bleak vision of the future'.[9] Price, a pupil in Tom's class, raises this issue and registers his concerns about an impending nuclear holocaust, which he uses as a context to argue that there is no point in studying the past, when civilization appears to be on the point of destruction: 'The only important thing about history, I think, sir, is that it's got to the point where it's probably about to end'.[10] This fear generates the establishment of the 'Anti-Holocaust Club' of which Price and some of his classmates are members, and whose motto is 'Fear is Here' (p. 333). Price's fears might be exaggerated, but they are genuine in the context in which he presents them. The idea of history ending also relates to the academic study of history, which, as suggested earlier, is a reference to Thatcherite policies that questioned the relevance of humanities subjects in state schools. This is represented in the novel by the threat that history as an academic subject is about to be dropped by the school, and this uncertainty about his professional future is a factor in Tom's breakdown. It is in opposition to both these senses of an end to history that Tom is keen to persuade his class that it is still a vital element, not only in understanding the past, but also how historical narratives (personal and social) have determined our identities in the present.

History, however, is shown to be a complex and multiple discourse and Tom's understanding of it rejects the idea of a monolithic official narrative of the past. This is reflected in the structure of the novel as a process of accretion of seemingly disparate stories which only gradually are shown to relate to each other. This combination of stories replaces the idea of a single determining, academic history:

So we closed our textbooks. Put aside the French Revolution. So we said goodbye to that old and hackneyed fairy-tale with its Rights of Man, liberty caps, cockades, tricolours, not to mention hissing guillotines, and its quaint notion that it had bestowed on the world a New Beginning.

I began, having recognized in my young but by no means carefree class the contagious symptoms of fear: 'Once upon a time . . .' (p. 7)

This shift in Tom's role from history teacher to storyteller is initiated by Price's rejection of history as relevant to the present, and the function of the two modes of narrative is identified as different. If history is concerned with a full revealing of the past and establishing a closed narrative, stories function in *Waterland* as a duty to retell, but in doing so defer closure, because in Tom's case, the impact of the 'truth' is too traumatic to bear. This sense of the endless deferral of stories is linked back to the idea of the end of history: 'But when the world is about to end there'll be no more reality, only stories [. . .] We'll sit down, in our shelter, and tell stories, like poor Schererazade, hoping it will never . . .' (p. 298). The missing 'end' from this sentence replicates the desire to resist the final point of the story, because the end is the thing that cannot be approached, represented as a dark secret in Tom's life that his narrative circles around. The 'real' story of the novel is the one that Tom finds most difficult to tell – his part in the death of his brother and in his wife's Mary's botched abortion, which many years later has led to her abduction of a child from a supermarket. These are the most important stories in the novel, but they are also the most difficult to tell.

This aspect of Swift's novel corresponds to one of the definitions of the relationship between postmodernism and the Kantian idea of the unpresentable as suggested by Jean-François Lyotard. According to Lyotard, the unpresentable refers to ideas that exist but, 'of which no presentation is possible'.[11] Postmodern art differs from modern in the way this idea is articulated, as he writes, 'The postmodern would be that which [. . .] puts forward the unpresentable in presentation itself; that which denies itself the solace of good forms'.[12] In the context of narrative fiction, this disruption of good forms relates to the self-reflexive scrutiny of the way in which the narrative is constructed as a means to suggest the existence of something that cannot be said directly. This has resonance with the situation in *Waterland*. For Tom, the unpresentable, the idea that is almost impossible to communicate, is the guilt that he feels with respect to his role in the death of his brother and Mary's abduction of the child. One of the ways in which Tom's difficulty in expressing his guilt is shown in the number of ellipses or gaps used throughout his narrative, for example, in the passage where he tries to explain to Dick the truth about the incestuous circumstances of his parentage. All attempts to convey this story seem inadequate: 'How can I put this into any other word? How can I preface, interpret, explain' (p. 323 – no question mark in the original). The drive to explain is thus forever frustrated because language is incapable of fully accounting for events that have led to Dick's existence. Unlike a traditional ethos of history that aims to reveal the truth, one of the functions of Tom's stories is to mask it through a series of prevarications and reworkings. This contradiction in the role of stories is at the heart of *Waterland*, the duty to bring to light the causes that have led to Mary's actions and the desire to keep secrets that, if revealed, will be harmful to those concerned. The novel is a confessional, but one where facing up to the guilt is balanced by the desire to turn away painful truths.

For Tom, this contradiction forms the basis of his psychological dilemma. He is a lover of history, but paradoxically, this love was developed as a response to the traumatic events of 1943 surrounding Dick and Mary. It is after this that Tom decides on a career in historical research and teaching, and it is research into his own family history that helps him to come to terms with the events in his own immediate past. However, the systematic uncovering of the hard facts pursued in academic history represents, in part, a diversion from his coming to terms with events from his personal life. As he explains to his class: 'And can I deny that what I wanted all along was not some golden nugget that history would at last yield up, but History itself: the Grand Narrative, the filler of vacuums, the dispeller of fears of the dark?' (p. 62). But he has reached a point in his life where this reliance on history as a positive bringing to the light of truth no longer works: hence the rejection of traditional methods of history teaching and the move to stories. Tom realizes that his life's work of researching the historical narratives of others has, in fact, been a displacement of the psychological imperative to repress his painful past. Tom's guilt only emerges towards the end of the story. But more than this, it is his initial desire to worm out secrets that has led to Dick discovering the truth about his birth, beginning a train of events that lead to his death.

Similar points of crisis are reached in the older family histories. In a moment of jealous madness, for example, Thomas Atkinson strikes his young wife Sarah, who from the resulting fall is rendered witless. This event is shrouded in secrecy and results in the guilt-ridden torment of Thomas, and in mythic tales of Sarah as having 'the gift to see and shape the future' (p. 83). Sarah lives on as a senseless mute but becomes associated by the Gildsey town folk as a reincarnation of St Gunnhilda, the patron saint of the town. Rumours of Sarah's supernatural qualities are re-enforced by the flood that immediately follows her death in 1874, during which her ghost is seen in the graveyard of St Gunnhilda's church (p. 103). Tom's narrative is equivocal on the veracity of this sighting, but her unworldly powers are supported by subsequent events in the text. During her long life she has occasional fits during which she warns of 'Smoke!, Fire!, Burning!' (p. 84), which anticipates the burning down of the Atkinson's brewery in 1914. It is at the time of the fire that a maid in Ernest Atkinson's house sees a second manifestation of Sarah's ghost.

This return of Sarah symbolically represents a return of repressed guilt that seems to hang over the Atkinsons, generated by Thomas's acts of violence against his wife. This family legacy of secreted and repressed stories that eventually return in acts of violence forms a series of parallels throughout the novel and antici-pates the events that surround Tom's life. It is Ernest Atkinson's madness that appears as a legacy of the family trait that results in his deluded belief that he should father a new Messiah and that the mother of this Messiah is to be his daughter (Tom and Dick's mother). It is this secret – that Dick is the issue of an incestuous father-daughter relationship – that is the story that it takes Tom so long to tell. As suggested earlier, the Atkinson family history also carries with it an analogy to the history of the British Empire from the mid-eighteenth century to the Second World War. The initial entrepreneurial skills of Josiah, William and Thomas result in the establishment of the Atkinsons' brewing empire, which is successfully continued by the Victorians George and Alfred. It is no coincidence that their empire finally falls in 1914 with the fire at the brewery, which parallels the great conflagration of the First World War, a conflict that marked the beginning of the end of Britain's position as the world's leading imperial power.

The novel, then, builds up its themes through the accumulation of symbolic and analogous stories and motifs. One of these motifs is beer, registered especially in the effects it produces on certain characters in the novel. The naming of the various ales that the Atkinson Brewery produce act as a form of historic document, for example, in the Jubilee, Empire and Coronation Ales that are produced to celebrate key moments in British history. Ernest, as a form of revenge on the town that has rejected his pacifist ideas prior to the First World War, produces the very strong Coronation Ale, which, when Dick drinks a bottle of it, results in his killing Freddie Parr. Dick's suicide is also accompanied by his drinking of several bottles of the over-strong ale. The role of alcohol as a form of Bacchanalian release is also noted at moments in the text, for example, in the scene that describes the fire at the Atkinson brewery: 'The crowd, indeed, eyes glazed as much by their intake of ale as by the glare of the flames, watched as if this were not their town brewery being burnt to the ground but some elaborate spectacle expressly arranged for their delight' (p. 174). Beer, then, acts as a dangerous conduit through which repressed stories and feelings return. Thomas, for example, is drunk when he hits Sarah. Alcoholism as a theme also affects many characters in the text such as Jack Parr, Freddie's father, who on one occasion in his job as a signalman narrowly avoids causing a train crash due to his excessive drinking; and Mr Lewis, the Headmaster at Tom's school, whose difficult job has driven him to drink.

A second linking motif is the eel, the natural history of which first appears to be another of Tom's digressions. This motif operates on a number of levels. Firstly, it reveals something of the contradictions in the Enlightenment project of scientific investigation, as it appears to elude the attempts by a series of scientists to identify its reproductive cycle. The chapter 'About the Eel' shows how many of the speculative theories that have been produced to explain its reproduction have subsequently been discredited. The natural history of the eel, therefore, simultaneously encapsulates and frustrates the desire for complete knowledge: 'Even today, when we know so much, curiosity has not unravelled the riddle of the birth and sex life of the eel. Perhaps these are things, like many others, destined to be learnt before the world comes to its end' (pp. 203–4). Secondly, the eel represents a phallic symbol, but ironically in that its reproductive cycle remains such a mystery and it appears to have no genitals. This aspect of the eel is registered most clearly in the episode that details the swimming competition, instigated by Mary, between Tom, Dick and Freddie Parr. The sexual context of the scene begins when Mary promises the winner of the competition a glimpse of her naked body. During this scene, Mary's adolescent sexual curiosity is stimulated by Dick's large erection. Although Dick wins the competition he does not claim his prize and the scene ends with a metaphorical sexual encounter when Freddie Parr drops a live eel into Mary's underwear. This is the beginning of Mary's relationship with Tom, but also with the innocent Dick. The older brother later catches and gives an eel to Mary, a scene that further establishes the phallic symbolism of the water creature (pp. 251–2). The sexual jealousy that thus ensues, which involves Freddie Parr because Dick mistakenly thinks that he rather than Tom is Mary's secret lover, results in Dick murdering Freddie. On a symbolic level, the curiosity that Mary has about Dick's penis parallels the scientific curiosity that the eel has engendered, although in the former case curiosity is seen to be a dangerous emotion resulting in the train of events that leads to the deaths of Freddie, Dick and Mary's unborn child. Dick's association with the eel, indicated in his swimming prowess, is restated at the end of the novel: 'Here indeed was a fish of a man', and his death is described in terms of a return to the sea, which shows him to be, 'Obeying Instinct' just as the eel returns to the sea to reproduce in some never discovered location (p. 357).

The contradiction between the desire to tell the truth and the desire to keep secrets is also presented symbolically in the landscape of the novel. The title of the novel, *Waterland*, encapsulates this

sense of contradiction in that it combines two contradictory physical states, whilst also refering to the Fenland location of the text, an
area of Britain where much of the land has been reclaimed from
marshland and given a physical, if somewhat precarious, solidity. As
the text keeps reminding the reader, however, the region is prone to
flooding, so that most solid of things in other areas, the ground, is
felt in the Fenlands to be unstable, ready to undermine you at any
time. An analogy is drawn here between the instability of the environment and the suspicion towards accepted histories. The very
geography of the setting suggests that the grounding of the character's understanding of the world can easily shift from beneath them.
As Daniel Lea argues: 'The processes of erosion and accretion that
render the Fen landscape so impalpable are equally applicable to
identity formation within that landscape'.[13]

Tom Crick is, in many ways, a typical tragic figure. His fatal flaw
is that his need to ask questions and to uncover the truth results in
his own downfall and the bleak fates of those he loves. Tom cannot
resist finding out what is in the box that was passed down to Dick
from his father, and once he knows its dark secret, he cannot resist
telling Dick the truth of his parentage. Tom's compunction to
reveal family secrets is set in contrast with his father, Henry Crick's
desire to keep things hidden, as seen in his attempts to stop Dick
learning to read. What appears initially to be an embarrassment on
Henry's part towards Dick's lack of mental capacities, turns out to
be an act of love as he wishes to protect Dick from the truth about
his birth:

> But don't shun *him* [Henry], Dick. Don't shun your own – I
> mean – He's the one who never wanted you to be educated.
> Your protector, your guardian. I'm the one who had to ask
> questions, who had to dig up the truth (my recipe for emer-
> gencies: explain your own way out). He would have kept you,
> happily, in the dark. (p. 324)

In one sense, Henry's attempts to keep things hidden emerge here
as the wiser response. But this challenges the whole nature of Tom's
belief in the need to explain, to uncover and to bring to light. The
morality of Tom's enlightenment imperative is complex, as the

revelation does not produce happiness but leads only to despair and death. In effect, then, the novel dramatizes a moral dilemma with respect to the existence of unpleasant truths: how far should one uncover a secret (however immoral) when it is clear that its disclosure will cause harm to those it concerns. The text presents this ethical conundrum without guiding the reader towards an answer and in its ending remains open on this issue.

A. S. BYATT, *POSSESSION: A ROMANCE* (1990)

A. S. Byatt's 1990 novel *Possession: A Romance* shares *Waterland*'s interest in the way narratives of the past affect people in the present. Byatt's novel interweaves two narratives, one in the late twentieth century, and one in the mid-nineteenth century. In the nineteenth-century narrative, Byatt creates two Victorian poets, Randolph Henry Ash and Christabel La Motte, and intersperses the novel with examples of their work. The twentieth-century narrative involves the main characters Roland Mitchell and Maud Bailey, both of whom are literary scholars. Roland is a post-doctoral research assistant working for the established literary critic James Blackadder, Maud is a lecturer at Lincoln University, and their two main research interests provide the basis for their meeting. Roland's PhD thesis has been on Randolph Ash and whilst researching his work in the library at the British Museum he comes across two versions of a letter that Ash has written to La Motte. Excited by his findings Roland uncharacteristically steals the two letters, not for financial gain, but for the intellectual excitement they generate. This provides the link to Maud Bailey as she is the leading British scholar on La Motte and Roland arranges to meet her to pursue his investigations. The subsequent research and uncovering of the previously hidden relationship between Ash and La Motte, and the parallel development of the relationship between Roland and Maud, provides the connected plot lines of the novel.

The various poems, stories and extracts by the Victorian characters act as a textual and historical hinge between the two narratives. Roland finds the letters in Randolph Ash's copy of Giambattista Vico's *The New Science* (1725) and this intertextual connection provides a theme for the novel. One of Vico's theories suggests that 'truth' is not only accessed by scientific fact and the language that science uses but that it can also be registered in the imaginary and literary motifs and symbols that a culture produces.[14] As Roland recognizes, the fact that Ash had been researching Vico for his poem 'Proserpina' shows that the he was interested in the idea that poetry can provide alternative expressions of truth to those represented in scientific discourse. This raises the question of the interpretation of works by Ash and La Motte that the text provides. As famous Victorian writers in the context of the novel, literary critics and historians have scrutinized their work. However, the prevailing interpretations promise to be overturned because of Roland's discovery. The reader is thereby encouraged to read the Victorian texts as critics and to make connections with what they discover about the lives of the two writers. As Vico's theory suggests, the 'truth' of the relationship between Ash and La Motte can be revealed not only in their personal correspondence but also through their imaginative and poetic writing.

To add to the complexity of discovering the truth about the relationship the novel juxtaposes different kinds of texts, which can be read differently once some of the facts about the writers' lives are revealed. One of the pleasures of the text is that a dramatic irony is established by the fact that the interpretations of the Victorian works by the dusty Blackadder and the voracious Cropper (a North American academic who acquires old English manuscripts for his own university library) will have to be completely re-assessed. The possession of the texts, as suggested by the title, relates, therefore, not only to ownership of the physical manuscripts but to knowledge about the meanings they produce and the lives of the authors that have produced them. By allowing the reader to see that these texts have not been accurately interpreted, a theme emerges in the novel that relates to poststructuralist understandings of literary criticism: that the prevailing interpretations of a text are never the final word. The poems of Ash and La Motte remain open to differing interpretations as they evade the desire by Blackadder and Cropper to close down the texts and to possess them by making every aspect fully knowable.

It is important to remember, however, that Byatt has written all of this – the main narrative as well as the poems attributed to Ash and La Motte. There is therefore a series of images, motifs and meaning that float across the various texts. One example of this process can be seen in the juxtaposition of La Motte's story 'The Glass Coffin' with the scene that precedes it in which Roland stays over at Maud's house for the first time. At the end of this section Maud's situation and character are described by means of attaching characteristics to La Motte. One example of this is in the way Maud's bathroom is described:

> He [Roland] moved gingerly inside the bathroom, which was not a place to sit and read or lie and soak, but a chill green glassy place, glittering with cleanness, huge dark green stoppered jars on water-green thick glass shelves, a floor tiled in glass tiles into whose brief and illusory depths one might peer, a shimmering shower curtain like a glass waterfall, a blind to match, over the window, full of watery lights.[15]

This passage appears to be a straightforward description of Maud's bathroom, but as well as revealing something about Maud's stand-offish character it also links to several motifs and themes in the novel. The bathroom space reminds us of the myth of Melusina, a myth that has inspired La Motte's poem 'The Fairy Melusina'. According to the myth Melusina is a mermaid who appears in public as a normal woman, but who in the private space of her bathroom reveals herself as a mermaid. This image of the 'real' identity of an individual being revealed in the bathroom is transferred to Maud. Melusina's true identity is only revealed when her lover spies her in her bathroom through a peephole. In the passage above this is represented by the gingerly moving Roland who is allowed access to Maud's private space. However, Maud's bathroom is not revealing of her 'true' self, as the Melusina myth suggests. It is discovered on the next page that Maud is not yet sure of her identity and therefore the cleanliness and minimalism of the bathroom serve in this case to conceal rather than reveal Maud's inner self.

This image of Maud as contained by exterior representations of herself is alluded to in La Motte's 'Glass Coffin' story that follows this passage. Roland reads the story after identifying that: 'Blanche Glover called Christabel the Princess. Maud Bailey was a thin-skinned Princess. He was an intruder into their female fast-nesses' (p. 58). In La Motte's fairy tale, the unlikely hero is not the usual prince but a tailor who, after choosing a glass key when offered three choices by the mysterious 'grey man', is sent on a mission where he eventually finds a sleeping princess. The princess is encased in a glass coffin, which reminds the hero of 'where a fast flowing stream comes to a little fall, how the water becomes glassy smooth'. Like Maud (and Christabel La Motte), the heroine of the fairy tale has 'gold hair [that] lay around her like a mantle'. This reminds us of the previous passage in which Maud had 'loosed from her shower cap all her yellow hair' (p. 57). The link between the emotionally repressed Maud and the princess in the story who lies in a coffin becomes clear at this point. The princess is described as a 'green ice egg', and she is awakened by the tailor, who opens her coffin with a (clearly phallic) glass key:

> And then he saw, in the side of the smooth box, which had no visible cleft or split, but was whole like a green ice egg, a tiny keyhole. And he knew that this was the keyhole for his won-drous delicate key, and with a little sigh he put it in and waited for what should ensue. And the little key slipped into the keyhole and melted, as it seemed into the glass body of the casket, so for a moment the whole surface was perfectly closed and smooth. And then, in a very orderly way, and with a strange bell-like tinkling, the coffin broke into a collection of long icicle splinters, that rang and vanished as they touched the earth. And the sleeper opened her eyes, which were as blue as periwinkle, or the summer sky, and the little tailor, because he knew this was what he must do, bent and kissed the perfect cheek. (p. 63)

This passage anticipates the 'awakening' of Maud by another unlikely hero, Roland, a hero who, like the tailor, acts on an intuitive choice (Roland steals the letters; the tailor chooses the glass key) and who is then set on an unknown quest that ultimately results in him encoun-tering a 'slumbering' princess. This situation not only relates to Maud and Roland, it is also analogous to Christabel's position before she encounters Randolph Ash and the fairy tale acts as a link between the two plots. The description of the princess' coffin as a green glass egg is taken up later in the text when Christabel in one of the private letters offers Ash the 'riddle of the egg'. The motif of the egg, of course, represents another image of an enclosed self-contained space that needs to be broken open before fruitful growth can occur.

The way, then, in which motifs are passed along the various kinds of text shows the complexity of Byatt's achievement in *Possession*. It also relates us back to another theme suggested by the reference to Giambattista Vico. Vico's model of history suggests that it moves in cycles rather than as a linear progression, and that it repeats itself. Vico was interested in the way that great civilizations go through periods of birth, ascendancy and decline, but this model chimes with *Possession* in the way that the discovery and description of the relationship between Ash and Christabel parallels the development of the relationship between Roland and Maud. The title of the novel indicates the genre in which it is written: a 'romance'. However, this reference should be understood as self-reflexive, if not ironic. The 'romantic' elements are clear in the parallel developing relationships of the two pairs of characters, but the novel also questions the way in which 'romance' represents a narrative code that determines to a certain extent not only the way the Victorian characters in the novel relate to each other, but also how romantic narrative structures also impinge on the 'realistic' contemporary love affair between Roland and Maud.

The novel does not only relate to the romance genre in its concerns with romantic love, it also includes other features of the genre, especially in its use of gothic situations and styles, which are often seen to encroach on its broadly realistic framework. The gothic as a genre works well with the novel's themes of showing the impact of the 'dead hand' on several of the contemporary characters, most notably in the scene in the graveyard towards the end of the novel in which the determined Cropper resorts to digging up the coffin of Randolph Ash to get hold of the secret that should have been left in the grave. In this scene the use of pathetic fallacy is so overdone as to parody the gothic style: 'The wind moved in the graveyard like a creature from another dimension, trapped and screaming. The branches of the yew and cedar gesticulated desperately' (p. 494). In a novel that pays close attention to literary style and the interpretation of style and meaning through the inclusion of the Victorian poets, this move to the gothic genre in the contemporary plot shows Byatt alerting the reader to the nature of fictions and their dependence on the language and style in which they are presented. Byatt cleverly adapts the style of the writing to the situation in which the characters find themselves. This can be seen in another earlier example in the text, the scene in which Maud and Roland first discover the secret letters between Ash and Christabel. The narrative at this point moves into the gothic style in its use of high emotion and suggestions of the uncanny in the figures of the dolls:

> They walked and walked, at first along tiled and bleakly lit corridors under electric lighting, and then along dusty carpets in dark shuttered places, and up a stone staircase and then further up a winding wooden stair, cloudy with dark dust. Maud and Roland neither looked nor spoke to each other. The little door was heavily panelled and had a heavy latch. They went in behind Sir George, who waved his huge cone of light around the dark, cramped, circular space, illuminating a semi-circular bay window, a roof carved with veined arches and mock-mediaeval ivy-leaves, felt-textured with dust, a box-bed with curtains still hanging, showing dull red under their pall of particles, a fantastically carved black wooden desk, covered with beading and scrolls, and bunches of grapes and pomegranates and lilies [. . .] a sudden row of staring tiny white faces, one, two, three, propped against a pillow. Roland drew his breath in minor shock: Maud said, 'Oh, the *dolls*' – and Sir George brought his light back from a blank mirror entwined with gilded roses and focussed it on the three rigid figures, semi-recumbent under a dusty counterpane, in a substantial if miniature four-poster bed. (p. 81)

This passage moves from the modernity of the 'electric lighting' to a gothic space of winding staircases and locked rooms. As the characters enter further into the closed off spaces of the country house, the reader moves closer to the secret at the heart of the text – not only to the discovery of the Ash and La Motte relationship, but to the heart of Maud's identity. The dolls are uncanny manifestations of Maud's inner self, an identity that, although she does not realise it at this stage, ultimately holds the key to her past. The apparatus of the gothic novel is, therefore, brought in at this stage to represent the theme of the search for the hidden identity at the heart of Maud's unconscious.

This passage begins to uncover the Victorian love story at the same time as it initiates the romance between Maud and Roland. Both romance plots are hampered by social and cultural codes, each of which has its respective historical context. In the Victorian narrative this is enforced by middle-class cultural codes of behaviour that police adulterous relationships, and in the case of Christabel and Blanche Glover, same-sex relationships. The contemporary period, however, is shown to be not simply a period in which these restrictions have been removed, but where a different set of restrictions now undermines the idea of romantic love, a set of cultural codes that impinges on the development of a sexual relationship just as much as Victorian conventions do for Ash and Christabel. In the contemporary narrative, feminist and poststructuralist theories, to which both Maud and Roland to differing extents subscribe, are seen to hamper the development of their romantic attachment. Maud, in particular, has been influenced by feminist theories and has developed her own sense of identity in relation to them. In the bathroom passage quoted earlier, Maud details the way in which her physical appearance is detached from her sense of self. When looking in the mirror she contemplates her image as 'a beautiful woman' but observes; 'The doll-mask she saw had nothing to do with her, nothing' (p. 57). She also describes how she had worn her hair cropped short as a way to accommodate her beauty within some of the positions within feminist thinking in the 1970s. This self-awareness is presented as debilitating as it has resulted in her being disconnected from the physicality of her body thereby making it difficult for her to enter into close physical and emotional relationships. As Katharine Tarbox has noted, the distance between the rationalism of literary criticism and the passionate enjoyment of reading has served as a feature of Byatt's writing: '[Byatt's] novels dwell on the failure of scholarship to contain and express the voice of passion'.[16]

The scepticism towards love functions as a bar to what is perceived as Roland and Maud's 'natural' urges, and for poststructuralist theory in particlaur, romantic love is reduced to another series of cultural narratives in which individuals might find themselves. As the novel explains: 'They were children of a time and culture which mistrusted love, "in love", romantic love, romance *in toto*, and which nevertheless in revenge proliferated sexual language, linguistic sexuality, analysis, dissection, deconstruction, exposure. They were theoretically knowing' (p. 423). To explain his emerging love for Maud, Roland falls back on his knowledge of critical theory by self-reflexively placing himself in a 'romance' narrative: 'He was in a Romance, a vulgar and a high romance simultaneously, a Romance was one of the systems that controlled him, as the expectations of Romance control almost everyone in the Western world, for better or worse, at some point or another' (p. 425). This is more than a playful metafictional device; it shows how postmodern self-awareness hampers Roland's feelings of love. In the romantic situation that develops with Maud his intellectual knowledge is far from an asset, it serves to contain him in a way that is analogous to the cultural restrictions placed on Ash and Christabel.

This questioning of the practical effects of contemporary theories is also related to Roland's understanding of the way writing and knowledge function. Roland eventually comes to a position by which he is forced to re-assess his poststructuralist beliefs about the nature of the relationship between writing and truth. He begins to accept that the way he has read texts in the past has been determined not by an emotional response but by a detached critical approach: 'There are readings – of the same text – that are dutiful, readings that map and dissect [. . .] Now and then there are readings which make the hairs on the neck, the non-existent pelt, stand on end and tremble' (p. 471). It is this second kind of reading that Roland experiences when re-reading one of Ash's poems in the light of his discoveries about the poet's personal life. He still recognizes that both kinds of reading are dependent on the context of the reader's situation, and that 'language was essentially inadequate' (p. 473), but his analytical temperament is nuanced by a new understanding that, 'the ways in which it *could* be said had become more interesting than the idea that it could not' (p. 473). This signals Roland's career move from literary criticism and scholarship to considering becoming a poet. In the context of the novel, criticism is limiting and self-serving in that it 'explains' that texts cannot be fully explained. In this sense poststructuralist criticism appears as biased in that it is in its own interest to suggest that criticism is unending. Poetry, on the other hand, comes to represent for Roland a form of language that might provide access to a kind of truth. This is similar to the position put forward by Vico, whose book, of course, contained Ash's drafted love letters. The poetic truth of romantic love is thereby passed on to Roland from Ash, and serves to make him question other forms of truth on which he has previously relied.

The plot of the novel, especially in its closing sections, also raises questions about the pursuit of literary criticism. Pursuit is an apt word in this context as the chase section at the end of the novel replicates the desire to disclose secrets and to track down meaning from a series of previously hidden events and associations. The novel turns self-consciously into a kind of literary detective fiction in the closing sections, and in detective fiction, the desire to know is the driving principle; as Maud says: 'We need the end of the story' (p. 498). This desire, however, is only partly satisfied. By the end of the contemporary story, Maud knows about her genealogical relationship to Ash and Christabel, but the epilogue upsets this sense of closure. For Maud and the other contemporaries it is assumed that Ash never knew his daughter, May, had survived, but the encounter between them in the epilogue (which remains unknown to the contemporaries) suggests that Ash did in fact realise that his daughter was still alive, despite the fact that Ellen felt it right not to pass on Christabel's final letter to him on his deathbed. This suggests that however far it is possible to interpret a text or an author's life there is always a supplement, an extra space in which the analysis can be pushed. In this way, then, the novel seems to agree partly with a poststructuralist approach to reading – that the meaning of a text can never be fully achieved and that a piece of literature will always remain open to further interpretations.

IAN MCEWAN, *ATONEMENT* (2001)

Atonement is McEwan's eighth novel, and like *Waterland* and *Possession* is interested in the relationship between history, memory and writing. One of the ways in which this is achieved is by using a metafictional frame. Unlike other classic framed narratives, however, such as *Wuthering Heights* (1847), *Heart of Darkness* (1899) and *Turn of the Screw* (1898), the framing does not become apparent until the novel's epilogue. The metafictional turn that McEwan provides at the end of the text forces the reader to re-assess the events of the preceding 350 pages. The central character is Briony Tallis, who at the opening of the novel is a thirteen-year-old girl who has ambitions to be a writer. The surprise of the ending is in part produced by the use of a third-person narration for most of the text, which on first reading creates an ironic distance, for example in Part One, towards Briony's over-romanticized emotional and aesthetic responses to the events she observes. The model for this form of narrative irony is taken from Jane Austen, and the epigram to the novel is from *Northanger Abbey* (1818), an illusion that combines a reference to the style, as well as the country house setting and the dangers of imposing an overly romanticized view of the world onto reality. McEwan has commented on his reasons for the allusion to Austen's novel as one of the guiding principles in *Atonement*:

> Catherine Morland, the heroine of Jane Austen's *Northanger Abbey*, was a girl so full of the delights of Gothic fiction that she causes havoc around her when she imagines a perfectly innocent man to be capable of the most terrible things. For many, many years I've been thinking how I might devise a hero or heroine who could echo that process in Catherine Morland, but then go a step further and look at, not the crime, but the process of atonement, and do it in writing – do it through story-telling, I should say.[17]

It is only later discovered that the three main parts of the novel are in fact an account written (and re-written) by Briony herself when she is much older, substituting the ironic narrative with one that is, in fact, closer to a kind of autobiographical novel whereby an external narrator comments on the beliefs and behaviour of an earlier self, a narrative framework that, for example, operates in traditional *Bildungsroman* novels like Charlotte Brontë's *Jane Eyre* (1847) and Charles Dickens's *Great Expectations* (1861). The whole novel then is, as McEwan suggests in the quotation above, an attempt to atone for actions by writing about them, and by turning them into a narrative.

The novel is divided into three parts, the first of which is set on a single day in 1935 at the country estate where Briony and her family live, including her father, who has a position in the government, her mother Emily, her sister Cecilia, and her brother Leon, as well as Robbie Turner, the son of the cleaning lady, who has been financially supported by her father after Robbie's own father absconded. On the day the events of the first part take place the family are being visited by their cousins Lola, and the twins Jackson and Pierrot whose parents are going through a divorce. After misreading the first stages of a love relationship between Robbie and Cecilia, Briony mistakenly accuses Robbie of attacking Lola by the lake in the grounds of the country house. She has observed Lola's attacker in the half-light and because of her feelings toward Robbie at this time mistakenly assumes that he is the culprit.

This first part is a kind of novel within a novel and is referred to later in the book as a fictional story, *Two Figures in the Fountain*, which Briony has sent to Cyril Connolly, a real historical figure who was the editor of *Horizon*, a literary magazine that began just before the Second World War.[18] The letter Briony receives from Connolly provides the first clues that the first part of the novel is in fact the re-written version of that story, as it includes the changes that Connolly has suggested such as correcting the reference to the location of the Bernini *Triton* (p. 18, p. 314).[19] Connolly's letter also provides a certain amount of irony in that he suggests that the girl narrator of the story should influence the relationship of the adults in some way: 'Might she come between them in some disastrous fashion' (p. 313). The letter also suggests that Briony's style 'owed a little too much to the techniques of Mrs Woolf'. This reference to the modernist techniques of Virginia Woolf has been alluded to by Briony previously in her thinking about becoming a writer: 'She had read Virginia Woolf's *The Waves* three times and thought that a great transformation was being worked in human nature itself, and that only fiction, a new kind of fiction, could capture the essence of the change' (p. 282). These bold claims for modernism in fiction are partly treated ironically here, as it is the detachment of art from real life that Briony fails to see at this point. Only later does she recognize the shortcomings of her adopted style: 'Did she really think she could hide behind some borrowed notions of modern writing, and drown her guilt in a stream – three streams! – of consciousness?' (p. 320). It is apparent, however, that Briony never completely drops her modernist style as there are passages in Part One that are similar to Woolf, for example, the action takes place over one day, a technique that Woolf uses in *Mrs Dalloway* (1925). In addition, some of the detailed description in Briony's internal monologue resonates with Woolf's style, for example, when she ponders the physical operation of bending her finger and the relationship her mind has to her physical actions (pp. 35–6).

Part Two continues this stream of consciousness style in the account of Robbie's experiences in France during the retreat of British troops to Dunkirk in the spring of 1940. That the modernist style continues suggests, once the metafictional twist is discovered, that it is indeed Briony who has also written this section, based on letters she has received from a Mr Nettles, who is presumably the character with the same name that accompanies Robbie across Northern France. It is through imagining Robbie's experiences that she begins to atone for the suffering she has caused him. Part Two also serves to debunk the myth of the heroic 'victory from defeat' that was imposed on the events surrounding Britain's withdrawal from France in the early parts of the Second World War. The events described in this section show a ramshackle and defeated army that is a mixture of heroic and more ambivalent acts of self-preservation. It also offers a parallel with Briony in its description of Robbie's feelings of guilt at abandoning a Flemish woman and her child he encounters during a Stuka attack, during which both are killed. When he reaches Dunkirk, Briony has Robbie considering whether to return north to 'ask the Flemish lady and her son if they held him accountable for their deaths' (p. 263). Eventually, however, he decides to try and get back to England to continue his relationship with Cecilia. His last words, 'you will not hear another word from me', are left ominously open, given what is later suggested about his fate in the epilogue (p. 265).

The third part provides a narrative of Briony's experience during the war in which she begins to assuage her guilt over her wrongful accusation of Robbie. Her experience of being trained as a nurse culminates in the events in the hospital when she first encounters the wounded returning from France, one of whom, she speculates might be Robbie (p. 298). The moment of atonement is actually displaced onto an eighteen-year-old French boy, Luc, who Briony comforts as he slips towards death. Luc is delirious and in her attempt to console him Briony accepts the fiction that she is his fiancée. Unlike the events in Part One, a fiction imposed upon reality is seen to have positive effects in that it eases the boy's death. It is after this event that Briony meets up once more with Cecilia and Robbie, and although the latter castigates her, she recognizes that she has experienced a certain amount of the suffering war causes: 'It was a pathetic form of comfort, that he could not know what she had seen' (p. 342). This final encounter represents a form of atonement, although one that is not fully achieved due to the fact that neither Robbie nor her sister will ever forgive her, and finally banish her from their lives. It is significant that in watching Cecilia and Robbie kiss, Briony 'had no wish to leave yet' suggesting that this moment is what she has needed to bring some kind of closure to her guilt, and in observing their kiss knows that her actions have not resulted in a complete break between the two lovers.

With the metafictional turn, however, it remains ambiguous how much of this Briony has romanticized and this introduces one of the central questions the novel asks: what are the ethical implications of fictionalizing the world? In Part One, much attention is paid to the way in which Briony, in her childlike way, is keen to miniaturize the world by imposing fixed and ordered narratives upon it. We are given an early indication of this in the neat and ordered way she arranges her toys, where, 'cowboys, deep-sea divers, humanoid mice – suggested by their even ranks and spacing a citizen's army awaiting orders' (p. 5). This desire to control is associated with the power Briony wishes to exert over the world around her and finds a perfect outlet in the stories she writes whereby, 'Her passion for tidiness was [. . .] satisfied, for an unruly world could be made just so' (p. 7). For Briony, frustration is caused by the fact that real life contaminates the purity, wholeness and order that can be obtained in her fictions and her first indication of this is when she attempts to stage her first play 'The Trials of Arabella'. In staging a play, she is forced to co-operate with others, and in doing so loses the control she craves over her creation. In dealing with her cousins Lola, Jackson and Pierrot she is subject to the ungovernable inconsistencies of real people who have their own anxieties and agendas. This experience alerts Briony to the possibility of the *otherness* of people, and the thought that she is not unique in having an inner life. As she muses to herself:

> Was being Cecilia just as vivid an affair as being Briony? Did her sister also have a real self concealed behind a breaking wave, and did she spend time thinking about it, with a finger held up to her face [sic]. Did everybody, including her father, Betty, Hardman? If the answer was yes, then the world, the social world, was unbearably complicated, with two billion voices, and everyone's thoughts striving in equal importance and everyone's claim on life as intense, and everyone thinking they were unique, when no one was. One could drown in irrelevance. (p. 36)

This marks a transition for Briony as she recognizes the complexity of the world and it marks a moment on her move towards maturity. For Briony the real world is complicated and muddled and will not behave like her miniature worlds. This is an unsettling feeling but it also involves a sense of the excitement of 'real' living. This culminates in her inability to understand the events she observes between Cecilia and Robbie at the fountain. The intimation of an adult world where actions take on meanings that cannot be comprehended fully represents an adolescent crisis for Briony to which she reacts by trying to impose her own narrative on the events. This fictional misreading of the real situation is exacerbated in her observation of the lovers in the library. Unfortunately, the narrative she imposes is drawn from her romanticized imagination, which fixes the main actors in simplified roles: Cecilia as the victim in need of protection and Robbie as the villain. The frustration at not being able to control the world in the way that she can control her fictions, therefore, carries the seeds of her misinterpretation of Robbie's relationship with Cecilia and the catastrophic outcome. As she tries to explain it to herself 'what she saw must have been shaped in part by what she already knew' (p. 123).

The novel, then, shows how romanticized accounts of real events can lead to dangerous misinterpretations. It is not only Briony who is susceptible to such misinterpretation; Cecilia and Robbie also fail to read the signs correctly in their relationship with each other. The organization of Part One into three stream of consciousness narratives emphasizes this process. One example is the way Cecilia and Robbie interpret differently a recent occasion when Robbie has removed his shoes and socks to enter the house. For Cecilia:

> Robbie had made a great show of removing his boots which weren't dirty at all, and then, as an afterthought, took his socks off as well, and tiptoed with comic exaggeration across the wet floor. Everything he did was designed to distance her. He was play-acting the cleaning lady's son come to the big house on an errand. (p. 27)

Robbie on the other hand sees the occasion differently:

> That was the day he had first noticed his awkwardness in her presence. Kneeling to remove his work shoes by the front door, he had become aware of the state of his socks – holed at toe and heel and, for all he knew, odorous – and on impulse had removed them. What an idiot he had felt, padding behind her across the hall and entering the library barefoot. (p. 84)

The discrepancy in these passages show how cultural codes are employed differently in the way in which people interpret each other's behaviour. For Cecilia, Robbie's actions are placed in a framework of a recognized cultural narrative: the resentful class-conscious parvenu in the aristocratic house. It is partly Robbie's status as a kind of class-crossing cuckoo that contributes to the willingness the Tallis family show in accepting Robbie is Lola's attacker. As Cecilia writes to Briony, 'I'm beginning to understand the snobbery that lay behind their stupidity' (p. 209). It is not only the Tallises that are susceptible, Robbie himself makes similar cultural presumptions in his (and Cecilia's) amazement that it is the wealthy, upper-class Peter Marshall who turns out to be the villain, and not Danny Hardman, the son of one of the Tallises's servants.

As Robbie reflects, once he discovers the truth, 'we owe an apology to Able Seaman Hardman' (p. 347). As Brian Finney has argued, one of the novel's themes is to show how the characters are suspect to the imposition of cultural fantasies, and that events serve to shake them out of their presumptions about others, whereby they are, 'expelled from the world they have constructed in their private fantasies into the unforgiving narrative of history, from narratives they concoct for their personal satisfaction to narratives concocted for them'.[20]

The novel also hints that Briony's naming of Robbie as Lola's attacker has a subconscious motivation. This has to do with a scene that occurred before the day described in Part One, but only later referred to as one of the memories given to Robbie in Part Two. An occasion is recalled when Briony was ten and before Robbie had gone off to university in which she had jumped in the estate's lake as a test to see whether Robbie would save her, after which she tells him she loves him. Robbie's subsequent rejection of her is seen as a potential, and perhaps repressed cause of her later keenness to denounce him, and it is perhaps significant that it is by the same lake that the attack on Lola takes place. Briony's repressed fantasy of a relationship with Robbie returns unconsciously when she sees Lola attacked several years later. The older Briony seems to understand that what was motivating the thirteen-year-old girl was the unconscious reaction to the rejection by Robbie of her adolescent romantic attraction to him. This is why the motivation is left out of the earlier text. It is only when Briony remembers this event that she can identify it as a cause for her attitude towards Robbie and show the way in which memory affects the interpretation of past events (see also p. 342 and pp. 231–2).

The importance of memory and its relationship with recording the past is a theme that returns in the epilogue. It is set in 1999, and we learn that Briony, now aged seventy-seven, has been diagnosed with vascular dementia, which means that her memory will progressively wither away along with 'language itself' (p. 355). This reveals the imperative behind her writing of the events contained in what we have previously read, which we now know represents the task set to her by Robbie to write down: 'Everything that led up to you saying you saw me by the lake'.[21] The initials and date at the end of Part Three suggest that this is the final draft of this letter of atonement: 'BT / London 1999' (p. 349). The three parts, then, are all part of Briony's attempt to atone for her actions and their consequences, but they are also an attempt to produce a written record of what happened.

The act of writing, therefore, provides a further complexity to the relationship between memory and the actual events. The first part shows how language is a slippery medium, and suggests the way in which the desire to record memories accurately is frustrated by the fact that language is not transparent or impartial, but already carries with it cultural signifiers and connotations that affect meaning. At one point in her thoughts Briony shows this, whilst in fact saying the opposite:

> By means of inking symbols onto a page, she was able to send thoughts and feelings from her mind to her reader's. It was a magical process, so commonplace that no-one stopped to wonder at it. Reading a sentence and understanding it were the same thing; as with the crooking of a finger, nothing lay between them. There was no gap during which the symbols were unravelled. You saw the word *castle*, and it was there, seen from some distance, with woods in high summer spread before it, the air bluish and soft with smoke rising from the blacksmith's forge, and a cobbled road twisting away into the green shade. (p. 37)

The ironic distance towards Briony allows us to see what she cannot; that her use of words leads her not into a straight system of communication, 'to send thoughts and feelings from her mind to her reader's', but in fact generate a series of meanings that are either subjective or loaded with culturally determined nuances and connotations that are not implicit in the words themselves, for example, in the train of romantic thoughts generated by the word *castle*. This is the lesson that Briony has still to learn at this point; that words are not as straightforward as they appear.

The ending, however, emphasizes the ethical implications of the relationship between truth and fiction and turns the desire to romanticize back onto the reader. It is suggested that closure can only be achieved by turning life into art. The paradox of this suggestion, however, is that this is the very approach that caused the problem in the first place. Although Briony achieves atonement for herself at the end, the novel itself remains less conciliatory, as we are left with the open ending, with the habit real life has of disrupting and destabilizing any attempt to impose order on it. There is, then, still an ironic distance in play at the end of the novel towards Briony. It is never fully explained ·whether the final meeting between Briony, Cecilia and Robbie ever took place within the realistic frame of the novel's events. However, as she states: 'If I really cared so much about facts, I should have written a different kind of book' (p. 360). Briony is still searching for a kind of emotional and aesthetic truth in her narrative, one that transcends mere facts. It is this impulse that persuades her to provide a wholeness to the story in the coming together of Cecilia and Robbie as the desired conclusion to a love story. The alternative circumstances she hints at, that 'Robbie Turner died of septacemia at Bray Dunes [and . . .] Cecilia was killed [. . .] by the bomb that destroyed Balham Underground' (p. 370) is too painful to write. The novel, then, asserts that the redemptive power of fiction allows it a certain licence with the truth, if the consequence of that licence is to produce a life-enhancing work. As Briony explains, 'Who would want to believe that they never met again?' (p. 371). The assertion towards the end of Part Three that, 'it was fixed in the unchangeable past' may not be corroborated by the epilogue, but it supplies an emotional truth that allows Briony to come to terms with her guilt (p. 348). It is in the fixing of the romantic story that the past gains a crystallization that is not available in real life.

SUMMARY OF KEY POINTS

- Traditional notions of history have been challenged by postmodern and poststructuralist theory. This has resulted in the pluralization of historical accounts, a focus on the inevitable bias of the agent constructing any historical text, and the role of language in writing about the past.
- An interest in the histories or 'genealogies' of previously marginalized communities and experience has shown how history is related to power relationships between people(s).

- Graham Swift is particularly concerned with the different ways of recounting the past, and in the relationship between social and political history and hidden personal and family narratives.
- *Possession* explores the relationship between nineteenth century and contemporary Britain in terms of the cultural forces acting upon individuals from both periods. Byatt frames this exploration in a self-conscious engagement with the genre of romance fiction.
- Ian McEwan is concerned with how writing transforms 'real' experience and the way in which a particularly romanticized view of the world can be both dangerous and soothing.

NOTES

1. Salman Rushdie, *Shame* (London: Picador, [1983] 1984), p. 124.
2. Jago Morrison, *Contemporary Fiction* (London: Routledge, 2003), p. 19.
3. Fredric Jameson, *Postmodernism, or, The Cultural Logic of Late Capitalism* (London: Verso, 1991), p. 18.
4. Linda Hutcheon, *A Poetics of Postmodernism: History, Theory, Fiction* (London: Routledge, 1988), p. 110.
5. Ibid., p. 89.
6. Hayden White, 'Introduction to Metahistory', in *Literature in the Modern World*, 2nd edn, ed. Dennis Walder (Oxford: Oxford University Press, 2004), pp. 444–9.
7. Beryl Bainbridge, *Young Adolf* (London: Duckworth, 1978); Julian Barnes, *Arthur and George* (London: Jonathan Cape, 2005).
8. Jameson, *Postmodernism*, pp. 16–31.
9. Daniel Lea, *Graham Swift* (Manchester: Manchester University Press, 2005), p. 76.
10. Graham Swift, *Waterland* (London: Picador, [1984] 1992), p. 7. All subsequent references in the text are to this edition.
11. Jean-François Lyotard, 'Answering the Question: What Is Postmodernism', trans. Régis Durand, in *The Postmodern*

Condition: A Report on Knowledge, trans. Geoff Bennington and Brian Massumi (Manchester: Manchester University Press, [1979] 1984), pp. 71–82, p. 78.

12. Ibid., p. 81.

13. Lea, *Graham Swift*, p. 82.

14. Giambattista Vico, *The New Science*, ed. Anthony Grafton, trans. David Marsh (Harmondsworth: Penguin, [1725] 2000).

15. A. S. Byatt, *Possession: A Romance* (London: Vintage, 1990), p. 56. All subsequent references in the text are to this edition.

16. Katharine Tarbox, 'Desire for Syzygy in the Novels of A. S. Byatt', in *The Contemporary British Novel since 1980*, ed. James Acheson and Sarah C. E. Ross (Basingstoke: Palgrave, 2005), pp. 177–88, p. 177.

17. Quoted in Peter Childs (ed.), *The Fiction of Ian McEwan: A Reader's Guide to Essential Criticism* (Basingstoke: Palgrave, 2006), p. 131.

18. Ian McEwan, *Atonement* (London: Vintage, [2001] 2002), p. 311. All subsequent references in the text are to this edition.

19. She also decides on Connolly's advice to change the vase from being Ming, although she chooses Meissen rather than Sevres or Nymphenburg as Connolly suggests as alternatives (p. 24, p. 313).

20. Brian Finney, 'Ian McEwan: *Atonement*', in *English Fiction Since 1984: Narrating a Nation* (Basingstoke: Palgrave, 2006), p. 93.

21. The metafictional conundrum the novel sets up means that it can never be known whether this instruction was really made by Robbie or Briony has projected it on to him.

CHAPTER 5

Narratives of Cultural Space

The importance of geographical location and different interpretations of cultural space has had a profound effect on the
British novel over the last few years. One of the factors in this
context is the shifting understanding of regional and national identity. Politically the United Kingdom is a unified state, but culturally
it is an amalgam of social, ethnic and national identities. The relationship between geographical space and the way discrete regions
are constructed in the collective imagination has proved fertile
ground for a number of recent novelists. The interrogation of the
concepts of Irishness, Welshness, Englishness and Scottishness, for
example, in a range of works by writers including Seamus Deane,
Niall Griffiths, Adam Thorpe, and Irvine Welsh (respectively) have
shown an increasing interest in interrogating what it means for an
individual to be attached to cultural discourses of national identity.[1]
The historical legacies of colonialism and diaspora have also
resulted in new cultural spaces in Britain, which correspond in
many ways to Stuart Hall's concept of 'new ethnicities' as discussed
in Chapter 2. This sense of cultural diversity has been explored
further with respect to other indicators of geographical location
such as the metropolis, cities, towns, suburbia and the 'country'.

This chapter looks at the importance of cultural and geographic
spaces in contemporary British fiction. The three novels covered
are Hanif Kureishi's *The Buddha of Suburbia* (1990), Iain Sinclair's
Downriver (1991) and Julian Barnes's *England, England* (1998), each

of which combines themes of cultural space with issues of form, identity and a political critique of certain aspects of British society that have been prominent during the period from the seventies onwards. Analysis of Kureishi's novel focuses on the representation of urban and suburban spaces with respect to issues of ethnic and sexual identity. Iain Sinclair's distinctive style of psychogeography is explored by focussing on a combination of narratives with a re-writing of the experience of passing through urban space set against a back-drop of East London in the 1980s. Julian Barnes's *England, England* considers the way in which national identity is culturally constructed and reproduced. It addresses the circulation of national stereotypes, the commodification of the nation and the relationship between personal and national identity.

HANIF KUREISHI, *THE BUDDHA OF SUBURBIA* (1990)

Unlike most of the novelists covered in this book, Hanif Kureishi published his first novel after gaining success in the theatre and as a screenwriter. His highly acclaimed play, TV drama and later film, *My Beautiful Laundrette* was produced in 1985 and was remarkable in its mixture of contemporary social commentary, sexual politics and youth culture. To a certain extent *The Buddha of Suburbia* continues to explore these themes, but the more expansive form of the novel allows Kureishi to develop these issues further and to allow greater insight into the internal thoughts, desires and anxieties of its main character. The text combines two genres, the *Bildungsroman* and the 'Condition of England' novel, but as with many of the works covered in this book, it brings these essentially nineteenth-century genres into a contemporary setting. As the main character declares at one point, after describing the violence and prejudice experienced in a modern state school: 'Fuck you, Charles Dickens, nothing's changed'.[2] Like Dickens's *Great Expectations*, Kureishi's novel traces the development from childhood to adulthood of a single character, in this case Karim Amir. Like Pip, in Dickens's novel, Karim passes through several social spheres, which allows Kureishi to comment on various issues of cultural politics including class, race, sexuality and gender. Karim's story spans the 1970s, beginning with him at high school and ending on the eve of Margaret Thatcher's first term of office in 1979. Alongside the political and social commentary, it traces the cultural history of Britain, especially in the importance of several popular musical forms and subcultures of the period, from the end of the influence of the hippie movement in Britain to the beginnings of New Wave in the late seventies.

One of the most important aspects of *The Buddha of Suburbia* is its attention to the cultural significance of place. The title alludes to one of these locations and a dialectical opposition is established between suburbia and the city. The novel begins in the suburbs, in Beckenham in South London, in which Karim feels a cloying tedium and restriction and increases his desire for 'trouble, any kind of movement, action and sexual interest' (p. 3). London, by contrast 'seemed like a house with five thousand rooms, all different' (p. 126). The bipartite structure of the novel reflects the movement from suburbia to the metropolis, with Part One titled 'In the Suburbs' and Part Two 'In the City'. However, the movement between these two cultural spaces is not as simple as this framework suggests as Karim passes back and forth between suburbia and the city, re-assessing his relationship to his each as the novel progresses. As Susan Brook has argued, 'The suburb [. . .] emerges as a space of in-betweenness, albeit of an unfashionable kind – of the lower middle classes, of middle England'.[3]

Alongside this urban–suburban relationship, the novel, then, deals with national and cultural contexts and, in particular, with the idea of Englishness in the late twentieth century alongside the meaning of Indianness for a series of characters who have either immigrated from India or are the children of immigrants. The context for this commentary on cultural geographies is grounded in the figure of Karim, who introduces himself as 'an Englishman born and bred, almost' but a 'funny kind of Englishman, a new breed as it were, having emerged from two old histories' (p. 3). Karim is the son of an Indian father who came to Britain in the 1950s and a white English mother. He is a hybrid figure, one who has influences from two ethnic backgrounds and it is in this sense that he perceives himself as 'a new breed'. This is reminiscent of Stuart Hall's concept of new ethnicities as discussed in the

Introduction, whereby the old racial categories that tended to fix people within monolithic groups such as black and white are losing their relevance in contemporary society. Karim also suggests that it is 'the odd mixture of continents and blood, of here and there, of belonging and not, that makes me restless and easily bored' (p. 3). Karim's hybridity marks him out as different despite being part of a predominantly suburban, English lower-middle-class culture at the beginning of the novel. In this sense, he occupies a liminal space with respect to mainstream English culture; he is both an insider and outsider and his experiences are to a large extent determined by his cultural inbetweenness.

One of the features of the novel is as a record of the kind of racism encountered in seventies Britain by characters from non-white ethnic backgrounds and it shows how racism takes several forms and can be found at all levels of society. The area where his cousin, Jamila, lives is 'full of neo-fascist groups' (p. 56) and there are several accounts of racially motivated physical attacks and intimidation, for example, the shop owned by Jamila's parents, Anwar and Jeeta, is attacked by racists. Later in the text, Changez, Jamila's husband, is set upon by a group of National Front supporters who attempt to carve 'NF' on his chest with razor blades (p. 224). Another example is the passage where Karim is informed by 'Hairy Back', the father of Helen, a white girl he starts to go out with, that: 'We don't want you blackies coming to the house'. Helen's father ejects him from their drive by setting his Great Dane on him, a scene that culminates in the dog ejaculating on Karim's back. This passage, although having an element of humour, symbolically represents a form of racial humiliation meted out to an outsider by a representative of the dominant culture.

These experiences come from the working and lower-middle-class environment where Karim grows up, but he finds that racism is also apparent in the so-called liberal middle and upper-middle-class circles in which he begins to move when he becomes an actor; although the forms the racism takes here are far more subtle. Karim's first acting job is in an adaptation of *The Jungle Book*, put on by the minor producer Shadwell. Karim is forced to play a cultural stereotype in his portrayal of Mowgli, which involves a series of cultural ironies by which he is 'blacked up' (because his skin is not quite dark enough) and forced to deliver his lines with a mock-Indian accent. The humiliation he feels in this role is part of the way in which Shadwell tries to return Karim to a subordinate position, effectively re-colonizing him, as his new 'English' identity is not deemed appropriate. One of the ironies, here, is that Shadwell claims that he wants the production to be more 'authentic' but it is clear that this kind of authenticity in practice results in Karim being reduced to a cultural stereotype. Although Karim tries to resist the process by 'suddenly relapsing into Cockney at odd times' (p. 158), the inauthentic position in which he is placed is recognized by both his father and Jamila; as the latter comments, 'It was disgusting, the accent and the shit you had smeared over you. You were just pandering to prejudices' (p. 157). Karim's experiences at the hands of Shadwell is an example of what Paul Gilroy has identified as 'cultural racism': a form of prejudice that does not focus directly on biology but attempts to re-establish a power relationship based on the perceived cultural practices engaged in by a particular ethnic group.[4]

The novel recognizes that the causes of racism are complex, but one of the reasons suggested is as a legacy of colonialism. The decline of the British Empire produces a residual sense of superiority amongst some of the white characters, exacerbated because the justification for this way of thinking is clearly undermined by the processes of decolonization in the years after the Second World War. As Karim's father explains: 'The whites will never promote us [. . .] they still think they have an Empire when they don't have two pennies to rub together' (p. 27). Shadwell, in considering Karim, emphasizes the ironies of this postcolonial situation whilst at the same time re-imposing a discourse based on racial difference:

What a breed of people two hundred years of imperialism has given birth to. If the pioneers from the East India Company could see you. What puzzlement there'd be. Everyone looks at you, I'm sure, and thinks: an Indian boy, how exotic, how interesting, what stories of aunties and elephants we'll hear now from him. And you're from Orpington. (p. 141)

Although Shadwell's tone is supercilious, he identifies one of the reasons behind the kind of racism Karim suffers: the contradictions and prejudices that are activated when old England meets this 'new breed' of Englishman (p. 3) are already determined by his appearance and his hybrid identity.

In reaction to these experiences of racism, Karim develops a desire for revenge that represents a backlash against the old colonial power. This can be seen in the pleasure he has in getting revenge on racists, such as the scene in which he gets his own back on 'Hairy Back': 'Had he known that four Pakis were resting their dark arses on his deep leather seats, ready to be driven by his daughter, who had just been fucked by one of them, he wouldn't have been a contented man' (p. 78). The use of the terms 'Pakis' and 'dark arses' shows Karim revelling in this idea of revenge by subverting the very language of the racists. As Jago Morrison writes: 'The comic effectiveness of scenes like this depends on our willingness to participate in a kind of ironic "post-racism"'.[5] Karim's father's actions are also motivated by a kind of post-colonial revenge, as he says at one point: 'You couldn't let the ex-colonialists see you on your knees, for that was where they expected you to be. They were exhausted now; their Empire was gone; their day was done and it was our turn' (p. 250). Karim's father, Haroon, is the suburban Buddha alluded to in the title and shows an ability to exploit cultural stereotypes to his own advantage. He takes on the image of the exotic mystic to get money out of the gullible, suburban, white middle class, and is, therefore, aware of the way in which cultural identities can be used to turn the exploitation back on the colonial centre. His position as a 'lapsed Muslim masquerading as a Buddhist', whilst at the same time continuing his day job as a suited civil servant, shows this fluidity of cultural identity and how it can be used for personal gain. Haroon, however, becomes increasingly convinced that his spiritual transformation is a way to escape the pressures placed on him by Western consumer capitalism, and inadvertently achieves a level of authenticity in his embracing of an Eastern religion.

Karim reflects on the effects of racism when considering the fate of Gene, the suicide ex-lover of Eleanor (the upper-class English woman with whom Karim has an affair). This reflection shows how broad cultural movements play themselves out in individual tragedies:

Sweet Gene, her black lover, killed himself because everyday, by a look, a remark, an attitude, the English told him they hated him; they never let him forget they thought him a nigger, a slave, a lower being. And we pursued our English roses as we pursued England; by possessing these prizes, this kindness and beauty, we stared defiantly into the eye of the Empire and all its self-regard [. . .] We became part of England and yet proudly stood outside it. But to be truly free we had to free ourselves of all the bitterness and resentment, too. (p. 227)

This passage shows both the effects of racism, but also the desire for revenge, played out in a sexual politics that tends to re-victimize white women as a reaction to the injustices of the colonial encounter. Kureishi, through Karim, suggests that this reaction is a form of colonialism in reverse and represents a continuation of an exchange of exploitation. However, it is suggested that only by rejecting the whole discourse of the superiority of the white colonial, which in turn generates the desire for revenge, that the legacy of colonialism can finally be removed. Events towards the end of the novel seem to suggest this move away from revenge to a deeper understanding that the idea of colonial superiority can now be recognized as an ideological fiction. Haroon, for example, in a reflective analysis of contemporary English culture, tells a magazine reporter that 'there has been no deepening in culture, no accumulation of wisdom, no increase in the way of the spirit' (p. 264). This represents a critique on the way in which English culture has suffered during the post-war period, both in the adoption of a consumer-led culture that culminates in the arrival of Thatcherism as the novel closes, but also in the refusal to accept that England is no longer a great imperial power. The way this is expressed, however, is as a form of sympathy for England, rather than a cause for revenge.

Alongside the critique of some of the characteristics of contemporary Englishness, Kureishi also challenges some of the cultural practices in Indian culture. Karim's uncle Anwar is one of the main targets for this criticism. Anwar is described as a more traditional Muslim than Karim's father, and appears to be going through an immigrant mid-life-crisis, which manifests itself in his trying to maintain a rapidly crumbling patriarchal power over his family. To keep his rebellious daughter Jamila in line he uses moral blackmail by going on hunger strike to make her marry the man he has chosen to be her husband. This represents an attempt by the older generation to impose Indian sensibilities on the new generation that have been brought up in England. Karim's dad explains, 'We old Indians come to like this England less and less and we return to an imagined India' (p. 74). The problem with this line of thinking, however, is that it negatively affects his family and ironically, Changez, the husband from India Anwar chooses for Jamila, disappoints his expectations by being lazy and unable to take over the work necessary to run the shop. As Bart Moore-Gilbert argues: 'At the root of Kureishi's objections to Anwar's "nativism" is its reliance on fixed and essentialist conceptions of identity which replicate precisely the assumptions that the author most deplores in the cultural nationalism of the host culture'.[6]

The description of Karim's father, Haroon, is also equivocal. In some ways, Karim respects his father's bravery in throwing off his old suburban life and taking on a new spiritual life with Eva, the woman with whom he has an affair. But Karim also blames Haroon for his treatment of his mother. His attitude to his father is sometimes reverential, but more often mocking as, for example, when he takes to calling him 'God' when he adopts the persona of an Eastern mystic. Karim's ambivalence towards his part-Eastern background is also registered through his critique of Indian culture as he observes it in his family; however, towards the end of the novel he begins to realize that: 'I did feel, looking at these strange creatures now – the Indians – that in some way these were my people, and that I'd spent my life denying or avoiding that fact' (p. 212).

This exploration of cultural identity is connected to the geographical contexts the novel employs. As discussed earlier, the geography of the book moves broadly from suburbia to the sophisticated urban spaces of London, but there are also descriptions of other cultural locations that reflect the state of the nation during the 1970s. There is, for example, the description of working-class housing estates in South London:

> The housing estates looked like makeshift prison camps; dogs ran around; rubbish blew about; there was graffiti. Small trees

had been planted with protective wire netting around them, but they'd all been snipped off anyway. The shops sold only inadequate and badly made clothes. Everything looked cheap and shabby. (p. 224)

The novel describes white working-class culture from a distance, and the one character from that group, Terry, is presented as being atypical. Karim recognizes that these are the areas that produce much of the right-wing sentiment that results in racially motivated violence that he and his family experience. The novel is aware, however, of the way in which these areas can be culturally misrepresented, especially by middle-class commentators. In his analysis of 1970s theatre, Karim comments:

The writers took it for granted that England, with its working class composed of slags, purple-nosed losers, and animals fed on pinball, pornography and junk-food, was disintegrating into terminal class struggle. These were the science-fiction fantasies of Oxford-educated boys who never left the house. The middle class loved it. (p. 207)

Kureishi identifies, here, a similarity in the way that the English middle classes reimpose stereotypes of both ethnic and white working-class culture, which serve to confirm prejudices even when on the surface they appear to be challenging them. The novel, however, is also keen to distance itself from the kind of romanticizing of the working classes that is an aspect of Terry's political outlook.

One of the other ways in which the novel tries to mark out a territory that challenges conventional notions of Englishness is through its discussion of subcultures based on popular music and fashion. Bart Moore-Gilbert has suggested that: 'For Kureishi pop epitomises the liberating energies of the "cultural revolution" which began in the 1960s'. However, the representation of different pop and rock styles in *The Buddha of Suburbia* is more complex and ambivalent than this suggests.[7] As a representative example of Asian-British youth, Karim and Jamila tend to look outside of Britain for their cultural influences, although not necessarily in places that register their ethnic background: 'sometimes we were French, Jammie and I, and other times we went black American' (p. 53). Karim, though, is more influenced by the British (and American-influenced) pop scene in the 1970s. The description of these subcultures and the relationship to them of individual characters represents a form of cultural history and reflects some of the social and political changes of the period, especially as it impacts on the generation to which Karim, Jamila and Charlie (Eva's son) belong.

The novel opens at the beginning of the 1970s when the bands that had come to prominence in the sixties (The Beatles, The Rolling Stones, The Kinks, The Faces and Pink Floyd are all referred to) are still the major pop cultural influence on the youths growing up in South London. This is at the end of the hippie generation and the idealism and promise that it offered seem now to be out of date, and also no longer relevant to Karim's geographical location. Helen, for example, wants to go and live in San Francisco, but by the beginning of the seventies as Karim notes, 'the kid's crusade was curdling now, everyone had overdosed' (p. 71). What emerges as the new musical influence is the advent of glam rock, and in particular, the figure of David Bowie who was a former pupil at Karim's school. In the context of the novel, the figure of Bowie promises not a new world order based on the collective and socialistic principles of hippiedom, but an individualist hedonism carrying with it the excitement of sexual excess. Charlie taps into each of the transitions in pop history recorded in the novel in a way that is emblematic of a throwaway pop culture that mirrors consumer capitalism's emphasis on the need to possess the next big thing. That Charlie is able to jettison past subcultural styles and take on new ones tells us something both of his character, but also the social and economic framework from which it arises. This is more pronounced in the arrival of punk in the mid-seventies. On seeing a punk band in a club in London, although initially sceptical, Charlie is by the end of the night seduced by the possibilities this new scene offers: 'The sixties have been given notice tonight. These kids we saw have assassinated all hope. They're the fucking future' (p. 131). Charlie is quick to adopt the new style and he changes the name of his band from 'Musn't Grumble' to 'The Condemned' and his own name to

Charlie Hero to reflect the angry, but often self-serving aspects of punk. In this section of the book, however, Charlie is shown to be exploiting punk rather than having any authentic claim to the social and cultural experiences that have produced it. Despite Karim's objection that 'we're not from the estates', Charlie is convinced that, 'suburban boys like us always know where it's at' (p. 132).[8] Charlie becomes a success as a punk artist due to his ability to exploit the latest trend, which makes up for his lack of talent. His real ability is to recognize the potential embedded within new subcultural trends and to adapt, chameleon-like to its main terms of signification. Charlie thus represents the process by which original and potentially subversive subcultural movements are quickly absorbed into consumer society and become part of the very establishment that the originators of the movement set themselves against.

This can be seen in the passage that describes Charlie's new punk attire, which, as Dick Hebdige has identified in punk, is a form of *bricolage* of cultural signifiers, each of which connotes some form of rebellion:

> He wore, inside out, a slashed T-shirt with a red swastika hand-painted on it. His black trousers were held together by safety-pins, paperclips and needles. Over this he had a black mackintosh; there were five belts strapped around his waist and a sort of grey linen nappy attached to the back of his trousers. The bastard was wearing one of my green waistcoats, too. (p. 152)[9]

This description identifies the political ambivalence of punk, a style that recycles fascist iconography alongside the rejection of consumer society through the use of safety pins and paperclips. Charlie's motives, however, are personal ambition and his inauthenticity represents the way in which punk very quickly became absorbed into dominant cultural mores. As with the misrepresentation of Indians and the working class, punk, as Charlie exploits it, is merely an indication of a culture that operates at a surface simulation of rebellion, without any depth to its potentially radical agenda.

The Buddha of Suburbia, then, offers a critique of the kind of consumer culture and individualism that was gaining credence in the seventies as a reaction to the sense of lost idealism promised by the cultural revolutions of the sixties. This kind of individualism becomes mainstream with the advent of Thatcherism in the 1980s. The historical context needs to be put in perspective here: although the novel is set during the seventies, it is published in 1990, when the legacies of Thatcherism had become more pronounced, but in hindsight were seen to have been developed in the previous decade. As Changez notes: 'Here, in this capitalism of the feelings no one cares for another person' (p. 215) and Karim becomes emblematic of this kind of selfish individualism. Most of the characters recognize this. Jamila informs him that: 'Actually, you've got no morality, have you?' (p. 157), whilst Eleanor recognizes that: 'You don't understand other people' (p. 198). Karim is aware of his shortcomings: 'I'm probably not compassionate or anything, I bet I'm a real bastard inside and don't care for anyone' (p. 104). Despite him being a charismatic and often likeable narrator, these judgements are recognized as accurate. His treatment of Changez, who he calls his friend and yet betrays on a number of occasions, is indicative of his general amorality. Karim partly begins to remedy his lack of feeling for others as he begins to mature towards the end of the text. As a symbol, however, he represents a 'new breed' not only in ethnic terms, but also in his lack of moral responsibility to others. The 1970s is represented as a decade in Britain where the dominant outlook represents a mixture of ambition and lethargy, a desire to achieve as much as possible, at the lowest possible cost in terms of effort. The exchange value, here, makes perfect economic sense, but results in a culture that places success above talent, and individual ambition above the development of meaningful human relationships. Charlie is the apotheosis of this, but it is also an important element in Karim's characterization: 'the spirit of the age among the people I knew manifested itself as general drift and idleness' (p. 94). This sense of drift stays with Karim throughout the text, despite his minor successes as an actor. By the end of the novel, he still appears directionless, and the attempt to complete the *Bildungsroman* narrative by reintegrating him into his family is unconvincing. The strengths of the novel lie its evocation of the way in which social, political and cultural forces of the 1970s impacted on the behaviour of individuals and created an essentially new culture, where the 'new breed', represented by Karim and Charlie, will flourish in the coming individualistic outlook of the 1980s. It is this decade that forms the basis for Iain Sinclair's critique of Thatcherism in *Downriver*.

IAIN SINCLAIR, *DOWNRIVER* (1991)

At the end of the first chapter of Iain Sinclair's novel *Downriver* there is a section where one character, Joblard, arranges twelve postcards to form a narrative that evokes Joseph Conrad's *Heart of Darkness* (1899). Each of the postcards is given its own itemized description, a process that effectively turns a visual medium into a linguistic one. In the last of the twelve accounts of the postcards, the photographer steps into his own frame allowing another to take the picture and the end of this account explains: 'He [the photographer] is the true author of this fiction that could, of course, be reassembled in any order, and read in whatever way suits the current narrator. These dim postcards are as neutral as a Tarot pack'.[10] This arrangement of narratives based on visual observation is a metaphor for the approach and structure of the book as a whole. *Downriver*, like the postcards, is arranged into twelve chapters and the book eschews the conventional narrative drive forward by presenting us with the idea that the organization is arbitrary and that the chapters could be read in more or less any order. Each of the chapters has its own theme and narrative, but the link with the other chapters does not follow a logic of sequential cause and effect. This replicates an experimental form that was used in the sixties by writers such as William Burroughs called 'cut-up', whereby the writer would produce a series of sentences or paragraphs, cut them into sections, and then rearrange them in an arbitrary order. *Downriver* pays homage to that tradition, although it must be stressed that in Sinclair's case there is a deeper sense of order established in the presentation of the chapters, despite giving the sense that they are arbitrary. Each of them involves a kind of frustrated search, whether for individuals such as Edith Cadiz in the third chapter 'Horse Spittle', or for the details behind a historical narrative such as the first train murder in Chapter 6, '*Eisenbahnangst*'. What also links the chapters is the unsettling and sometimes threatening presence of the River Thames. It is also the Thames that offers life and death, and represents a transcendent natural force that is disinterested in the fate of the people that line its shores.[11] It is the Thames that is referred to in the title and this provides us with the location for most of the book, 'down' river referring to the East End of London and out towards the Docklands and the Isle of Dogs, the scene of major architectural, social and cultural changes in the 1980s. It is also the changes in these East London locations that provide the main political context of the book.

Sinclair began his literary career as a poet and this poetic sensibility is carried into his lush descriptions of character and landscape. Take, for example, the following passage, which describes the history of illegal importation of exotic animals into London's docklands:

> Marmosets, lemurs, genets, tamarins and sugar gliders were brought ashore, covertly, and traded from public houses along the Highway. Across the tables of the Old Rose bundles were passed. From under stiff seamen's jerseys, small hot lives were drawn, living hearts. The locals adopted them without certificates or rabies clearance, without quarantine. The tamed exotics enriched their primal soot. (p. 33)

This passage includes rhetorical devices and sound effects that mark out Sinclair's poetic approach to prose narrative, for example, the alliterative 's' sounds in the list of animals; the shift to the passive tense in the second sentence; the use of punctuation to control the flow of the sentences, and the use of metonymy in 'living hearts'. The last sentence provides a rhythmic quality that is almost iambic pentameter, and uses the evocative, yet economical metaphor of the life of the East Londoners as 'primal soot'. Sinclair's style abounds with such poetic devices, and this tends to slow down the pace of reading, as attention has to be paid to the organization of words as well as their meaning. In this sense, Sinclair works in a tradition of prose writing that has allegiances with the modernist experimentalists of the early and mid-twentieth century, writers such as Henry James, Joseph Conrad, James Joyce, D. H. Lawrence and Virginia Woolf.

Sinclair combines this attention to the flow of language with a gothic sensibility, especially seen in his description of characters and setting. At one point the narrator refers to the narrative style as 'Baroque Realist', which captures the sense of an exaggerated observation of reality. Most of his characters are on the margins of society; they are grotesques that are just about people it might be possible to encounter in real life. Take, for example, this description of Jon Kay, the captain of a boat, the narrator and his companion Joblard take on the Thames:

> This creature, our self-inflicted Ahab, hitched his pants and lurched, bow-legged, towards us. He couldn't make up his mind whether he wanted to be a cowboy or an Indian. He had the bronze skin of a reservation Apache, and the last non-institutionalized Frank Zappa moustache on the planet. A shockwave of snakecurl hair had been tipped over him: like well-mashed seaweed. (p. 327)

The cultural incongruity of this figure – the Americanized physical characteristics and clothing of a character appearing on a dilapidated wharf in East London – exemplifies Sinclair's technique in character description. Nearly all of the characters the narrator encounters seem to be out of place in the environment in which they are located. They are alienated figures who exist in a dark underworld of violence and squalor, and often represent some aspect of a lost culture in a London that is rapidly changing around them. Most of them are oddly déclassé: impoverished booksellers, actors, photographers and film-makers who are struggling to make a living in Thatcher's Britain, a nation where it is suggested there has been a wholesale devaluation of artistic culture and where books, once the arbiters of cultural value are reduced merely to economics and evaluated on their physical condition and saleability rather than the knowledge or literary merit they might contain. In one passage, for example, the bookseller Iddo Okoli, checks out the 'rationalization' of a bookshop which was 'reshelving its stock into a builder's skip [. . .] He nominated a dozen or so, on the grounds of weight and size' (pp. 12–13).

As in the postcard analogy mentioned earlier, much of the narrative of *Downriver* involves lengthy descriptions of visual aspects of London, its architecture and landscapes, as well as the grotesque figures that people the city. The kind of city that is represented in Sinclair's novel is different from the broadly realistic descriptions in *The Buddha of Suburbia*. Sinclair's vision is a postmodern image of London and it is necessary, therefore, to expand a little on the concept of the postmodern city in order to understand a little better what is going on in *Downriver*. One of the most important theorists of postmodernism in a geographical and urban context is David Harvey. In *The Condition of Postmodernity* (1990), Harvey describes the postmodern city as, 'necessarily fragmented, a "palimpsest" of past forms superimposed upon each other, and a "collage" of current uses'.[12] Here, Harvey stresses the postmodern city's multiple functions, its heteroculture. He goes on to define the city as unplanned and argue that postmodern architects view urban space as independent and autonomous. This is in opposition to the modernist notion of space as something to be manipulated for social purposes, as subservient to a master conception of the uses of an overarching project. Modernist cities are, thereby, international in character, and tend towards homogeneity, while postmodern cities, Harvey suggests, have architecture that responds to local conditions and needs, and are, therefore, responsive to particular spaces and communities. This notion of the city as unplanned, and essentially uncontrollable, links in with older constructions and myths of the urban landscape as dangerous and unpredictable. This is the kind of city represented in *Downriver* and it is in these older constructions of the urban environment, where crime and the darker sides of human existence can run rampage, that forms the basis of Sinclair's use of grotesque characters.

In *Downriver* there are real and imaginary representations of the city. London is never simply an objective location and the textuality of the city is stressed, as if London were a series of overlapping narratives, some from the present, others evoking the past. This narrative process inevitability leads to the questioning of the representations of the urban experience, and the nature of any 'reality' of the city. The narrator, who is provocatively called Iain Sinclair, is a complex figure that both is and is not the author, and it is through this complex narrator that we 'read' the urban landscape. *Downriver* represents the fragmented nature of London; there are different worlds within the city, which are at times presented realistically, but at times as fantasy, as for example in the following: 'Mother London herself was splitting into segments, the overlicked shell of a chocolate tortoise. Piggy hands grabbed the numbered counters from the table. The occult logic of "market forces" dictated a new geography' (p. 265). It is the narrator who acts as the guide through the labyrinth and offers an interpretation of the different situations and characters encountered. More often than not, however, the narrator is also lost: 'the townscape would not settle into any recognizable pattern. Disturbingly, everything was *almost* familiar – but from the wrong period. I was navigating with a map whose symbols had been perversely shifted to some arcane and impenetrable system' (p. 51). This represents the experience of travelling through the city as 'arcane and impenetrable', partly as the result of the narrator's spontaneous and uncontrolled engagement with a myriad of older narratives and histories. For Sinclair, passing through the city is like the act of writing it down. The narrator, as he walks or travels through London is constantly making associations of place and text, and he is stimulated, through semiotic readings, into numerous digressions that are in fact reproduced as the writing of the text itself. Because of the intellectual nature of the narrator (a journalist, researcher and ex-bookseller) the associations thrown up by the city tend to be intertextual and literary: 'I knew what the Isle of Dogs meant. An unlucky place, anathematized by Pepys; and identified by William Blake with the Dogs of Leutha, whose only purpose was to destroy their masters' (p. 269). The novel, then, is partly generated by other, previously written stories, both fictional and non-fictional, for example, in the references to *Heart of Darkness*, to the sinking on the Thames of the Victorian pleasure steamer 'Princess Alice', to *Alice in Wonderland* (1865) and to Jack the Ripper: all of which are suggested by specific places and which link together into a complex intertextual web. The novel is a kind of palimpsest of previous texts, stories and legends, reminiscent of Harvey's description of the postmodern city.

The figure of the narrator-writer, therefore, is crucial. The narrator initially appears as the modernist observer, the *flâneur* who walks through the city recording his experiences and observations. Iain Sinclair, the narrator as distinct from Iain Sinclair the author, acts initially as an impartial observer. However, this impartiality begins to be questioned as the text moves forward. Whilst describing the fantastic events on the 'Isle of Doges' the narrator states, 'I was beginning to have some slight misgivings about my oft-stated policy of witnessing anything and everything, taking whatever was put in front of me. Those excuses would stand no longer [. . .] We have to take full responsibility for what we choose to see' (p. 292). Here, the narrator registers his transition from providing an objective and impartial account to a position of that emphasizes perspectivism and a postmodern scepticism towards the possibility of any claim to objective truth. As the novel progresses the narrator's reliability is further undermined:

> my story was pure fiction. And my fiction was corrupted by its desire to tell a story. Lies, all lies. The text was untrustworthy [. . .] But still I shouted BELIEVE ME! I developed, on the instant, a theory of the shunting of place by time [. . .] The validity of received emotion migrates through all civil and temporal boundaries. (p. 357)

In this passage, although the narrator is questioned, it relies on the 'validity of received emotion' as a truth claim for the narration.

These recurring metafictional occasions begin to deconstruct the role of the narrator. Sinclair, as narrator, becomes less and less confident of his role as the text proceeds and as the narrative he presents gets increasingly out of control, just as the London he is writing about is becoming more and more unfathomable and fragmented. Eventually the narration of the novel is taken over by one of Sinclair's fictional characters, Joblard, a move which self-consciously foregrounds the metafictional nature of the text. As Joblard explains, 'now he [Sinclair] wants me to collude in this cheap trickery (this dreary post-modernist fraud) by writing as if I truly were that person he has chosen to exploit [. . .] I will write *my version* of him writing as me' (p. 380). This move also replicates the re-positioning of the photographer within the frame of the photograph in the first chapter, as noted earlier. This represents a typical postmodernist technique of having a story within a story, or perhaps more accurately in this case, a narration within a narration, to the point where there is no longer any recourse to an objective reality. All the text can do in this situation is to offer a limited and partial discourse of the city. What Sinclair, the author, is representing here is a break-down of the authorial voice, whilst alluding to that breakdown as a postmodernist ploy, itself part of an established literary prac-tice. All things are reduced to the text, and the textuality of the text, including the representation of the city. The novel is metaphorically out of control, as is the London it is describing.

Although Sinclair's book represents a postmodern engagement with the city, there are a set of concrete political and social contexts referred to in the text that suggest why the city appears to be in such a state of fluidity. One of these contexts is the impact of Thatcherism on the landscape of London, and, in particular, the deleterious effects consumerism had on some of the more run down parts of the city. As Peter Brooker has noted, the East End was an area of particular res-onance in eighties culture, 'sandwiched between the City and Canary Wharf, twin monuments to finance and property speculation', and thus provides a rich location for Sinclair's critique of Thatcherism.[13] Sinclair refers to Thatcher's government as 'The Widow and her Gang' and the political outlook of the book is clearly critical of the urban and social policies introduced in the 1980s. Despite the claim referred to earlier that the descriptions of the city should be under-stood to be 'as neutral as a Tarot pack' (p. 29), Sinclair has an agenda, and much of the political critique is focussed on the unscrupulous and underhanded dealings involved in the development of so-called 'riverside opportunities' in East London in the eighties. According to Sinclair, this form of urban 're-generation' involved a corrupt col-laboration between property developers and government which saw established communities uprooted and replaced by expensive, yet poor-quality housing:

These bespoke 'riverside opportunities' are so many stock points; painted counters. They are sold before they are inhabited. Investors shuffle the deeds to other investors, and take their profits. The empty spaces appreciate. Now thrive the chippies.

I met one such in the rain [. . .] 'They target you,' he told me, 'at forty doors a session. Hang 'em high, and hang 'em fast. Then double-check the show flat. I'm in work for years – repairing the damage.' (p. 54)

This system of corruption is fuelled by the media and local press that present incompatible accounts of the benefits and demerits of the area in the same publication: 'a calculated splicing together of the most surreal samples of proletarian life, with an ever expanding, colour-enhanced section on property speculation' (pp. 65–6). This is designed to scare away the current, poorer dwellers of the area, whilst at the same time attempting to attract more prosperous inhabitants for the future developments. It is these inconsistencies in the presentation of the same area that Sinclair identifies as the work of a political agenda symptomatic of Thatcherite economics.

Resistance to these economic measures is also identified, for example, in the Wapping print workers strike of 1986, during which: 'The riverside acres were a battleground, a no man's land; barricaded, fought to the point of inertia, by private armies and absentee War Lords' (p. 48). Here, the language evokes the combination of past and present, for example, in the use of 'barricades', 'standing armies' and the phrase 'absentee War Lords' (instead of landlords) which provides images of the contemporary industrial conflict as a kind of mediaeval dispute. Sinclair, however, is also critical of the nature of some of the political opposition at this time:

The great shame, and dishonour, of the present regime is its failure to procure a decent opposition. Never have there been so many complacent dinner parties, from Highbury to Wandsworth Common, rehearsing their despair [. . .] The worse things got, the more we rubbed our hands. We were safely removed from any possibility of power: blind rhetoric without responsibility. (p. 73)

This passage criticizes the intellectual Left (which includes the narrative voice) and suggests that the ineffectiveness of the opposition has contributed to the success of Thatcherite policies. *Downriver*, then, is both a critique of Thatcherism and of the form of resistance taken amongst sections of the Left during the period. Like Martin Amis's *London Fields*, this is presented with a sense of millennial doom and imminent catastrophe. Some of the scenes, for example, take place in 'The World's End' pub and there is a sense throughout the novel of the passing away of several groups (such as the Tilbury Group) as well as the disappearance and death of several characters. These people are untraceable but live on as ghostly figures populating the imagination as a series of underground narratives, some historical, some fictional – figures such as Todd Silleen, Adam Tenbrücke, Edith Cadiz and David Rodinsky.

Sinclair's novel, then, has a complex narrative structure and self-consciously employs a rich rhetorical and stylistic use of language. These formal devices enhance the evocation of a dark psychogeography of the East End of London, an area that is rich in historical narratives, but is shown to be suffering from the economic policies of the 1980s. The political context of Thatcherism in the 1980s also provides the basis for Julian Barnes's commentary on national identity, *England, England*.

JULIAN BARNES, *ENGLAND, ENGLAND* (1998)

Julian Barnes's 1998 novel is centred on the creation of a theme park based on a collection of all things that are traditionally associated with the concept of Englishness. It traces the planning and development of the park, eponymously called 'England, England', and its eventual construction, which involves the taking over, wholesale, of the Isle of Wight. The novel's theme is clearly related to the way in which the nation is constructed and exists in the collective imagination of not only its inhabitants, but also the rest of the world. In preparation for the theme park, market research is carried out to identify what constitutes Englishness for the (mainly foreign) consumer. The results of this research is presented in the novel in the form of 'Fifty Quintessences of Englishness', and includes such signifiers of national identity as the Royal Family, Big Ben, Manchester United and Robin Hood.[14] The project is the brain-child of Sir Jack Pitman (Pitco Industries), who represents a parody of a Thatcherite entrepreneur whose success has been established by the time of the main events of the novel, and for whom the theme park is his final project.

The novel is divided into three sections: 'England', 'England, England' and 'Albion', each of which has a distinctive narrative style that to some extent tries to mirror its subject matter. Barnes's text interweaves an analysis of the nation with an exploration into the way in which individual identities are constructed. This is focused through the main character in the novel, Martha Cochrane. Martha is eventually employed as Sir Jack Pitman's adviser, given the provocative title of 'Appointed Cynic'. The first section of the novel is concerned with her childhood, and provides an indication to the cause of her later cynicism. Her earliest memory is of doing a jigsaw puzzle made up of the counties of England. The process of constructing and re-constructing the nation is central to this image, but this is also overlaid with the development of Martha's individual identity in that she recounts how each time she did the jigsaw, her father would playfully hide one piece (usually a piece from the heart of England) and then supply it at the end (pp. 4–6). The image of the father providing the final piece is thus presented in terms of both completing the nation, but also of completing and fulfilling Martha's identity. Crucially, when he leaves her mother, she imagines he has taken the last piece of the jigsaw with him. This defining metaphor for the incompleteness of Martha's character is projected throughout the rest of the book and profoundly marks her adulthood as unsatisfied, unfulfilled and incomplete. This situation provides a link between a personal and national psychology and the jigsaw becomes a symbolic expression of the psyche of both Martha and the collective consciousness of the nation. The first section of Barnes's novel, then, emphasizes the overlapping themes of personal memory, national history and geographic space. Although Martha recounts the story of this memory, it is stressed that firstly, memories are always unreliable, and secondly, that articulating a memory as an ordered narrative is bound up with the construction of identity. Martha produces her memory as a narrative to give it form and meaning, which allows her to articulate it not only to others, but also to herself.

English history is similarly turned into a narrative by the teacher Martha remembers at school who would encourage her pupils to recite mantras of English history, with rhyme and hand claps:

55BC (clap clap) Roman Invasion
1066 (clap clap) Battle of Hastings
1215 (clap clap) Magna Carta
1512 (clap clap) Henry the Eighth (clap clap)
     Defender of Faith (clap clap). (p. 11)

This educational strategy succeeds in implanting within the pupils a logical order (or grand narrative) of English history, one that is poeticized through rhythm and rhyme. This fixes itself in Martha's memory and thereby becomes one of the ways in which she 'knows herself' as throughout the book Martha repeatedly questions self-understanding by comparing personal to national identity. Towards the end of the second section of the novel (also called 'England, England'), Martha ponders the question: 'An individual's loss of faith and a nation's loss of faith, aren't they much the same?' (p. 243). The combination of part-fictionalized and con-structed narratives of the self and of the nation are seen as insepa-rable indices in the formation of identity. That these narratives are based on memories is also crucial to the novel's exploration of the way in which the nation is produced. As Sarah Henstra has argued, in *England, England*, 'memory is a sign that only ever points back to another sign'.[15] The text stresses that memories are, in fact, essentially unreliable, and that they are constructed and re-constructed:

If a memory wasn't a thing but a memory of a memory of a memory, mirrors set in parallel, then what the brain told you now about what it claimed had happened then would be coloured by what had happened in between. It was like a country remembering its history: the past was never just the past, it was what made the present able to live with itself. The same went for individuals [. . .] an element of propaganda, of sales and marketing, always intervened between the inner and the outer person. (p. 6)

Here, the combination of the unreliability of memory (and the necessary element of fictional re-construction involved) with the language of consumerism and commodities, parallels the way in which England is re-constructed in the second part of the book, in the theme park.

Part II is concerned with the ideas of replicas, simulations and simulacra that form the theoretical basis for the project of 'England, England'. It is also concerned with the way in which the nation is commodified and re-presented as a marketable, reified object. This again involves a process of turning the nation into a narrative, which can then be told (and sold) to consumers, who buy both the story and the commodities associated with it. When developing the project, Sir Jack relies on the marketing consultant Jerry Batson, whose narrative articulates this sense of the nation as commodity:

> 'You – we – England – my client – is – are – a nation of great age, great history, great accumulated wisdom. Social and cultural history – stacks of it, reams of it – eminently marketable, never more so than in the current climate. Shakespeare, Queen Victoria, Industrial Revolution, gardening, that sort of thing. If I may coin, no copyright a phrase, *We are already what others may hope to become.* This isn't self-pity, this is the strength of our position, our glory, our product placement. We are the new pioneers. We must sell our past to other nations as their future!' (pp. 39–40)

The cultural, economic and fantasy space that is created as 'England, England' is also perceived as a paradigm of a pure capitalist environment: a place where the mixed economy of post-war England has finally been replaced by the triumph of the market. A financial analyst in the book comments:

> 'It's [the theme park] a pure market state. There's no interference from government because there *is* no government. So there's no foreign or domestic policy, only economic policy.

It's a pure interface between buyers and sellers without the market being skewed by central government.' (p. 183)

The second part also parodies the postmodern effects of a total victory of the market economy articulated through an 'end of history' image, in particular, the end of the history of England ('There was no history except Pitco history' p. 202). The accumulation of paradigmatic images of England's past – the Royal Family, Dr Johnson, Nell Gwynn, the Battle of Britain pilots, et cetera – results in the removal of any sense of a future England, and the cultural space of the theme park reduces history to the immediate present and to the ephemeral transience of the now. In this way it reflects Fredric Jameson's concerns about the way postmodern culture threatens to 'weaken historicity' as discussed in Chapter 4. This critique of postmodernism is dramatized most clearly in the figure of the French intellectual who Sir Jack invites to speak to the project team. This intellectual theorizes the contemporary preference for the replica over the real, the simulacrum over the original, and is a clear parody of theorists such as Jean Baudrillard. In fact, the French philosopher in the novel presents us with an argument that is an adaptation of Baudrillard's theories on simulacra.[16] Baudrillard identifies what he calls the 'third order of simulacra' as that being most closely related to postmodernism, which is the stage when: 'It is no longer a question of imitation, nor of reduplication, nor even of parody. It is rather a question of substituting signs of the real for the real itself'.[17] There is a clear comparison here with what the French theorist says in Barnes's novel:

'It is well established – and indeed it has been incontrovertibly proved by many of those I have earlier cited – that nowadays we prefer the replica to the original. We prefer the reproduction to the work of art itself, the perfect sound and solitude of the compact disc to the symphony concert in the company of a thousand victims of throat complaints, the book on tape to the book in the lap [. . .] the world of the third millennium is inevitably, is ineradicably modern, and that it is our intellectual duty to submit to that modernity, and to dismiss as sentimental and inherently fraudulent all yearnings for what is dubiously called the "original".' (pp. 53–5)

The irony, of course, is that the theories of Baudrillard, the post-68 *enfant terrible* of the Left, are here being invoked for the support of Sir Jack Pitman's capitalist project. Baudrillard's critique of postmodern culture is recycled as a celebration of the market economy.

What remains ambiguous, however, is how far the novel dismisses the French critic's ideas. The end of the chapter in which he appears details how the great philosopher is flown in, gives his speech, stops off in London to buy fishing waders, flies and a quantity of aged Caerphilly with his conference fee, and then flies off to his next international conference. But despite satirizing this contemporary high-flying intellectual, the ideas expressed in the first part of the novel concerning the unreliability of memory and the impossibility of recovering any sense of an original or authentic representation of the past fit well with the postmodern theorizing of the French intellectual. What is being satirized is not the ideas or theories themselves, but the way in which they have been incorporated into a commodity culture – where intellectualism has become a commodity in the pay of corporate projects such Pitman's theme park. In fact, Dr Max, the English historian in the novel, who in many ways represents an English academic tradition in opposition to poststructuralist continental theory, ultimately agrees with much of what the French theorist says:

'[. . .] is it not the case that when we consider such lauded and fetishized concepts as, oh, I throw a few out at random, Athenian democracy, Palladian architecture, desert-sect worship of the kind that still holds many in thrall, there *is* no authentic moment of beginning, of purity, however hard their devotees pretend. We may choose to freeze a moment and say it all "began" then, but as an historian I have to tell you that such labelling is intellectually indefensible. What we are looking at is almost always a replica, if that is the locally fashionable term, of something earlier.' (p. 132)

It is Dr Max and Martha's discussion of a particularly natural-looking English landscape that precipitates this moment, and the focus on the artificiality of 'nature' emphasizes the sense in which England as both a geographical and historical concept is dependent on the artificial manipulation of time and place, rather than essential and permanent. The artificial construction of England, England, therefore, is presented as an extreme case of the processes involved in any construction of what appears to be the natural world. The idea of the nation and of national identity is always artificial, with no authentic moment of beginning. This is reminiscent of the Marxist critic Benedict Anderson's description of modern nations as 'imagined communities'. According to Anderson, the nation is '*imagined* because the members of even the smallest nation will never know most of their fellow-members, meet them, or even hear of them, yet in the minds of each lives the image of their communion [. . .] it is imagined as a *community*, because, regardless of the actual inequality and exploitation that may prevail in each, the nation is always conceived as a deep, horizontal comradeship' (italics in original).[18] Although Anderson is not a postmodernist, his ideas about the imagined nature of the nation concur with postmodernism's sense of the artificiality of constructed grand narratives such as that represented by the cultural discourse of Englishness. Although Barnes's novel does not celebrate this sense of England as merely an artificial construct, it is more accurate to see the novel not as a critique of postmodernity, but as a lament that the theories underpinning postmodernism are likely to be the most accurate for the contemporary world.

The novel, then, laments the fact that it is impossible to identify an authentic place of origin for the nation or for personal memory, whilst it simultaneously critiques those who celebrate this position. It presents the preference for the replica alongside the psychological desire for the original, and, in fact, these are presented as the same thing. What Martha discovers in the last section of the book is that the desire to recover a lost past – a garden show, our image of rural England, Cornish smugglers, Robin Hood – is in fact a desire not for the original or the authentic (because there is no original), but for the artificial construction of these objects and signs that are products of the imagination. Paradoxically, it is these artificial copies that appear authentic to our memories of the past. To use Baudrillard's phrase, it is the hyperreal that is recovered, because to talk of the reality of a memory becomes non-sensical.[19] If the past is a series of memories of constructed images, then recovering those reconstructed images operates as a kind of recovery of what masquerades as the authentic. The novel, therefore, is a lament not for lost Englishness, but for the fact that the 'real' past can never be recouped, as it is always artificial. As James J. Miracky argues, 'Just when one suspects that Barnes is validating postmodern theory, he incorporates elements that reach for an authentic human experience of the real ultimately leaving the novel positioned somewhere between homage and parody of the dominance of the "hyperreal" '.[20]

The form of the novel is interesting in this context. In terms of narrative modes, the novel can best be described as hybrid. The first section, 'England', appears to use what literary critic Catherine Belsey calls a classic realist mode.[21] There is a third-person narrator, who presents the narrative with what appears to be little self-consciousness in terms of the mode of address used. In addition, what Belsey calls a 'hierarchy of discourses' is established with Martha as the central consciousness of this section. There is a recognizable, even familiar social setting located in a post-war English past. The fact, however, that Part II shifts from this realist mode to what might be described as postmodernist, emphasizes the constructedness of the first section. There is a clear case of form attempting to parallel content in Barnes's novel. The first section is presented as realist because it is concerned with an evocation of a traditional English past. The form of the writing, therefore, evokes the sense of that past as much as the details it supplies us with. This, of course, is different from saying that it is un-self-conscious writing: Barnes uses a realist form because it seems most appropriate to the subject matter in that part. As Matthew Pateman has suggested, Barnes appears to be, 'deploying the strategies of simulacra, inauthenticity, and fake in order to tell a story of simulacra, inauthenticity, and fake'.[22]

The second part is more distinctly postmodern in style. It uses situations and characters that become increasingly grotesque and unbelievable, including the metamorphoses of the actors playing, for example, Dr Johnson, Robin Hood and the Cornish smugglers in the theme park, as the identity of their adopted characters actually takes over their consciousness. There are a variety of different textual forms in the second part – for example, the French intellectual's speech, and a newspaper review of the theme park – and there are knowing side references to contemporary theorists such as Baudrillard and Michel Foucault. The elements of parody, pastiche, magic realism and knowing self-referentiality mark out the section as postmodern in style. This mode of narration fits well with its subject matter: the presentation of the postmodern theme park. It could also be argued that this section represents a departure from a form associated with an English literary tradition. Postmodernism, despite many British novelists using the form, is still most associated with American novelists, both North and South. The encroachment of this foreign mode into the text, therefore, parallels Sir Jack's Disneyfication of England on the Isle of Wight.

In this context, the final section of the book, 'Albion', seems formally to return us to a more recognizably English form – the pastoral elegy. The elegy, in this case, is for the passing of the old England, but also for Martha, who now appears as an old woman. 'Old England', as it is now called, is represented as a pastoral idyll and it is as if the market economy has been drained off into the theme park on the Isle of Wight leaving behind a pre-capitalist society on the mainland. In terms of form, however, the situation is not as straightforward as it appears. The opening description of the pastoral scene is exaggerated to the point of parody (p. 241), and fictionalized narratives still supply the main way by which identity is formed. This latter point is represented in the character of Jez Harris (formerly Jack Oshinsky) who was formerly a junior legal expert with an American electronics firm, but who has now adopted the persona of an English yokel who provides made-up 'tales of witchcraft and superstition, of sexual rites beneath a glowing moon and the trance slaughter of livestock' (p. 243). The artificiality that fuels the second section contaminates the third, and Jez's tales form an artificial narrative of Englishness in much the same way as the theme park.

The novel, then, addresses issues of national identity by undermining the basis on which they have rested in the past. If there ever was a grand narrative of Englishness, then the novel is keen to undermine the philosophical basis on which such a story was produced. It does not celebrate, however, what Jean-François Lyotard describes as 'incredulity towards grand narratives'.[23] Rather, it wistfully reflects on what appears to be a simpler, if naïve version of Englishness, without the complexities of postmodern experience.

SUMMARY OF KEY POINTS

- Contemporary British fiction is keen to explore the cultural representation of geographical spaces, especially in relation to the urban environment and national identity.
- The relationship between narrative fiction and the representation of space has proved a fruitful area in terms of formal experimentation in the novel.
- Postmodernism and postcolonialism in fiction have both served to loosen traditional discourses of Englishness.
- The changes made to social and cultural landscapes have provided a good source for fiction that is critical of social and political changes over the last thirty years.

NOTE

1. See, for example, Seamus Deane's *Reading in the Dark: A Novel* (London: Jonathan Cape, 1996); Niall Griffiths's *Sheepshagger* (London: Jonathan Cape, 2001); Adam Thorpe's *Ulverton* (London: Secker & Warburg, 1992); and Irvine Welsh's *Trainspotting* (London: Secker & Warburg, 1993).
2. Hanif Kureishi, *The Buddha of Suburbia* (London: Faber and Faber, 1990), p. 63. All subsequent references in the text are to this edition.
3. Susan Brook, 'Suburban Space in *The Buddha of Suburbia*', in *British Fiction of the 1990s*, ed. Nick Bentley (London: Routledge, 2005), pp. 209–25, p. 216.
4. Paul Gilroy, *There Ain't No Black in the Union Jack: The Cultural Politics of Race and Nation* (London: Hutchinson, 1987).

5. Jago Morrison, *Contemporary Fiction* (London: Routledge, 2003), p. 184.
6. Bart Moore-Gilbert, *Hanif Kureishi* (Manchester: Manchester University Press, 2001), pp. 133–4.
7. Ibid., p. 115.
8. The band Karim and Charlie see are a fictional version of *The Sex Pistols*; the singer's aggressive attitude on stage and his 'carrot topped hair' is a clear reference to Johnny Rotten. Charlie's exploitation of the punk subculture is an analogy to the way in which Malcolm McLaren, *The Sex Pistols*'s manager moved the band away from its original anarchic politics to the lure of 'filthy lucre'. See Julien Temple's film *The Filth and the Fury*, dir. Julien Temple (Film Four, 2000).
9. See Dick Hebdige, *Subculture: The Meaning of Style* (London: Routledge, [1979] 1988), pp. 100–27.
10. Iain Sinclair, *Downriver* (London: Vintage, [1991] 1995), p. 29. All subsequent references in the text are to this edition.
11. The references to Joseph Conrad and his novel *Heart of Darkness* have a particular resonance here. Conrad's novel opens on the Thames, and although set at the beginning of the twentieth century, when London was arguably the greatest metropolis on earth, Marlow, the narrator of the book, invokes his audience to consider that London has also, 'been one of the dark places of the earth': Conrad, *Heart of Darkness* (Harmondsworth: Penguin, [1902] 1973), p. 29. The sense that the river is both contemporary and outside of history is something that *Downriver* shares with *Heart of Darkness*.
12. David Harvey, *The Condition of Postmodernity: An Enquiry into the Origins of Cultural Change* (Oxford: Blackwell, 1990), p. 66.
13. Peter Brooker, *Modernity and Metropolis: Writing, Film, and Urban Formations* (London: Routledge, 2002), p. 97.
14. Julian Barnes, *England, England* (London: Picador, [1998] 1999), pp. 83–5. All subsequent references in the text are to this edition.
15. Sarah Henstra, 'The McReal Thing: Personal/National Identity in Julian Barnes's *England, England*', in *British Fiction of the 1990s*, ed. Bentley, pp. 95–107, p. 97.
16. Jean Baudrillard, *Simulations* (New York: Semiotext(e), 1983).

17. Ibid., p. 4.
18. Benedict Anderson, *Imagined Communities* (London: Verso, 1991), p. 7.
19. Baudrillard, *Simulations*.
20. James J. Miracky, 'Replicating a Dinosaur: Authenticity Run Amok in the "Theme Parking" of Michael Crichton's *Jurassic Park* and Julian Barnes's *England, England'*, *Critique: Studies in Contemporary Fiction* 45(2) (2004), 163–71, 165.
21. Cathereine Belsey, *Critical Practice* (London: Routledge, [1980] 1987), pp. 67–84.
22. Matthew Pateman, *Julian Barnes* (Plymouth: Northcote House, 2002), p. 75.
23. Jean-François Lyotard, *The Condition of Postmodernity: A Report on Knowledge*, trans. Geoff Bennington and Brian Massumi (Manchester: Manchester University Press, [1979] 1984).

Conclusion

One of the points that this book has tried to suggest is the healthy state of contemporary British fiction, despite, as Jago Morrison has noted, fears about the anticipated demise of the novel at the beginning of the 1970s.[1] One of the concerns for proponents of literary fiction throughout most of the twentieth century was the feeling that first film, and then television, would replace the novel as the primary media in presenting narratives to an interested and engaged public. What we have seen over the last thirty years or so, however, is that the novel has continued to flourish alongside other more popular forms of narrative. In many ways the novel has not been an alternative, but has gone hand-in-hand with these newer forms of narrative as can be seen by the number of contemporary novels that have been adapted for the small and big screen. Of the novels covered in this book, several have been successfully adapted for television, such as *Oranges Are Not the Only Fruit* (1990), *The Buddha of Suburbia* (1993) and *White Teeth* (2002), whilst several have been turned into films such as *Waterland* (1992), *Fever Pitch* (1997), *Possession* (2002), *Atonement* (2007) and *Brick Lane* (2007). Narrative fiction and filmic and televisual adaptations have often fed off each other, creating a cultural circularity in which readers and viewers accept the contexts in which both are consumed. This has been part of a general cultural trend in Britain during the period in which the old opposition between high and popular culture has become increasingly blurred. This can be seen, for example, in writers such as Nick Hornby, Hanif Kureishi and Courttia Newland, who have, in their own way, combined literary fiction with an interest in popular cultural practices and forms such as football and rock and pop music.

In a national context, there was an understanding in the 1970s and early 1980s that British fiction had become overly provincial in the period from the end of the modernist period, which had produced a literature that was inward looking. Other national literatures, especially the post-war American novel, had been more successful in tapping into the global zeitgeist. This is not to say that fiction that deals with the quotidian and regional is necessarily limiting, and as examples from this book have shown, the everyday and provincial can form the basis for profound philosophical and ethical explorations, as in the fiction of Alasdair Gray, Graham Swift and Jeanette Winterson. In fact, since the 1960s, British fiction has shown a capability to be inclusive towards themes and trends from other parts of the world. The range and scope of the national novel has benefited, in this context, from Britain's specific colonial history, which has influenced several writers such as Zadie Smith, Monica Ali and Salman Rushdie. This openness to other literatures has also been important for formal experimentation. Foreign influences have continued to enhance the indigenous production of literature in Britain with many writers incorporating styles that have perhaps originated elsewhere. Angela Carter and Salman Rushdie, for example, have engaged with magic realism, a mode developed mainly by South American writers, whilst Martin Amis and Iain Sinclair have looked to North America for their influences, both poetic and novelistic. Sinclair's style, for example, owes a lot to the American Beat writers of the 1950s and 60s, whilst Amis's main influences are Vladimir Nabokov and Saul Bellow.

One of the exciting aspects of studying contemporary fiction, a feature that differs from other periods of literary history, is the immediacy of the relationship between the writing and reading of fiction, and literary criticism. Most of the authors covered in this book are still alive and continue to publish fiction, and it is possible (although sometimes difficult) to speak to them directly about their work. The range of primary texts, then, is continually increasing, with both established authors continuing to add to their corpus and the emergence of new writers. This may be one of the reasons for the increased popularity of contemporary literature courses on university and school syllabuses. As Philip Tew, in research carried out for the English Subject Centre, has identified, 'contemporary fiction is a growing area in literary and cultural studies both in the UK and internationally'.[2] Contemporary British fiction, in particular, promises to be an area of literary studies that continues to be vibrant and exciting.

The constantly evolving and expanding nature of contemporary fiction, however, has its own problems for literary criticism, especially in terms of the selection of primary texts that can be regarded as the main works within the field. Most periods of literary history have an established canon of works that are studied on undergraduate and postgraduate courses. If you were studying British Romantic poetry, for example, you might expect to find the poetry of William Blake, William Wordsworth, Samuel Taylor Coleridge, Percy Shelley, Lord Byron and John Keats (and perhaps John Clare) as well as, more recently, the addition of a range of women poets such as Anna Barbauld, Charlotte Smith and Joanna Baillie. This list of writers is fairly well established, although it has to be said that the canon of past literary periods has been greatly influenced by critical theories associated with Marxism, feminism, postcolonialism and queer theory over the last forty years or so. Contemporary fiction is different in that only recently can anything as authoritative as a canon of contemporary fiction be said to have emerged. My own work in this area, and Philip Tew's research referred to above, have attempted to identify certain trends to speculate on who might be included in a canon of contemporary British fiction.[3] Certain authors do seem to be achieving canonical status, at least in terms of the impact higher education and academic research has on that process. These authors include (with relevance to this book) Martin Amis, Zadie Smith, Salman Rushdie, Angela Carter, Jeanette Winterson, Graham Swift, A. S. Byatt, Hanif Kureishi and Julian Barnes.

In addition to the identification of particular authors it is also possible to identify trends within contemporary British fiction in terms of subject matter and formal techniques. As the organization of this book suggests, the contemporary field has particular interests in addressing questions about the nature of writing fiction and the role of language in that process; issues around ethnicity, national identity and the legacies of postcolonialism; the construction of gender and sexual identity; the way in which history and narratives of the past affect the present, and the problems involved in attempting to record that past accurately; and the way in which cultural spaces and geographies impact on people's lives. Each of these topics has proved to be a fruitful source for British fiction over the last forty years. It is, of course, dangerous to predict the thematic directions that the novel might take in the future, as can be seen by the 'end of the novel' commentators in the late 1960s and early 1970s. However, certain recent political and cultural events such as the legacies of the 9/11 attacks and the so called 'war on terror' can be assumed to provide source material for fiction in the coming years. One of the areas that has been overlooked by this book is the concern with the environment, an area that looks likely to stimulate (and frustrate) interested parties for the foreseeable future. The contemporary ecological novel might very well establish itself as a genre within its own right in Britain. Political events around the world also suggest that issues raised by postcolonialism will continue to provide material for investigations in the encounters between different cultures, systems of belief and ideologies.

Richard Bradford in his book *The Novel Now* (2007) suggests that one of the issues facing contemporary fiction is the relationship between what might be called a general readership and the way the study of contemporary fiction is undertaken in academia. One of his concerns is the role of literary theory in the institutional study of literature. He writes, 'The lexicon, mannerisms and intellectual hauteur of literary theory are now endemic features of the critical writing of all but a small minority of academics [. . .] its own preoccupations have effectively alienated both from its alleged subject, literature, and the body of individuals who are that subject's lifeblood, intelligent ordinary readers'.[4] Bradford makes a serious point and the aspects of literary theory he identifies can be observed in some quarters. He relies, however, on an assumption that the language of academia and that of 'intelligent ordinary readers' represent distinct and oppositional discourses. There is perhaps some justification for this. In practice, however, the best discussions about fiction, whether in the seminar room or the living room tend to move between the 'general' and the 'theoretical' and involve practical criticism of both the fiction and the social environment in which it has been produced. In this way a circulatory flow can be established between these so-called distinct discourses. It would be difficult to imagine, for example, discussing the work of Martin Amis, A. S. Byatt, Angela Carter or Julian Barnes without there being recourse at some stage to ideas related to critical theory. Part of this circulation between fiction, theory and criticism is the incorporation of theoretical ideas in the novels themselves such as the indirect references to Michel Foucault and Jean Baudrillard in Julian Barnes's *England England*. Rather than a cause for concern, the relationship between the intelligent general reader and literary theory has always been and should continue to be a stimulating and intriguing encounter.

In terms of narrative form, what has emerged from this book is the variety of literary modes that continue to be used in British fiction. In Chapter 1, we looked at David Lodge's intriguing image of the novelist at a formal crossroads at the beginning of the 1970s, whereby the paths open appeared to be a choice between realism or modernism.[5] In fact, fiction in Britain in the years after 1970 has developed along a series of routes. There has been increased experimentation in the novel, such as that associated with postmodern narrative techniques, which in itself includes a range of different approaches to fiction. Other novelists have continued to work in a mostly realist mode. In addition hybrid categories have evolved such as magic realism and historiographic metafiction, as well as the realignment as serious literature of such popular forms as science fiction, the detective novel and romance. In fact, the range of formal modes used in contemporary fiction has pluralized beyond Lodge's dichotomy. The novelist at the end of the first decade of the twenty-first century appears to be standing not at a crossroads but at a far more complicated intersection that offers routes in several directions.

NOTES

1. Jago Morrison, *Contemporary Fiction* (London: Routledge, 2003), pp. 3–8.

2. Philip Tew and Mark Addis, 'Final Report: Survey on Teaching Contemporary British Ficton', *English Subject Centre* (2007) http://www.english.heacademy.ac.uk/explore/projects/archive/contemp/contemp1.php. Accessed 31 October 2007.
3. Nick Bentley, 'Developing the Canon: Texts, Themes and Theories in Teaching Contemporary British Fiction', in *Teaching Contemporary British Fiction: Anglistik & Englischunterricht* Special Issue, 69, ed. Steve Barfield et al. (Heidelberg: Universitätsverlag, 2007), 27–45.
4. Richard Bradford, *The Novel Now* (Malden, MA: Blackwell, 2007), pp. 245–6.
5. David Lodge, *The Novelist at the Crossroads* (London: Routledge, 1971).

Student Resources

INTERNET RESOURCES

Contemporary British Fiction

www.contemporarywriters.com
www.artandculture.com/cgi-bin/WebObjects/ACLive.woa/wa/
movement?id=439
www.artandculture.com/cgi-bin/WebObjects/ACLive.woa/wa/
movement?id=559
http://vos.ucsb.edu/
www.k-state.edu/english/westmank/literary/contempbrit_
resources.html

Individual Authors

Monica Ali
        www.authortrek.com/monica_ali_page.html
Martin Amis
        www.martinamisweb.com
Julian Barnes
        www.julianbarnes.com
        www.salon.com/weekly/interview960513.html
A. S. Byatt
        www.asbyatt.com

www.literaryhistory.com/20thC/Byatt.htm
www.sjsu.edu/depts/jwss/mesher/annotations/
possession/posshome.html
Angela Carter
www.angelacartersite.co.uk
Alasdair Gray
www.alasdairgray.co.uk
www.lanark1982.co.uk
Nick Hornby
www.nickhornby.net/
Hanif Kureishi
www.hanifkureishi.com
www.literaryhistory.com/20thC/Kureishi.htm
Ian McEwan
www.ianmcewan.com
www.literaryhistory.com/20thC/McEwan.htm
Courttia Newland
www.myvillage.co.uk/urbanfactor/courttianewland.htm
Salman Rushdie
www.subir.com/rushdie.html
www.literaryhistory.com/20thC/Rushdie.htm
Iain Sinclair
www.literarylondon.org/london-journal/september2005/
index.html
Zadie Smith
www.authortrek.com/zadiesmithpage.html
Graham Swift
www.usp.nus.edu.sg/post/uk/gswift/gsworks.html
Jeanette Winterson
www.jeanettewinterson.com

QUESTIONS FOR DISCUSSION

Introduction: Historical and Theoretical Contexts 1975–2005

- How can the relationship between cultural movements and fiction be identified?

- What are the major political transitions and events in British history in the last thirty years?
- Is class still a useful social category?
- How has society's understanding of femininity and masculinity changed over the last forty years?
- How have immigration, multiculturalism and devolution affected the identities of Britishness?

Chapter 1 Narrative Forms: Postmodernism and Realism

- What are the major stylistic features associated with postmodernism?
- What are the major stylistic features associated with realism?
- How do each of the texts covered in this chapter explore the way in which identities are formed and maintained in society?
- How, and why, do *London Fields* and *Poor Things* question the authority of the author? Why do they include a number of narrative levels?
- Why does Zadie Smith choose to use a conventional realist mode?

Chapter 2 Writing Contemporary Ethnicities

- What are the specific historical and geographical contexts that are informing each postcolonial novel in this chapter?
- In what ways have postcolonial writers tried to manipulate narrative forms and techniques, and to what effect?
- Why is the language in which novelists write a particular issue for postcolonial writers?
- What is the relationship between postcolonialism and Britain's contemporary status as a multicultural society?
- How have novelists used narrative and language techniques to convey the experiences of immigration and living in Britain as part of a minority ethnic community?

Chapter 3 Gender and Sexuality

- What does Simone de Beauvoir mean when she writes: 'I am not born a woman, I become one'?

- How are psychoanalytic theories useful in thinking about gender and sexual identity?
- Why is the *Bildungsroman* form particularly useful in narratives about discovering sexual identity?
- How does *The Passion of New Eve* encourage readers to examine the way in which gender is constructed by society?
- How do attitudes to sexuality relate to religion in Jeanette Winterson's *Oranges Are Not the Only Fruit*?
- How does *Fever Pitch* approach changing codes of masculinity in terms of class?

Chapter 4 History, Memory and Writing

- What is the difference between history and the 'past'?
- What is the relationship between differing kinds of history: such as 'official', social, political, family, personal and literary histories?
- Why does Tom Crick take so long to tell his story in *Waterland*?
- Which of the characters are freer to express their love in *Possession*: the Victorians or the contemporaries?
- Where does Briony's fiction begin and end in *Atonement*?

Chapter 5 Narratives of Cultural Space

- How are ethnic and national identities represented in the novels covered in this chapter?
- How is narrative voice used in each text to convey the experience of moving through urban and suburban landscapes?
- How does *The Buddha of Suburbia* use the *Bildungsroman* form to contrast urban and suburban identities?
- In *Downriver*, how does Iain Sinclair develop a political critique through his analysis of geographical space and historical context?
- How is the relationship between individual and national identity conveyed in *England, England*?

ALTERNATIVE PRIMARY TEXTS

Introduction: Historical and Theoretical Contexts 1975–2005

- Kingsley Amis, *The Old Devils* (London: Hutchinson, 1986).
- Martin Amis, *Money: A Suicide Note* (London: Jonathan Cape, 1984).
- Pat Barker, *Union Street* (London: Virago, 1982).
- Nicholas Blincoe, *Acid Casuals* (London: Serpent's Tail, 1995).
- Jonathan Coe, *The Closed Circle* (London: Viking, 2004).
- Helen Fielding, *Bridget Jones's Diary* (London: Picador, 1996).
- Alan Hollinghurst, *The Line of Beauty* (London: Chatto & Windus, 2004).
- James Kelman, *How Late it Was, How Late* (London: Secker & Warburg, 1994).
- Hanif Kureishi, *The Black Album* (London: Faber and Faber, 1995).
- David Lodge, *Changing Places* (London: Secker & Warburg, 1975).
- Bernard MacLaverty, *Grace Notes* (London: Jonathan Cape, 1997).
- Will Self, *Dorian* (London: Viking, 2002).
- Sam Selvon, *Moses Ascending* (Oxford: Heinemann, 1975).
- Fay Weldon, *The Lives and Loves of a She Devil* (London: Hodder & Stoughton, 1983).

Chapter 1 Narrative Forms Postmodernism and Realism

- Janice Galloway, *The Trick is to Keep Breathing* (Edinburgh: Polygon, 1989).
- A. L. Kennedy, *Now That You're Back* (London: Jonathan Cape, 1994).
- Doris Lessing, *The Fifth Child* (London: Jonathan Cape, 1988).
- David Mitchell, *Cloud Atlas* (London: Sceptre, 2004).
- Salman Rushdie, *Midnight's Children* (London: Jonathan Cape, 1981).
- Will Self, *How the Dead Live* (London: Bloomsbury, 2000).
- Ali Smith, *Hotel World* (London: Hamish Hamilton, 2001).

Chapter 2 Writing Contemporary Ethnicities

- Buchi Emecheta, *Kehinde* (London: Heinemann, 1994).
- Diana Evans, *26a* (London: Chatto & Windus, 2005).
- Andrea Levy, *Small Island* (London: Review, 2004).
- V. S. Naipaul, *The Enigma of Arrival* (London: André Deutsch, 1987).
- Caryl Phillips, *Cambridge* (London: Bloomsbury, 1991).
- Caryl Phillips, *A Distant Shore* (London: Secker & Warburg, 2004).
- Sam Selvon, *Moses Ascending* (Oxford: Heinemann, 1975).

Chapter 3 Gender and Sexuality

- Janice Galloway, *The Trick is to Keep Breathing* (Edinburgh: Polygon, 1989).
- Alan Hollinghurst, *The Swimming Pool Library* (London: Chatto & Windus, 1998).
- John King, *The Football Factory* (London: Jonathan Cape, 1996).
- Emma Tennant, *Hotel de Dream* (London: Gollancz, 1976).
- Sarah Waters, *Fingersmith* (London: Virago, 2002).
- Fay Weldon, *The Lives and Loves of a She Devil* (London: Hodder & Stoughton, 1983).

Chapter 4 History, Memory and Writing

- Peter Ackroyd, *Hawksmoor* (London: Hamish Hamilton, 1985).
- Martin Amis, *Time's Arrow* (London: Jonathan Cape, 1991).
- Beryl Bainbridge, *Every Man for Himself* (London: Duckworth, 1996).
- J. G. Ballard, *Empire of the Sun* (London: Gollancz, 1984).
- Pat Barker, *The Regeneration Trilogy*
  - *Regeneration* (London: Viking, 1991).
  - *The Eye in the Door* (London: Viking, 1993).
  - *The Ghost Road* (London: Viking, 1995).
- Kazuo Ishiguro, *The Remains of the Day* (London: Faber and Faber, 1989).
- Jane Rogers, *Mr Wroe's Virgins* (London: Faber and Faber, 1991).

- Jeanette Winterson, *Sexing the Cherry* (London: Jonathan Cape, 1989).

Chapter 5 Narratives of Cultural Space

- Peter Ackroyd, *Hawksmoor* (London: Hamish Hamilton, 1985).
- J. G. Ballard, *Kingdom Come* (London: Fourth Estate, 2006).
- Seamus Deane, *Reading in the Dark: A Novel* (London: Jonathan Cape, 1996).
- Niall Griffiths, *Sheepshagger* (London: Jonathan Cape, 2001).
- Will Self, *The Book of Dave* (London: Viking, 2006).
- Adam Thorpe, *Ulverton* (London: Secker & Warburg, 1992).
- Irvine Welsh, *Trainspotting* (London: Secker & Warburg, 1993).

General

Monica Ali, *Alentjo Blue* (London: Doubleday, 2006).

Martin Amis, *The Information* (London: Jonathan Cape, 1995).

J. G. Ballard, *Millennium People* (London: Flamingo, 2003).

Julian Barnes, *Flaubert's Parrot* (London: Jonathan Cape, 1984).

Julian Barnes, *A History of the World in 10½ Chapters* (London: Jonathan Cape, 1989).

Julian Barnes, *Arthur and George* (London: Jonathan Cape, 2005).

A. S. Byatt, *The Virgin in the Garden* (London: Chatto & Windus, 1978).

A. S. Byatt, *Still Life* (London: Chatto & Windus, 1985).

A. S. Byatt, *Babel Tower* (London: Chatto & Windus, 1996).

Angela Carter, *The Bloody Chamber* (London: Gollancz, 1979).

Angela Carter, *Nights at the Circus* (London: Chatto & Windus, 1984).

Angela Carter, *Wise Children* (London: Chatto & Windus, 1991).

Jonathan Coe, *What a Carve Up!* (London: Viking, 1994).

Jonathan Coe, *The Rotters' Club* (London: Viking, 2001).

John Fowles, *A Maggot* (London: Jonathan Cape, 1985).

Alasdair Gray, *Lanark* (Edinburgh: Canongate, 1981).

Nick Hornby, *High Fidelity* (London: Gollancz, 1995).

Nick Hornby, *How To Be Good* (London: Viking, 2001).

Kazuo Ishiguro, *When We Were Orphans* (London: Faber and Faber, 2000).

Doris Lessing, *The Good Terrorist* (London: Jonathan Cape, 1985).

Ian McEwan, *The Cement Garden* (London: Jonathan Cape, 1978).

Ian McEwan, *The Child in Time* (London: Jonathan Cape, 1987).

Ian McEwan, *Black Dogs* (London: Jonathan Cape, 1992).

Ian McEwan, *Saturday* (London: Jonathan Cape, 2005).

Ian McEwan, *On Chesil Beach* (London: Jonathan Cape, 2007).

Courttia Newland, *The Scholar: a West Side Story* (London: Abacus, 1998).

Salman Rushdie, *Shalimar the Clown* (London: Jonathan Cape, 2005).

Iain Sinclair, *Radon Daughters* (London: Jonathan Cape, 1994).

Iain Sinclair, *Landor's Tower* (London: Granta, 2001).

Iain Sinclair, *Dining on Stones* (London: Hamish Hamilton, 2004).

Zadie Smith, *On Beauty* (London: Hamish Hamilton, 2005).

Graham Swift, *The Sweet Shop Owner* (London: Allen Lane, 1980).

Graham Swift, *Shuttlecock* (London: Allen Lane, 1981).

Graham Swift, *Last Orders* (London: Picador, 1996).

Sarah Waters, *Tipping the Velvet* (London: Virago, 1998).

Jeanette Winterson, *The PowerBook* (London: Jonathan Cape, 2000).

GLOSSARY

Bildungsroman

A German term referring to the 'novel of development', a narrative in which the main character develops from childhood or adolescence into adulthood. Sometimes called the 'coming of age' or rite of passage story. Typically it follows the adventures of an orphaned character who eventually finds themselves reintegrated into the society from which they were at first excluded. It was popular in the nineteenth century in particular, with examples such as Charles Dickens's *Great Expectations*, *Nicholas Nickleby* and *David Copperfield*, and Charlotte Brontë's *Jane Eyre* and *Villette*. The narrative tends to be in the first person with the main protagonist relating their story at some point in the future and looking back on their former selves. Many contemporary novels use a *Bildungsroman* framework but subvert or parody the form to suggest that the contemporary world no longer allows the neat conclusions available to the nineteenth-century hero. Such contemporary examples include Angela Carter's *The Passion of New Eve* and Hanif Kureishi's *The Buddha of Suburbia*.

Bricolage

A formal style that combines signs or symbols taken from different areas and put together apparently randomly to create a new configuration. One of the more relevant examples in contemporary culture is punk fashion which combined political symbols, such as union jacks and swastikas, with ripped clothing, nappies and safety pins. Dick Hebdige, in particular, has written on the *bricolage* style of punk in his book *Subcultures: The Meaning of Style*.

Consumerism

Refers to a distinct phase in socio-economics after the Second World War in Western societies. It represents a move from production to consumption as the driving force in a nation's economics. Because of this shift it is often associated with the post-industrial age.

Defamiliarization

A literary technique identified by the Russian Formalist critic Viktor Shklovsky in the 1910s. It relates to the way in which an everyday event or object is described in such a way as to make it appear strange or unusual. It is identified as one of the ways in which literature functions to persuade the reader to ask questions about their everyday practices, and in some cases the social, political and ideological frameworks in which they operate. Many contemporary novelists use the technique in this way such as Alasdair Gray in *Poor Things* and Monica Ali in *Brick Lane*.

Eclecticism

A term associated with an art form or cultural space in which elements, symbols or commodities from a wide range of cultures are placed side-by-side. Jean-François Lyotard has identified eclecticism as one of the primary indicators of postmodernity. Perhaps one of the most visible examples is the food court in a contemporary shopping centre where you might find an American burger bar, a Chinese take-away, a fish and chip shop and a sushi restaurant next to each other in an equalizing consumer space.

Diaspora

A term originally from the Bible that related to the exodus of the Jews led by Moses out of Egypt to the Promised Land. In modern times, it has come to represent the migration of a significant amount of people from one area of the world to another. In a contemporary British context, it is often related to the Caribbean and the South East Asian diasporas, whereby groups of people moved to Britain from these areas and established distinct communities. This process has been one of the most important factors in the development of a multicultural Britain.

Grand Narrative

In a seminal work, *The Conditions of Postmodernity*, Jean-François Lyotard argued that postmodernism represented an 'incredulity towards metanarratives'. These metanarratives were based on scientific and rationalist thought established during the Enlightenment, and can also be called grand narratives. The term refers to any system of belief or ideology that establishes a fixed set of criteria to understand the way in which the world works and how people should operate within it. The term has, therefore, been associated with a range of discourses including the major religions, patriarchy, science, 'official' history, Marxism and the idea of the rational self.

Heteroglossia

A term coined by the Russian foramlist and Marxist critic Mikhail Bakhtin to refer to the multiple codes, accents, registers and styles of speech existing within a single language at any moment in society.

He argues that within the social practice of language two opposing forces are constantly fighting each other. One of these is heteroglossia, the other is monoglossia, which tends towards unity in language, and which can be seen in the way dominant authorities in a given society try to impose a singular notion of 'official' language. In the context of the English language, examples of monoglossia could be the 'Queen's English' or 'Received Pronunciation'. According to Bakhtin, the novel is the ideal literary space in which to articulate the multifarious nature of language as it operates in everyday practice, because it can introduce a range of characters from different social, cultural and regional backgrounds, each with their own distinctive forms of dialogue.

Hybridity

A term that refers to the combination of two (or more) cultural influences in the creation of a third distinct category. It has often been used in an ethnic context to refer to the way in which individuals or cultural practices combine to form a dual heritage identity. The critical theorist Homi Bhabha, in particular, has written on the concept. For him, one of the important characteristics of the hybrid situation is that neither of the constituent parts takes precedence over the other. This is particularly important in the context of a hybridity based on the interaction of colonizing and colonized subjects. Several contemporary writers have engaged with the idea including Hanif Kureishi, Salman Rushdie and Zadie Smith.

Hyperreal

A term coined by the postmodernist theorist Jean Baudrillard to refer to the way in which contemporary culture operates in a world where signs, images and simulacra are taken to represent reality, but which, in fact, have no original referent in the real world. The idea is often associated with the mass production of cultural objects, such as MP3 files of a single track, each identical, but none of which can be said to be the original. The term has also been related to a style of art and literature, in which characters, objects or events are described or presented in such a way that they are exaggerated beyond the conventional form of realism. This attempts to express the strangeness of living in contemporary Western societies. This approach can be seen, for example, in the characters used by film-makers such as David Lynch and David Cronenberg. In a contemporary British fiction context, Martin Amis's characters in *London Fields* could be described as hyperreal due to the novel's exaggerated representations of stereotypes.

Intertextuality

A term referring to the way in which any one literary (or other) text might refer to another text. In a poststructuralist context, it refers to the way in which language relies on conventions and recognized syntax to show that any sentence, to be understood, refers intertextually to all other sentences that have been constructed. It can also refer to the way in which any individual text relies on the existence of all other texts – that a novel or poem cannot exist in isolation, and part of its production of meaning relies on the fact that other novels and poems exist. The term has tended, however, in literary studies, to refer more generally to the way texts allude to, reflect back or parody another named text, for example, the way that Jeanette Winterson uses the Bible and *Jane Eyre* as intertexts in her *Oranges Are Not the Only Fruit*, or in Zadie Smith's novel *On Beauty* which is partially patterned on E. M. Forster's *Howards End*.

Linear and Non-Linear Narrative

Linear narrative is one of the structural conventions of the realist novel. It is based on the assumption that events occur one after the other in a logical order and that each event has some causal relationship with the events that precede and follow it. Postmodern narrative techniques have often upset this framework by using non-linear structures, thus problematizing the logical relationship between events that you might expect to find in the realist mode. For example, events can be presented in an order that jumps between historical time frames as, for example, in A. S. Byatt's *Possession: A Romance* which has two narrative plots running side by side: one set in the nineteenth century and one in the late twentieth. Another way in which a linear narrative can be disrupted is by using a 'spiral' narrative as Jeanette Winterson claims to do in *Oranges Are Not the Only Fruit*. In Ian McEwan's *Atonement*, what appears on first reading to be a linear narrative is disrupted by the epilogue which forces the reader to question the representation of all the events and characters that have been thus far presented as realistic.

Metafiction

A term relating to fiction that self-reflexively and self-consciously announces itself as fiction. It typically draws attention to the use of narrative conventions and techniques and thereby parodying or critiquing them. Although metafiction is nothing new and examples can be found from the eighteenth century (such as Lawrence Stern's *Tristram Shandy*) it has been closely associated with postmodernist fiction. Examples include Martin Amis's *London Fields* and Alasdair Gray's *Poor Things*.

Magic Realism

A style of narrative fiction developed originally from certain Latin American writers such as Jorge Luis Borges, Gabriel Garcia Marquez and Alejo Carpentier. As the term suggests, it constitutes a mixture of realistic scenarios with characters and events drawn from a non-realistic or fantastic context. In contemporary British fiction, writers such as Angela Carter, Salman Rushdie and Jeanette Winterson have often been associated with the form.

Multiculturalism

A term relating to the way in which a nation is made up of communities in which distinct ethnic, cultural or religious codes of behaviour are practised. The term is often contentious and is politicised in relation to other concepts such as Britishness, which is sometimes seen as its opposite, sometimes complementary.

Palimpsest

A writing practice related mainly to the nineteenth century by which, because of the scarcity of paper, a letter writer might complete a page in the normal way, then turn the page sideways and continue writing across the original text. This can then be repeated diagonally. It has come to refer metaphorically to the way in which narrative texts can be layered in terms of meaning, and that a literary description is produced in such a way that it generates several ways of being interpreted.

Parody and Pastiche

Both of these terms relate to a style of writing that takes a previous style, form or genre and either critically or comically emphasizes some if its features. Parody tends to refer to the way in which the style being commented upon is made to seem foolish in some way and presumes that a better or more accurate approach could have been taken. Pastiche tends to adopt a style without the critical edge shown in parody, so that the style is mimicked without suggesting better alternatives. This is the sense in which the critic Fredric Jameson understands the terms and suggests that pastiche, in particular, is a representative form of postmodernism with its depthless recycling of past genres without a fixed ethical grounding from which to launch a critique. Linda Hutcheon, however, suggests that postmodern style is closer to parody, as although no alternative ideal form might be possible, the critical approach of postmodernism serves to create a critique of the conventions and ideologies of the form being parodied.

Patriarchy

A social, political and cultural system whereby men are regarded as the dominant gender. In addition, the father is privileged as the head of the family and by extension, male members of society are seen as the heads of communities and nations. Patriarchy usually relates to economic power, but also to a range of discourses such as politics, religion, philosophy and ethics. Patriarchy is thereby targeted by those who lose out in this power relationship, most typically women or the young. Young males, for example, might want to challenge the power of a particular father, but not to challenge the power of fathers generally, as they will one day inherit the position. Feminism, on the other hand, serves to break down patriarchy and replace its unfair ways of organizing personal, familial and social relationships.

Phallocentrism

A system of power or cultural significance based on the phallus as the determining factor. It is therefore often associated with patriarchal societies and is seen as a target for feminism. It is a term that has been used often in French feminist theory in particular. In the context of contemporary British fiction, Angela Carter and Jeanette Winterson have explored the concept.

Politics of Difference

A broad concept that relates to a range of political movements that challenge inequalities in society in terms of class, gender, sexuality and age. Ernesto Laclau and Chantal Mouffe, for example, have suggested that a 'chain of equivalence' can exist between different marginalized groups, so that, for example, working-class white heterosexual men and black lesbian women from any class could potentially unite against the dominant forces in society, because they can recognize the other's position. In practice, however, this is often not the case as groups privilege their self-interests above those of other marginalized groups.

Postcolonialism

A term referring to an intellectual and academic practice that is concerned to study the effects of colonization on nations and peoples that were former colonies. It tends to refer to those countries that were colonies of European nations in the period from the mid-sixteenth century to the middle of the twentieth century. It can also refer to the period after a colony gains independence. In a British context, it is most often used to refer to nations that gained independence from the British Empire in the period after the Second World War.

Postmodernism

A complex term, that most often relates to the artistic practices that have become increasingly dominant in art and culture from the 1960s onwards in Western societies. As can be seen by the term itself, it offers a critical dialogue with modernism, a form of art and culture prominent in the 1920s and 1930s. Postmodernism tends to take an ironic or cynical approach to all art, even that which is done in its name. It is often the art form most associated with consumer capitalism, although the approach varies amongst artists and writers. Some of them celebrate the release from grand narratives such as religion and patriarchy. Others see consumer society as a system that devalues art and social relationships and use postmodern literary techniques to produce a critique of postmodernity.

Postmodernity

A periodizing term suggesting that a set of social, economic and philosophical paradigms have been established from roughly the end of the Second World War that distinguish (usually Western) civilization from modernity. These include theories associated with a post-industrial society and the move to an economics based on consumption rather than production. One of the philosophical tenets of postmodernism is that all claims to truth should be treated with scepticism. This is replaced, philosophically, by a model where a range of discourses (political, social and ideological) communicate with each other, but with none of them claiming absolute authority over the others.

Subaltern

Originally a military term, a subaltern refers to anyone who is lower in rank. It has been used by Gayatri Spivak to refer to a series of marginalized or minority positions related to class, race and gender. A branch of critical theory called Subaltern Studies was developed in the 1980s by a number of South Asian scholars, and aimed to interrogate the way in which cultural discourses and ideologies served to perpetuate inequalities in society with respect to the social categories identified above.

Thatcherism

An economic and ideological term related to the policies pursued by Margaret Thatcher's Conservative government during her time in office from 1979 to 1990, and continued to a certain extent by John Major into the mid 1990s. It stands for a *laissez faire* approach to economics and away from state intervention in the market. It is, therefore, in opposition to the economic theories of John Maynard Keynes, which advocated a mixed economy of private and state run industries, and had been the prevailing system adopted in Britain from the end of the Second World War. Thatcherism championed the accumulation of individual wealth and conspicuous consumption, whilst it set about dismantling many of the social welfare policies that had been established by Clement Attlee's 1945 Labour government. Thatcherism was responsible for the denationalization of several nationalized industries such as British Gas, British Rail and British Telecom. It also set itself to challenge the power of the Trade Unions which culminated in a number of bitter struggles in the 1980s such as the Miner's Strike and the Wapping Print Worker's Strike. Thatcherism has close affinities with Reaganomics, a similar economic ideology named after the U. S. President Ronald Reagan. In a British context, many novelists, such as Martin Amis, Julian Barnes, Alasdair Gray, Hanif Kureishi and Iain Sinclair, have offered a critique of the effects of Thatcher's policies in the 1980s and into the 1990s.

GUIDE TO FURTHER READING

Contemporary British Fiction

Acheson, James and Sarah C. E. Ross (eds), *The Contemporary British Novel since 1980* (Basingstoke: Palgrave, 2005).

Armit, Lucie, *Contemporary Women's Fiction and the Fantastic* (Basingstoke: Macmillan, 2000).

Bell, Ian A. (ed.), *Peripheral Visions: Images of Nationhood in Contemporary British Fiction* (Cardiff: University of Wales Press, 1995).

Bentley, Nick (ed.), *British Fiction of the 1990s* (London: Routledge, 2005).

Bradbury, Malcolm, *The Modern British Novel 1878–2001*, 2nd edn (Harmondsworth: Penguin, 2001).

Bradford, Richard, *The Novel Now: Contemporary British Fiction* (Malden, MA: Blackwell, 2007).

Brannigan, John, *Orwell to the Present: Literature in England, 1945– 2000* (Basingstoke: Palgrave, 2003).

Childs, Peter, *Contemporary Novelists: British Fiction since 1970* (Basingstoke: Palgrave, 2005).

Connor, Steven, *The English Novel in History, 1950–1995* (London: Routledge, 1996).

Craig, Cairns, *The Modern Scottish Novel: Narrative and the National Imagination* (Edinburgh: Edinburgh University Press, 1999).

D'Haen, Theo and Hans Bertens (eds), *Postmodern Studies 7: British Postmodern Fiction* (Amsterdam: Rodopi, 1994).

Duncker, Patricia, *Sisters and Strangers: An Introduction to Contemporary Feminist Fiction* (Oxford: Blackwell, 1992).

Eagleton, Mary, *Figuring the Woman Author in Contemporary Fiction* (Basingstoke: Palgrave, 2005).

Ferrebe, Alice, *Masculinity in Male-Authored Fiction, 1950–2000: Keeping it Up* (Basingstoke: Palgrave, 2005).

Finney, Brian, *English Fiction Since 1984: Narrating a Nation* (Basingstoke: Palgrave, 2006).

Gasiorek, Andrzej, *Post-War British Fiction: Realism and After* (London: Arnold, 1995).

Greaney, Michael, *Contemporary Fiction and the Uses of Theory* (Basingstoke: Palgrave, 2006).

Haffenden, John, *Novelists in Interview* (London: Methuen, 1985).

Head, Dominic, *The Cambridge Introduction to Modern British Fiction, 1950–2000* (Cambridge: Cambridge University Press, 2002).

Lane, Richard J., Rod Mengham and Philip Tew (eds), *Contemporary British Fiction* (Cambridge: Polity, 2003).

Leader, Zachary, *On Modern British Fiction* (Oxford: Oxford University Press, 2002).

Lee, Alison, *Realism and Power: Postmodern British Fiction* (London: Routledge, 1990).

Lee, A. Robert (ed.), *Other Britain, Other British: Contemporary Multicultural Fiction* (London: Pluto, 1995).

Massie, Alan, *The Novel Today* (London: Longman, 1990).

Mengham, Rod (ed.), *An Introduction to Contemporary Fiction: International Writing in English since 1970* (Cambridge: Polity, 1999).

Mengham, Rod and Philip Tew (eds), *British Fiction Today* (London: Continuum, 2006).

Middleton, Peter and Tim Woods, *Literatures of Memory: History, Time and Space in Postwar Writing* (Manchester: Manchester University Press, 2000).

Monteith, Sharon, Jenny Newman and Pat Wheeler, *Contemporary British and Irish Fiction: An Introduction Through Interviews* (London: Arnold, 2004).

Morrison, Jago, *Contemporary Fiction* (London: Routledge, 2003).

Palmer, Paulina, *Contemporary Women's Fiction: Narrative Practice and Feminist Theory* (New York: Harvester Wheatsheaf, 1989).

Prillinger, Horst, *Family and the Scottish Working-Class Novel, 1984–1994: A Study of Novels by Janice Galloway, Alasdair Gray, Robin Jenkins, James Kelman, A. L. Kennedy, William McIlvanney, Agnes Owens, Alan Spence and George Friel* (Frankfurt am Main: Peter Lang, 2000).

Proctor, James, *Dwelling Places: Postwar Black British Writing* (Manchester: Manchester University Press, 2003).

Rennison, Nick, *Contemporary British Novelists* (London: Routledge, 2004).

Sesay, Kadija (ed.), *Write Black, Write British: From Post Colonial to Black British Literature* (Hertford: Hansib, 2005).

Shaffer, Brian W., *Reading the Novel in English 1950–2000* (Malden, MA: Blackwell, 2006).

Smyth, Edmund (ed.), *Postmodernism and Contemporary Fiction* (London: Batsford, 1991).

Stevenson, Randall, and Gavin Wallace (eds), *The Scottish Novel since the Seventies: New Visions, Old Dreams* (Edinburgh: Edinburgh University Press, 1993).

Stevenson, Randall, *The Last of England? Vol 12, The Oxford English Literary History, 1960–2000* (Oxford: Oxford University Press, 2004).

Taylor, D. J., *After the War: The Novel and English Society since 1945* (London: Chatto and Windus, 1993).

Tew, Philip, *The Contemporary British Novel* (London: Continuum, 2004).

Todd, Richard, *Consuming Fictions: The Booker Prize and Fiction in Britain Today* (London: Bloomsbury, 1996).

Waugh, Patricia, *Harvest of the Sixties: English Literature and its Backgrounds, 1960–1990* (Oxford: Oxford University Press, 1995).

Worthington, Kim L., *Self as Narrative: Subjectivity and Community in Contemporary Fiction* (Oxford: Oxford University Press, 1996).

Gender and Sexuality

Alexander, Marguerite, *Flight from Realism: Themes and Strategies from Postmodernist British and American Fiction* (London: Hodder Arnold, 1990).

Beauvoir, Simone de, *The Second Sex*, ed. and trans. H. M. Parshley (London: Jonathan Cape, [1949] 1953).

Birke, Lynda, *Feminism and the Biological Body* (Edinburgh: Edinburgh University Press, 1999).

Butler, Judith, *Gender Trouble: Feminism and the Subversion of Identity* (London: Routledge, 1990).

Chapman, Rowena and Jonathan Rutherford (eds), *Male Order: Unwrapping Masculinity* (London: Lawrence and Wishart, 1988).

Cixous, Hélène, 'The Laugh of the Medusa', in *Literature in the Modern World*, 2nd edn, ed. Dennis Walder (Oxford: Oxford University Press, 2004), pp. 291–301.

Cixous, Hélène, 'The Newly Born Woman', in *Literary Theory: An Anthology*, 2nd edn, ed. Julie Rivkin and Michael Ryan (Malden, MA: Blackwell, 2004), pp. 348–54.

Doan, Laura, *The Feminist Postmodern* (New York: University of Columbia Press, 1994).

Foucault, Michel, *The History of Sexuality, Volume I*, trans. Robert Hurley (London: Penguin, [1976] 1990).

Friedan, Betty, *The Feminine Mystique* (London: Penguin, 1963).

Gallop, Jane, *Feminism and Psychoanalysis* (Basingstoke: Macmillan, 1982).

Grosz, Elizabeth, *Jacques Lacan: A Feminist Introduction* (London: Routledge, 1990).

Haraway, Donna, 'A Manifesto for Cyborgs: Science, Technology and Socialist Feminism in the 1980s', in *Feminism/Postmodernism*, ed. Linda J. Nicholson (London: Routledge, 1990), pp. 190–233.

Hite, Molly, *The Other Side of the Story: Structures and Strategies of Contemporary Feminist Narratives* (Ithaca, NY: Cornell University Press, 1989).

Irigaray, Luce, *This Sex Which Is Not One* (New York: Cornell University Press, [1977] 1985).

Irigaray, Luce, 'The Power of Discourse and the Subordination of the Feminine', in *Literary Theory: An Anthology*, 2nd edn, ed. Julie Rivkin and Michael Ryan (Malden, MA: Blackwell, 2004), pp. 795–8.

Jackson, Stevi and Jackie Jones (eds), *Contemporary Feminist Theories* (New York: New York University Press, 1998).

Knights, Ben, *Writing Masculinities: Male Narratives in Twentieth-Century Fiction* (London: Macmillan, 1999).

Kristeva, Julia, 'Revolution in Poetic Language', in *The Kristeva Reader*, ed. Toril Moi (Oxford: Blackwell, 1986), pp. 89–136.

Lea, Daniel and Berthold Schone (eds), *Posting the Male: Masculinities in Post-War and Contemporary Literature* (Amsterdam: Rodopi, 2003).

Marks, Elaine and Isabelle de Courtivron (eds), *New French Feminisms: An Anthology* (Brighton: Harvester Press, 1981).

Meaney, Geraldine, *(Un)like Subjects: Women, Theory, Fiction* (London: Routledge, 1993).

Moers, Ellen, *Literary Women* (London: Women's Press, 1978).

Moi, Toril, *Sexual/Textual Politics* (London: Methuen, 1985).

Moi, Toril (ed.), *The Kristeva Reader* (Oxford: Blackwell, 1986).

Nicholson, Linda J. (ed.), *Feminism/Postmodernism* (London: Routledge, 1990).

Plant, Sadie, *Zeroes and Ones: Digital Women and the New Technoculture* (New York: Doubleday, 1997).

Rowbotham, Sheila, *Women, Resistance and Revolution* (New York: Vintage, 1974).

Sedgwick, Eve Kosofsky, *Between Men: English Literature and Male Homosocial Desire* (New York: Columbia University Press, 1985).

Sedgwick, Eve Kosofsky, *Epistemology of the Closet* (London: Harvester Wheatsheaf, 1991).

Showalter, Elaine, *A Literature of Their Own: British Women Novelists from Brontë to Lessing* (Princeton, NJ: Princeton University Press, 1977).

Sinfield, Alan, *Cultural Politics – Queer Reading* (London: Routledge, 1994).

Tripp, Anna (ed.), *Gender* (Basingstoke: Palgrave, 2000).

Waugh, Patricia, *Feminine Fictions: Revisiting the Postmodern* (London: Routledge, 1989).

Waugh, Patricia, 'Postmodernism and Feminism?', in *Contemporary Feminist Theories*, ed. Stevi Jackson and Jackie Jones (New York: New York University Press, 1998), pp. 177–92.

Woolf, Virginia, *A Room of One's Own* (London: Hogarth, 1929).

Woolf, Virginia, 'To Cambridge Women', in *Literature in the Modern World*, 2nd edn, ed. Dennis Walder (Oxford: Oxford University Press, 2004), pp. 91–6.

Postcolonialism

Ahmed, Aijaz, *In Theory: Classes, Nations, Literatures* (London: Verso, 1992).

Anderson, Benedict, *Imagined Communities* (London: Verso and New Left Books, 1983).

Ashcroft, Bill, Gareth Griffiths and Helen Tiffin (eds), *The Post-Colonial Studies Reader* (London: Routledge, 1995).

Ashcroft, Bill, Gareth Griffiths and Helen Tiffin, *The Empire Writes Back* (London: Routledge, 1989).

Ato, Quayson, *Postcolonialism: Theory, Practice or Process?* (Cambridge: Polity, 2000).

Bhabha, Homi K., *The Location of Culture* (London: Routledge, 1984).

Bhabha, Homi K. (ed.), *Nation and Narration* (London: Routledge, 1990).

Boehmer, Elleke, *Colonial and Postcolonial Literature: Migrant Metaphors* (Oxford: Oxford University Press, 1995).

Brydon, Diana (ed.), *Postcolonialism: Critical Concepts in Literary and Cultural Studies* (London: Routledge, 2000).

During, Simon, 'Postmodernism or Post-Colonialism Today', in *Postmodernism: A Reader*, ed. Thomas Doherty (New York: Harvester, 1993), pp. 448–62.

Fanon, Frantz, *The Wretched of the Earth*, trans. Constance Farrington (Harmondsworth: Penguin, 1967).

Fanon, Frantz, *Black Skin, White Masks*, trans. Constance Farrington (New York: Grove Press, [1952] 1967).

Gilroy, Paul, *There Ain't No Black in the Union Jack: The Cultural Politics of Race and Nation* (London: Hutchinson, 1987).

Hall, Stuart et al. (eds), *Resistance Through Rituals: Youth Subcultures in Postwar Britain* (London: Hutchinson, 1976).

Hall, Stuart, 'Old and New Identities, Old and New Ethnicities', in *Culture, Globalization and the World-System*, ed. Anthony D. King (Basingstoke: Macmillan, 1991), pp. 41–68.

Harrison, Nicholas, *Postcolonial Criticism: History, Theory and the Work of Fiction* (Cambridge: Polity, 2003).

Hill, Tracey, and William Hughes (eds), *Contemporary Writing and National Identity* (Bath: Sulis Press, 1995).

hooks, bell, 'Postmodern Blackness', in *Modern Literary Theory*, 4th edn, ed. Philip Rice and Patricia Waugh (London: Edward Arnold, 1992), pp. 362–8.

Loomba, Ania, *Colonialism/Postcolonialism* (London: Routledge, 1998).

McLeod, John, *Beginning Postcolonialism* (Manchester: Manchester University Press, 2000).

McLeod, John, *Postcolonial London: Rewriting the Metropolis* (London: Routledge, 2003).

Masden, Deborah (ed.), *Postcolonial Literatures* (London: Pluto, 1999).

Moore-Gilbert, Bart, *Postcolonial Theory: Contexts, Practices, Politics* (London: Verso, 1997).

Nasta, Susheila, *Home Truths: Fictions of the South Asian Diaspora* (Basingstoke: Palgrave, 2002).

Said, Edward, *Orientalism: Western Conceptions of the Orient* (Harmondsworth: Penguin, [1978] 1991).

Said, Edward, *Culture and Imperialism* (London: Chatto & Windus, 1993).

Thieme, John (ed.), *Postcolonial Literatures in English* (London: Edward Arnold, 1996).

Thieme, John, *Post-Colonial Contexts: Writing Back to the Canon* (London: Continuum, 2002).

Williams, Patrick and Laura Chrisman (eds), *Colonial Discourse / Postcolonial Theory* (New York: Columbia University Press, 1994).

Young, Robert, *Colonial Desire* (London: Routledge, 1995).

Young, Robert J. C., *Postcolonialism: A Very Short Introduction* (Oxford: Oxford University Press, 2003).

Young, Robert J. C., *Postcolonialism: An Historical Introduction* (Oxford: Blackwell, 2000).

Postmodernism

Alexander, Marguerite, *Flight from Realism: Themes and Strategies from Postmodernist British and American Fiction* (London: Hodder Arnold, 1990).

Baker, Stephen, *The Fiction of Postmodernity* (Edinburgh: Edinburgh University Press, 2000).

Baudrillard, Jean, *Simulacra and Simulation*, trans. Sheila Faria Glaser (Ann Arbor, MI: University of Michigan Press, 1995).

Baudrillard, Jean, *Simulations* (New York: Semiotext(e), 1983).

Bertens, Hans, *The Idea of the Postmodern: A History* (London: Routledge, 1995).

Brooker, Peter (ed.), *Modernism/Postmodernism* (London: Longman, 1988).

Connor, Steven, *Postmodernist Culture: An Introduction to Theories of the Contemporary* (Oxford: Blackwell, 1989).

Currie, Mark, *Postmodern Narrative Theory* (Basingstoke: Macmillan, 1998).

D'Haen, Theo and Hans Bertens (eds), *Postmodern Studies 7: British Postmodern Fiction* (Amsterdam: Rodopi, 1994).

Doan, Laura, *The Feminist Postmodern* (New York: University of Columbia Press, 1994).

Doherty, Thomas (ed.), *Postmodernism: A Reader* (New York: Harvester, 1993).

During, Simon, 'Postmodernism or Post-Colonialism Today', in *Postmodernism: A Reader*, ed. Thomas Doherty (New York: Harvester, 1993), pp. 448–62.

Eagleton, Terry, *The Illusions of Postmodernism* (Oxford: Blackwell, 1996).

Foster, Hal (ed.), *Postmodern Culture* (London: Pluto Press, 1985).

Gibson, Andrew, *Towards a Postmodern Theory of Narrative* (Edinburgh: Edinburgh University Press, 1996).

Gibson, Andrew, *Postmodernism, Ethics and the Novel: From Leavis to Levinas* (London: Routledge, 1999).

hooks, bell, 'Postmodern Blackness', in *Modern Literary Theory*, 4th edn, ed. Philip Rice and Patricia Waugh (London: Edward Arnold, 1992), pp. 362–8.

Harvey, David, *The Condition of Postmodernity: An Enquiry into the Origins of Cultural Change* (Oxford: Blackwell, 1990).

Hutcheon, Linda, *A Poetics of Postmodernism: History, Theory, Fiction* (London: Routledge, 1988).

Hutcheon, Linda, *The Politics of Postmodernism* (London: Routledge, 1989).

Jameson, Fredric, *Postmodernism, or the Cultural Logic of Late Capitalism* (London: Verso, 1991).

Jenkins, Keith (ed.), *The Postmodern History Reader* (London: Routledge, 1997).

Lee, Alison, *Realism and Power: Postmodern British Fiction* (London: Routledge, 1990).

Lyotard, Jean-François, *The Postmodern Condition: A Report on Knowledge*, trans. Geoff Bennington and Brian Massumi (Manchester: Manchester University Press, [1979] 1984).

Jean-François Lyotard, 'Answering the Question: What Is Postmodernism', trans. Régis Durand, in *The Postmodern Condition: A Report on Knowledge*, trans. Geoff Bennington and

Brian Massumi (Manchester: Manchester University Press, [1979] 1984), pp. 71–82.

McRobbie, Angela, *Postmodernism and Popular Culture* (London: Routledge, 1994).

McHale, Brian, *Postmodernist Fiction* (London: Methuen, 1987).

Malpas, Simon (ed.), *Postmodern Debates* (Basingstoke: Palgrave, 2001).

Nicholson, Linda J. (ed.), *Feminism/Postmodernism* (London: Routledge, 1990).

Pefanis, Julian, *Heterology and the Postmodern: Bataille, Baudrillard, and Lyotard* (Durham, NC: Duke University Press, 1991).

Sarup, Madan, *An Introductory Guide to Post-structuralism and Postmodernism* (Brighton: Harvester, 1988).

Sim, Stuart, *Irony and Crisis: A Critical History of Postmodern Culture* (New York: Totem, 2002).

Sim, Stuart (ed.), *The Routledge Companion to Postmodernism* (London: Routledge, 2004).

Smethurst, Paul, *The Postmodern Chronotype: Reading Space and Time in Contemporary Fiction* (Amsterdam: Rodopi, 2000).

Smyth, Edmund, *Postmodernism and Contemporary Fiction* (London: Batsford, 1991).

Waugh, Patricia, *Feminine Fictions: Revisiting the Postmodern* (London: Routledge, 1989).

Waugh, Patricia, *Practising Postmodernism, Reading Modernism* (London: Edward Arnold, 1992).

Waugh, Patricia (ed.), *Postmodernism: A Reader* (London: Hodder Arnold, 1998).

Woods, Tim, *Beginning Postmodernism* (Manchester: Manchester University Press, 1999).

General Literary and Cultural Theory

Althusser, Louis, 'Ideology and Ideological State Apparatuses', in *Lenin and Philosophy and Other Essays*, trans. Ben Brewster (London: New Left Books, 1971), pp. 122–73.

Bakhtin, Mikhail, *Rabelais and His World*, trans. Helene Iswolsky (Bloomington, IN: Indiana University Press, [1965] 1984).

Bakhtin, M. M., 'Discourse in the Novel', in *The Dialogic Imagination: Four Essays by M. M. Bakhtin*, ed. and trans. Caryl Emerson and Michael Holquist (Austin, TX: University of Texas Press, 1981), pp. 259–422.

Barthes, Roland, 'Introduction to the Structural Analysis of Narratives', in *Image, Music, Text*, trans. Stephen Heath (London: Fontana, 1977), pp. 79–124.

Barthes, Roland, 'The Death of the Author', in *Image, Music, Text*, trans. Stephen Heath (London: Fontana, 1977), pp. 142–8.

Belsey, Catherine, *Critical Practice* (London: Routledge, [1980] 1987).

Belsey, Catherine, *Desire: Love Stories in Western Culture* (Oxford: Blackwell, 1994).

Bennett, Andrew and Nicholas Royle, *An Introduction to Literature, Criticism and Theory: Key Critical Concepts*, 3rd edn (Hemel Hempstead: Harvester Wheatsheaf, 2004).

Bloom, Clive and Gary Day (eds), *Literature and Culture in Modern Britain: Volume Three: 1956–1999* (Harlow: Longman, 2000).

Brooker, Peter, *Modernity and Metropolis: Writing, Film, and Urban Formations* (Basingstoke: Palgrave, 2002).

Brooks, Cleanth, *The Well-Wrought Urn: Studies in the Structure of Poetry* (New York: Harcourt, Brace and World, 1947).

Chatman, Seymour, *Story and Discourse: Narrative Structure in Fiction and Film* (Ithaca, NY: Cornell University Press, 1978).

Clarke, Gary, 'Defending Ski-Jumpers: A Critique of Theories of Youth Subcultures', in *The Subcultures Reader*, ed. Ken Gelder and Sarah Thompson (London: Routledge, 1997), pp. 175–80.

Cohen, Phil, 'Subcultural Conflict and Working-Class Community', in *The Subcultures Reader*, pp. 90–9.

Deleuze, Gilles and Felix Guattari, *Kafka: Toward a Minor Literature*, trans. Dana Polan (Minneapolis, MN: University of Minnesota Press, 1986).

Derrida, Jacques, *Acts of Literature*, trans. Derek Attridge (London: Routledge, 1992).

Dipple, Elizabeth, *The Unresolvable Plot: Reading Contemporary Fiction* (London: Routledge, 1988).

Eagleton, Terry, *Literary Theory*, 2nd edn (Oxford: Blackwell, 1996).

Easthope, Anthony, *Englishness and National Culture* (London: Routledge, 1999).

Eliot, Anthony, *Psychoanalytic Theory: An Introduction* (Oxford: Blackwell, 1994).

Foucault, Michel, *The Order of Things: An Archaeology of the Human Sciences*, trans. Alan Sheridan Smith (London: Routledge, 1970).

Foucault, Michel, 'Nietzsche, Genealogy, History', in *Language, Counter-Memory, Practice* (Oxford: Blackwell, 1977), pp. 139–64.

Foucault, Michel, *Power/Knowledge: Selected Interviews and Other Writings 1972–77*, ed. Colin Gordon (London: Harvester, 1980).

Freud, Sigmund, *Beyond the Pleasure Principle*, ed. and trans. James Strachey (New York: W. W. Norton, [1929] 1975).

Fukuyama, Francis, *The End of History and the Last Man* (London: Hamish Hamilton, 1992).

Furst, Lilian R. (ed.), *Realism* (Harlow: Longman, 1992).

Gane, Mike, *Baudrillard: Critical and Fatal Theory* (London: Routledge, 1991).

Goring, Paul, Jeremy Hawthorn and Domhall Mitchell, *Studying Literature: The Essential Companion* (London: Arnold, 2001).

Hall, Stuart, 'The Question of Cultural Identity', in *Modernity and Its Futures*, ed. Stuart Hall, David Held and Tony McGrew (Cambridge: Polity, 1992), pp. 274–316.

Hawkes, Terence, *Structuralism and Semiotics* (London: Routledge, 1977).

Hawthorn, Jeremy, *Studying the Novel*, 5th edn (London: Hodder Arnold, 2005).

Hebdige, Dick, *Subculture: The Meaning of Style* (London: Routledge, [1979] 1988).

Jackson, Rosemary, *Fantasy: The Literature of Subversion* (London Methuen, 1981).

Kellner, Douglas, *Jean Baudrillard: From Marxism to Postmodernism and Beyond* (Cambridge: Polity, 1989).

Leavis, F. R., *The Great Tradition* (London: Chatto and Windus, 1947).

Lodge, David, *The Novelist at the Crossroads* (London: Routledge, 1971).

Lodge, David, 'The Novelist at the Crossroads', in *The Novel Today: Contemporary Writers on Modern Fiction*, ed. Malcolm Bradbury (London: Fontana/Collins, 1977), pp. 84–110.

Lodge, David, *The Modes of Modern Writing: Metaphor, Metonymy and the Typology of Modern Literature* (London: Edward Arnold, 1979).

Lodge, David, *After Bakhtin: Essays on Fiction and Criticism* (London: Routledge, 1990).

Lovell, Terry, *Consuming Fiction* (London: Verso, 1987).

McQuillan, Martin et al. (eds), *Post-Theory: New Directions in Criticism* (Edinburgh: Edinburgh University Press, 1999).

McQuillan, Martin (ed.), *The Narrative Reader* (London: Routledge, 2000).

Morley, David and Kuan-Hsing Chen (eds), *Stuart Hall: Critical Dialogues in Cultural Studies* (London: Routledge, 1996).

Moore-Gilbert, Bart and John Seed, *Cultural Revolution?: The Challenge of the Arts in the 1960s* (London: Routledge, 1992).

Norris, Christopher, *Deconstruction* (London: Routledge, 1991).

Payne, Michael, *Reading Theory: An Introduction to Lacan, Derrida and Kristeva* (Oxford: Blackwell, 1993).

Pearce, Lynne, *Reading Dialogics* (London: Arnold, 1994).

Pope, Rob, *The English Studies Book* (London: Routledge, 1998).

Readings, Bill, *Introducing Lyotard* (London: Routledge, 1991).

Richards, I. A., *Practical Criticism: A Study of Literary Judgment* (New York: Harcourt, Brace and World, [1929] 1967).

Rice, Philip, and Patricia Waugh, *Modern Literary Theory*, 4th edn (London: Edward Arnold, 1992).

Rimmon-Kenan, Shlomith, *Narrative Fiction; Contemporary Poetics* (London: Methuen, 1983).

Rivkin, Julie and Michael Ryan (eds), *Literary Theory: An Anthology*, 2nd edn (Malden, MA: Blackwell, 2004).

Rogers, David and John McLeod (eds), *The Revision of Englishness* (Manchester: Manchester University Press, 2004).

Royle, Nicholas, *The Uncanny* (Manchester: Manchester University Press, 2003).

Shklovsky, Viktor, 'Art as Technique', in *Literary Theory: An Anthology*, 2nd edn, ed. Julie Rivkin and Michael Ryan (Malden, MA: Blackwell, 2004), pp. 15–21.

Sim, Stuart (ed.), *Post-Marxism: A Reader* (Edinburgh: Edinburgh University Press, 1998).

Sinfield, Alan, *Literature, Politics and Culture in Postwar Britain* (Oxford: Basil Blackwell, 1989).

Spivak, Gayatri, 'Can the Subaltern Speak', in *Marxism and the Interpretation of Culture*, ed. by Cary Nelson and Lawrence Grossberg (London: Macmillan, 1988), pp. 271–313.

Vice, Sue (ed.), *Psychoanalytic Criticism* (Cambridge: Polity, 1996).

Waugh, Patricia, *Metafiction: The Theory and Practice of Self-conscious Fiction* (London: Methuen, 1984).

Wimsatt, W. K., Jr, *The Verbal Icon* (Lexington, KY: University of Kentucky Press, 1954).

Wright, Elizabeth, *Psychoanalytic Criticism* (London: Routledge, 1984).

Young, Robert, *White Mythologies: Writing History and the West* (London: Routledge, 1990).

Žižek, Slavoj, *Enjoy Your Symptom: Jacques Lacan in and out of Hollywood* (London: Routledge, 1992).

Monica Ali

Cormack, Alistair, 'Migration and the Politics of Narrative Form: Realism and the Postcolonial Subject in *Brick Lane*', *Contemporary Literature*, 47 (4) (2006), 695–721.

Haq, Kaiser, 'Monica Ali', in *South Asian Writers in English*, ed. Fakrul Alam (Detroit, MI: Thomson Gale, 2006), pp. 20–4.

Lewis, Paul, 'Brick Lane Film Protests Force Film Company to Beat Retreat', *The Guardian*, 27 July 2006.

Marx, John, 'The Feminization of Globalization', *Cultural Critique*, 63 (2006), 1–32.

Matthew Taylor, 'Brickbats Fly as Community Brands Novel "Despicable" ', *The Guardian*, 3 December 2003, p. 5.

Martin Amis

Brook, Susan, 'The Female Form, Sublimation, and Nicola Six', in *Martin Amis: Postmodernism and Beyond*, ed. Gavin Keulks (Basingstoke: Palgrave, 2006), pp. 87–100.

Childs, Peter, 'Martin Amis: Lucre, Love, and Literature', in *Contemporary Novelists: British Fiction since 1970* (Basingstoke: Palgrave, 2005), pp. 35–57.

Dern, John A., *Martians, Monsters and Madonna: Fiction and Form in the World of Martin Amis* (New York: Peter Lang, 2000).

Diedrick, James, 'The Fiction of Martin Amis: Patriarchy and its Discontents', in *Contemporary British Fiction*, ed. Richard J. Lane, Rod Mengham and Philip Tew (Cambridge: Polity, 2003), pp. 239–55.

Diedrick, James, *Understanding Martin Amis*, 2nd edn (Columbia, SC: University of South Carolina Press, 2004).

Keulks, Gavin, *Father and Son: Kingsley Amis, Martin Amis and the British Novel Since 1950* (Madison, WI: University of Wisconsin Press, 2003).

Keulks, Gavin (ed.), *Martin Amis: Postmodernism and Beyond* (Basingstoke: Palgrave, 2006).

McEwan, Ian, 'Interview with Martin Amis', Guardian Conversations (London: ICA Video/Trilion, 1988).

Reynolds, Margaret and Jonathan Noakes, *Martin Amis: The Rachel Papers, London Fields, Time's Arrow, Experience* (London: Vintage, 2003).

Tew, Philip, 'Martin Amis and Late-twentieth-century Working-class Masculinity: *Money* and *London Fields*', in *Martin Amis: Postmodernism and Beyond*, ed. Gavin Keulks (Basingstoke: Palgrave, 2006), pp. 71–86.

Tredell, Nicolas, *The Fiction of Martin Amis: A Reader's Guide to Essential Criticism* (Cambridge: Icon Books, 2000).

Julian Barnes

Guignery, Vanessa, *The Fiction of Julian Barnes* (Basingstoke: Palgrave, 2006).

Henstra, Sarah, 'The McReal Thing: Personal/National Identity in Julian Barnes's *England, England*', in *British Fiction of the 1990s*, ed. Nick Bentley (London: Routledge, 2005), pp. 95–107.

Miracky, James J., 'Replicating a Dinosaur: Authenticity Run Amok in the "Theme Parking" of Michael Crichton's *Jurassic*

Park and Julian Barnes's *England, England*, *Critique: Studies in Contemporary Fiction* 45 (2) (2004), 163–71.

Moseley, Merritt, *Understanding Julian Barnes* (Columbia, SC: University of South Carolina Press, 1997).

Nunning, Vera, 'The Invention of Cultural Traditions: The Construction and Deconstruction of Englishness and Authenticity in Julian Barnes's *England, England*, *Anglia* 119 (1) (2001), 58–76.

Rubinson, Gregory J., *The Fiction of Rushdie, Barnes, Winterson, and Carter: Breaking Cultural and Literary Boundaries in the Work of Four Postmodernists* (Jefferson, NC: McFarland, 2005).

Pateman, Matthew, *Julian Barnes* (Plymouth: Northcote House, 2002).

A. S. Byatt

Alfer, Alexa and Michael J. Noble (eds), *Essays on the Fiction of A. S. Byatt: Imagining the Real* (Westport, CT: Greenwood Press, 2001).

Alban, Gillian M. E., *Melusine the Serpent Goddess in A. S. Byatt's Possession and in Mythology* (New York: Lexington Books, 2003).

Burgass, Catherine, *A. S. Byatt's Possession: A Reader's Guide* (New York: Continuum International, 2002).

Campbell, Jane, *A. S. Byatt and the Heliotropic Imagination* (Waterloo: Wilfrid Laurier University Press, 2004).

Elam, Diane, 'Postmodern Romance', in *Postmodernism Across the Ages*, ed. Bill Readings and Bennet Schaber (New York: Syracuse University Press, 1993), pp. 216–30.

Kelly, Kathleen Coyne, *A. S. Byatt* (New York: Twayne Publishers, 1996).

Reynolds, Margaret and Jonathan Noakes, *A. S. Byatt: The Essential Guide* (London: Vintage, 2004).

Tarbox, Katharine, 'Desire for Syzygy in the Novels of A. S. Byatt', in *The Contemporary British Novel since 1980*, ed. James Acheson and Sarah C. E. Ross (Basingstoke: Palgrave, 2005), pp. 177–88.

Todd, Richard, *A. S. Byatt* (Plymouth: Northcote House, 1997).

Wallhead, Celia M., *The Old, The New and The Metaphor: A Critical Study of the Novels of A. S. Byatt* (Atlanta: Minerva Press, 1999).

Angela Carter

Bristow, Joseph and Trev Lynn Broughton (eds), *Infernal Desires of Angela Carter* (London: Longman, 1997).

Clark, Robert, 'Angela Carter's Desire Machine', *Women's Studies: An Interdisciplinary Journal* 14(2) (1987), 147–61.

Day, Aidan, *Angela Carter: The Rational Glass* (Manchester: Manchester University Press, 1998).

Eaglestone, Robert, 'The Fiction of Angela Carter: The Woman Who Loved to Retell Stories', in *Contemporary British Fiction*, ed. Richard J. Lane, Rod Mengham and Philip Tew (Cambridge: Polity, 2003), pp. 195–209.

Easton, Alison (ed.), *Angela Carter* (Basingstoke: Macmillan, 2000).

Gamble, Sarah, *Angela Carter* (Edinburgh: Edinburgh University Press, 1997).

Gamble, Sarah (ed.), *The Fiction of Angela Carter: A Reader's Guide to Essential Criticism* (Basingstoke: Palgrave, 2001).

Gamble, Sarah, *Angela Carter: A Literary Life* (Basingstoke: Palgrave, 2005).

Lee, Alison, 'Angela Carter's New Eve(lyn): De/Engendering Narrative', in *Ambiguous Discourse: Feminist Narratology and British Women Writers*, ed. Kathy Mezei (Chapel Hill, NC: University of North Carolina Press, 1996), pp. 238–49.

Morrison, Jago, 'Angela Carter: Genealogies', in *Contemporary Fiction* (London: Routledge, 2003), pp. 155–78.

Munford, Rebecca (ed.), *Re-Visiting Angela Carter: Texts, Contexts, Intertexts* (Basingstoke: Palgrave, 2006).

Peach, Linden, *Angela Carter* (Basingstoke: Macmillan, 1998).

Rubinson, Gregory J., *The Fiction of Rushdie, Barnes, Winterson, and Carter: Breaking Cultural and Literary Boundaries in the Work of Four Postmodernists* (Jefferson, NC: McFarland, 2005).

Sage, Lorna, *Angela Carter* (Plymouth: Northcote House, 1994).

Sage, Lorna (ed.), *Flesh and the Mirror: Essays on the Art of Angela Carter* (London: Virago, 1994).

Stoddart, Helen, *Angela Carter's Nights at the Circus* (London: Routledge, 2007).
Wisker, Gina, *Angela Carter* (London: Hodder and Stoughton, 2003).

Alasdair Gray

Bernstein, Stephen, *Alasdair Gray* (Lewisburg, PA: Bucknell University Press, 1999).
Crawford, Robert, and Thom Nairn (eds), *The Arts of Alasdair Gray* (Edinburgh: Edinburgh University Press, 1991).
Kaczvinsky, Donald P., ' "Making Up for Lost Time": Scotland, Stories, and the Self in Alasdair Gray's *Poor Things*', in *Contemporary Literature* 42(4), (2001), 775–99.
Lumsden, Alison, 'Innovation and Reaction in the Fiction of Alasdair Gray', in *The Scottish Novel since the Seventies: New Visions, Old Dreams*, ed. Randall Stevenson and Gavin Wallace (Edinburgh: Edinburgh University Press, 1993), pp. 115–26.
Miller, Gavin, *Alasdair Gray: The Fiction of Communion* (Amsterdam: Rodopi, 2005).
Moores, Phil (ed.), *Alasdair Gray: Critical Appreciations and a Bibliography* (Boston Spa: The British Library, 2002).

Nick Hornby

Moseley, Merritt, 'Nick Hornby, English Football and *Fever Pitch*', *Aethlon: The Journal of Sport Literature* 11(2) (1994), 87–95.
Stein, Thomas Michael, 'Rewriting Tony Blair's "Vision of Modern Britain": Fictions by Martin Amis, Julian Barnes, Nick Hornby and Fay Weldon', *Anglistik und Englischunterricht* 65 (2003), 193–206.

Hanif Kureishi

Ball, John Clement, 'The Semi-Detached Metropolis: Hanif Kureishi's London', *Ariel* 27(4) (1996), 7–27.
Brook, Susan, 'Hedgemony? Suburban Space in *The Buddha of Suburbia*', in *British Fiction of the 1990s*, ed. Nick Bentley (London: Routledge, 2005), pp. 209–25.

Carey, Cynthia, '*The Buddha of Suburbia* as a Post-Colonial Novel', *Commonwealth Essays and Studies* 4 (1997), 119–25.

Childs, Peter, 'Hanif Kureishi: In Black and White', in *Contemporary Novelists: British Fiction since 1970* (Basingstoke: Palgrave, 2005), pp. 141–59.

Doyle, Waddick, 'The Space Between Identity and Otherness in Hanif Kureishi's *The Buddha of Suburbia*', *Commonwealth Essays and Studies* 4 (1997), 110–18.

Finney, Brian, 'Hanif Kureishi: *The Buddha of Suburbia*', in *English Fiction since 1984: Narrating a Nation* (Basingstoke: Palgrave, 2006), pp. 124–38.

Gallix, Francois (ed.), *The Buddha of Suburbia* (Paris: Elipses, 1997).

Hashmi, Alamgir, 'Hanif Kureishi and the Tradition of the Novel', *International Fiction Review* 19(2) (1992), 77–82.

Iloma, Anthony, 'Hanif Kureishi's *The Buddha of Suburbia*', in *Contemporary British Fiction*, ed. Richard J. Lane, Rod Mengham and Philip Tew (Cambridge: Polity, 2003), pp. 87–105.

Kaleta, Kenneth C., *Hanif Kureishi: Postcolonial Storyteller* (Austin, TX: University of Texas Press, 1998).

Moore-Gilbert, Bart, *Hanif Kureishi* (Manchester: Manchester University Press, 2001).

Morrison, Jago, 'After "Race": Hanif Kureishi's Writing', in *Contemporary Fiction* (London: Routledge, 2003), pp. 155–78.

Oubechou, Jamel, 'The Barbarians and Philistines in *The Buddha of Suburbia*', *Commonwealth Essays and Studies* 4 (1997), 101–9.

Ranasinha, Ruvani, *Hanif Kureishi* (Plymouth: Northcote House, 2002).

Thomas, Susie (ed.), *Hanif Kureishi: A Reader's Guide to Essential Criticism* (Basingstoke: Palgrave, 2005).

Yousaf, Nahem, *Hanif Kureishi's The Buddha of Suburbia* (London: Continuum, 2002).

Ian McEwan

Byrnes, Christina, *The Work of Ian McEwan: A Psychodynamic Approach* (Nottingham: Paupers' Press, 2002).

Childs, Peter, ' "Fascinating Violation": Ian McEwan's Children', in *British Fiction of the 1990s*, ed. Nick Bentley (London: Routledge, 2005), pp. 123–34.

Childs, Peter, 'Ian McEwan: The Child in Us All', in *Contemporary Novelists: British Fiction since 1970* (Basingstoke: Palgrave, 2005), pp. 160–79.

Childs, Peter (ed.), *The Fiction of Ian McEwan: A Reader's Guide to the Essential Criticism* (Basingstoke: Palgrave, 2006).

Finney, Brian, 'Ian McEwan: *Atonement*', in *English Fiction since 1984: Narrating a Nation* (Basingstoke: Palgrave, 2006), pp. 87–101.

Finney, Brian, 'Briony's Stand Against Oblivion: The Making of Fiction in Ian McEwan's *Atonement*', *Journal of Modern Literature* 27(3) (2004), 68–82.

Harold, James, 'Narrative Engagement with *Atonement* and *The Blind Assassin*', *Philosophy and Literature* 29(1) (2005), 130–45.

Hidalgo, Pilar, 'Memory and Storytelling in Ian McEwan's *Atonement*', *Critique: Studies in Contemporary Fiction* 46(2) (2005), 82–91.

Malcolm, David, *Understanding Ian McEwan* (Columbia, SC: University of Columbia Press, 2002).

Phelan, James, 'Narrative Judgements and the Rhetorical Theory of Narrative: Ian McEwan's *Atonement*', in *A Companion to Narrative Theory*, ed. James Phelan and Peter J. Rabinowitz (Malden, MA: Blackwell, 2005), pp. 322–36.

Ryan, Kiernan, *Ian McEwan* (Plymouth: Northcote House, 1994).

Slay, Jack Jr, *Ian McEwan* (New York: Twayne, 2000).

Tönnies, Merle, 'A New Self-Conscious Turn at the Turn of the Century? Postmodernist Metafiction in Recent Works by 'Established' British Writers', *Anglistik und Englischunterricht* 66 (2005), 57–82.

Courttia Newland

Arana, R. Victoria, 'Courttia Newland's Psychological Realism and Consequentialist Ethics', in *Write Black, Write British: From Post Colonial to Black British Literature*, ed. Kadija Sesay (Hertfordshire: Hansib, 2005), pp. 86–106.

Davis, Geoffrey, '"Me – I'm a Black British Londoner": An Interview with Courttia Newland', in *Staging New Britain: Aspects of Black and South Asian British Theatre Practice*, ed. Geoffrey V. Davis and Anne Fuchs (Brussels: Peter Lang, 2006).

Roberts, Maureen, 'Does the Writer Have a Responsibility to Their Community? Courttia Newland and Jacob Ross', in *Wasafiri: The Transnational Journal of International Writing* 41 (2004), 3–7.

Salman Rushdie

Appignanesi, Lisa and Sara Maitland (eds), *The Rushdie File* (London: Fourth Estate, 1989).

Baker, Stephen, 'Salman Rushdie: Self and the Fiction of Truth', in *Contemporary British Fiction*, ed. Richard J. Lane, Rod Mengham and Philip Tew (Cambridge: Polity, 2003), pp. 145–57.

Ben-Yishai, Ayelet, 'The Dialectic of Shame: Representation in the Metanarrative of Salman Rushdie's *Shame*', *Modern Fiction Studies* 48(1) (2002), 194–215.

Brennan, Timothy, *Salman Rushdie and the Third World: Myths of the Nation* (Basingstoke: Macmillan, 1989).

Blake, Andrew, *Salman Rushdie: A Beginner's Guide* (London: Hodder and Stoughton, 2001).

Childs, Peter, 'Salman Rushdie: A Long Geographical Perspective', in *Contemporary Novelists: British Fiction since 1970* (Basingstoke: Palgrave, 2005), pp. 180–200.

Cundy, Catherine, *Salman Rushdie* (Manchester: Manchester University Press, 1996).

Fletcher, M. D., *Reading Rushdie: Perspectives on the Fiction of Salman Rushdie* (Amsterdam: Rodopi, 1994).

Goonetilleke, D.C.R.A., *Salman Rushdie* (Basingstoke: Macmillan, 1998).

Grant, Damian, *Salman Rushdie* (Plymouth: Northcote House, 1999).

Morrison, Jago, 'Imagining Nations: Salman Rushdie', in *Contemporary Fiction* (London: Routledge, 2003), pp. 133–54.

Raza, Hima, 'Unravelling Sharam: Narrativisation as a Political Act in Salman Rushdie's *Shame*', *Wasafiri: The Transnational Journal of International Writing* 39 (2003), 55–61.

Rubinson, Gregory J., *The Fiction of Rushdie, Barnes, Winterson, and Carter: Breaking Cultural and Literary Boundaries in the Work of Four Postmodernists* (Jefferson, NC: McFarland, 2005).

Teverson, Andrew, 'Salman Rushdie and Aijaz Ahmad: Satire, Ideology and *Shame*', *Journal of Commonwealth Literature* 39(2) (2004), 45–60.

Iain Sinclair

Bond, Robert, and Jenny Bavidge (eds), 'The Iain Sinclair Special Edition', *Literary London: Interdisciplinary Studies in the Representation of London* 3(2) (2005) [no pagination].

Brooker, Peter, 'Iain Sinclair: The Psychotic Geographer Treads The Border-Lines', in *British Fiction of the 1990s*, ed. Nick Bentley (London: Routledge, 2005), pp. 226–37.

Mengham, Rod, 'The Writing of Iain Sinclair: "Our Narrative Starts Everywhere"', in *Contemporary British Fiction*, ed. Richard J. Lane, Rod Mengham and Philip Tew (Cambridge: Polity, 2003), pp. 56–67.

Murray, Alex, 'Exorcising the Demons of Thatcherism: Iain Sinclair and the Critical Efficacy of a London Fiction', *Literary London: Interdisciplinary Studies in the Representation of London* 3(2) (2005), [no pagination].

Potter, Rachel, 'Culture Vulture: The Testimony of Iain Sinclair's *Downriver*', in *Parataxis*, 5 (1993), 40–8.

Watson, Ben, 'Iain Sinclair: The Right Kind of Schizophrenia (a Note on *Downriver*)', *Literary London: Interdisciplinary Studies in the Representation of London* 3(2) (2005), [no pagination].

Wolfreys, Julian, 'Londonography: Iain Sinclair's Urban Graphic', *Literary London: Interdisciplinary Studies in the Representation of London* 3(2) (2005), [no pagination].

Zadie Smith

Botting, Fred, 'From Excess to the New World Order', in *British Fiction of the 1990s*, ed. Nick Bentley (London: Routledge, 2005), pp. 21–41.

Childs, Elaine, 'Insular Utopias and Religious Neuroses: Hybridity Anxiety in Zadie Smith's White Teeth', *Proteus: A Journal of Ideas* 23(1) (2006), 7–12.

Childs, Peter, 'Zadie Smith: Searching for the Inescapable', in *Contemporary Novelists: British Fiction since 1970* (Basingstoke: Palgrave, 2005), pp. 201–16.

Head, Dominic, 'Zadie Smith's *White Teeth*: Multiculturalism for the Millennium', in *Contemporary British Fiction*, ed. Richard J. Lane, Rod Mengham and Philip Tew (Cambridge: Polity, 2003), pp. 106–19.

Moss, Laura, 'The Politics of Everyday Hybridity: Zadie Smith's *White Teeth*', *Wasifiri: The Transnational Journal of International Writing* 39, (2003), 1–17.

Sell, Jonathan P. A., 'Chance and gesture in Zadie Smith's *White Teeth* and *The Autograph Man*: a model for multicultural identity', *Journal of Commonwealth Literature* 41(3) (2006), 27–44.

Squires, Claire, *Zadie Smith's White Teeth: A Reader's Guide* (London: Continuum, 2002).

Thompson, Molly, ' "Happy Multicultural Land'? The Implications of an 'Excess of Belonging' in Zadie Smith's White Teeth" ', in *Write Black, Write British: From Post Colonial to Black British Literature* ed. Kadija Sesay (Hertford: Hansib, 2005), pp. 122–40.

Walters, Tracey L., ' "We're All English Now Mate Like It or Lump It": The Black/Britishness of Zadie Smith's *White Teeth*', in *Write Black, Write British: From Post Colonial to Black British Literature*, ed. Kadija Sesay (Hertford: Hansib, 2005), pp. 314–22.

Graham Swift

Acheson, James, '*Historia* and guilt: Graham Swift's *Waterland*', *Critique: Studies in Contemporary Fiction* 47(1) (2005), 90–100.

Alphen, Ernest van, 'The Performativity of Histories: Graham Swift's *Waterland* as a Theory of History', in *The Point of*

Theory, ed. M. Bal and I. Boer (Amsterdam: Amsterdam University Press, 1994), pp. 202–10.

Bényei, Tamás, 'The Novels of Graham Swift: Family Photos', in *Contemporary British Fiction*, ed. Richard J. Lane, Rod Mengham and Philip Tew (Cambridge: Polity, 2003), pp. 87–105.

Berlatsky, Eric, ' "The swamps of myth . . . and empirical fishing lines": Historiography, Narrativity, and the "Here and Now" in Graham Swift's *Waterland*', *Journal of Narrative Theory* 36(2) (2006), 254–92.

Childs, Peter, 'Graham Swift: Past Present', in *Contemporary Novelists: British Fiction since 1970* (Basingstoke: Palgrave, 2005), pp. 237–54.

Cook, Rufus, 'The Aporia of Time in Graham Swift's Waterland', *Concentric: Literary and Cultural Studies* 30(1) (2004), 133–48.

Cooper, Pamela, 'Imperial Topographies: The Spaces of History in *Waterland*', *Modern Fiction Studies* 42(2) (1996), 371–96.

DeCoste, Damon Marcel, 'Question and Apocalypse: The Endlessness of *Historia* in Graham Swift's *Waterland*', *Contemporary Literature* 43(2) (2002), 377–99.

Irish, Robert K., ' "Let me tell you": About Desire and Narrativity in Graham Swift's *Waterland*', *Modern Fiction Studies* 44(4) (1998), 917–34.

Lea, Daniel, *Graham Swift* (Manchester: Manchester University Press, 2005).

McKinney, Robert, 'The Greening of Postmodernism: Graham Swift's *Waterland*', *New Literary History* 28(4) (1997), 821–32.

Powell, Katrina M, 'Mary Metcalf's Attempt at Reclamation: Maternal Representation in Graham Swift's *Waterland*', *Women's Studies: An Interdisciplinary Journal* 32(1) (2003), 59–77.

Schad, John (1992), 'The End of the End of History: Graham Swift's *Waterland*', *Modern Fiction Studies* 38(4) (1992), 911–25.

Jeanette Winterson

Andermahr, Sonya, 'Cyberspace and the Body: Jeanette Winterson's *The.PowerBook*', in *British Fiction of the 1990s*, ed. Nick Bentley (London: Routledge, 2005), pp. 108–22.

Bailey, Peggy Dunn, 'Writing "Herstory": Narrative Reconstruction in Jeanette Winterson's *Oranges Are Not the Only Fruit*', *Philological Review* 32(2) (2006), 61–78.

Carter, Keryn, 'The Consuming Fruit: Oranges, Demons, and Daughters', *Critique: Studies in Contemporary Fiction* 40(1) (1998), 15–23.

Childs, Peter, 'Jeanette Winterson: Boundaries and Desire', in *Contemporary Novelists: British Fiction since 1970* (Basingstoke: Palgrave, 2005), pp. 25–73.

DeLong, Anne, 'The Cat's Cradle: Multiple Discursive Threads in Jeanette Winterson's *Oranges Are Not the Only Fruit*', *LIT: Literature Interpretation Theory* 17(3–4) (2006), 263–75.

Makinen, Merja, *The Novels of Jeanette Winterson* (Basingstoke: Palgrave, 2005).

Grice, Helena and Tim Woods (eds), *I'm Telling You Stories: Jeanette Winterson and the Politics of Reading* (Amsterdam: Rodopi, 1998).

Meyer, Kim Middleton, 'Jeanette Winterson's Evolving Subject', in *Contemporary British Fiction*, ed. Richard J. Lane, Rod Mengham and Philip Tew (Cambridge: Polity, 2003), pp. 210–25.

Morrison, Jago, 'Jeanette Winterson: Re-Membering the Body', in *Contemporary Fiction* (London: Routledge, 2003), pp. 95–114.

Onega, Susana, *Jeanette Winterson* (Manchester: Manchester University Press, 2006).

Palmer, Paulina, 'Jeanette Winterson and the Lesbian Postmodern: Story-Telling, Performativity and the Gay Aesthetic', in *The Contemporary British Novel since 1980*, ed. James Acheson and Sarah C. E. Ross (Basingstoke: Palgrave, 2005), 203–16.

Reynolds, Margaret, *Jeanette Winterson* (Plymouth: Northcote House, 1998).

Reynolds, Margaret and Jonathan Noakes (eds), *Jeanette Winterson: The Essential Guide* (London: Vintage, 2003).

Rubinson, Gregory J., *The Fiction of Rushdie, Barnes, Winterson, and Carter: Breaking Cultural and Literary Boundaries in the Work of Four Postmodernists* (Jefferson, NC: McFarland, 2005).

Index

NEW from Edinburgh University Press

Edinburgh Critical Guides to Literature
Series editors: **Martin Halliwell** and **Andy Mousley**

Already published in the *Edinburgh Critical Guides to Literature* series:

Gothic Literature
Andrew Smith, University of Glamorgan

2007, 224 pp, Pb, 978 0 7486 2370 9, £14.99
Hb, 978 0 7486 2369 3, £60.00

Asian American Literature
Bella Adams, Liverpool Hope University College

April 2008, 248 pp, Pb, 978 0 7486 2272 6, £15.99
Hb, 978 0 7486 2271 9, £50.00

Contemporary American Drama
Annette Saddik, New York City College of Technology, CUNY

2007, 224 pp, Pb, 978 0 7486 2494 2, £15.99
Hb, 978 0 7486 2493 5, £60.00

Canadian Literature
Faye Hammill, Strathclyde University

2007, 172 pp, Pb, 978 0 7486 2162 0, £15.99
Hb, 978 0 7486 2161 3, £60.00

Shakespeare
Gabriel Egan, Loughborough University

2007, 256 pp, Pb, 978 0 7486 2372 3, £14.99
Hb, 978 0 7486 2371 6, £50.00

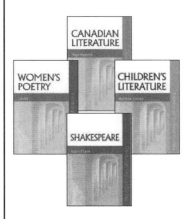

Women's Poetry
Jo Gill, Exeter University

2007, 224 pp, Pb, 978 0 7486 2306 8, £15.99
Hb, 978 0 7486 2305 1, £50.00

Children's Literature
Matthew Grenby, Newcastle University

April 2008, 256 pp, Pb, 978 0 7486 2274 0, £15.99
Hb, 978 0 7486 2273 3, £50.00

NEW from Edinburgh University Press

Edinburgh Critical Guides to Literature
Series editors: **Martin Halliwell** and **Andy Mousley**

Forthcoming in the *Edinburgh Critical Guides to Literature* series:

Renaissance Literature
Siobhan Keenan, De Montfort University

This concise introduction to the literature of an exciting and influential period opens with an overview of the historical and cultural context in which English Renaissance literature was produced, and a discussion of its subsequent critical reception.

The volume includes detailed readings of Spenser's *The Faerie Queene*; Milton's 'Lycidas'; Sidney's *Astrophil and Stella*; Shakespeare's sonnets, *Venus and Adonis* and *Hamlet*; Marlowe's *Tamburlaine*; Jonson's *The Alchemist*; Sir Francis Bacon's Essays, and more.

September 2008, 288 pp, Pb, 978 0 7486 2584 0, £16.99
Hb, 978 0 7486 2583 3, £50.00

Crime Fiction
Stacy Gillis, Newcastle University

Crime Fiction discusses British and American crime fiction from the eighteenth century to the beginning of the twenty-first. Gillis discusses writers, concepts and issues and explores the ways in which such diverse texts as *The Leavenworth Case*, *The Murder of Roger Ackroyd*, *A Rage in Harlem*, and *Postmortem* can be read in the light of critical approaches.

March 2009, 256 pp, Pb, 978 0 7486 2319 8, £15.99
Hb, 978 0 7486 2320 4, £50.00

Restoration and Eighteenth-Century Literature
Hamish Mathison, University of Sheffield

This introduction maps the emergence of the novel onto changes in poetry, drama and popular print. Mathison discusses Milton's *Paradise Lost*, Pope's *The Rape of the Lock*, Behn's *Oroonoko*, Defoe's *Robinson Crusoe*, Sterne's *Tristram Shandy*, as well as examples of restoration drama, satire, song, popular and print culture.

March 2009, 224 pp, Pb, 978 07486 2377 8, £15.99
Hb, 978 0 7486 2376 1, £50.00

Scottish Literature
Gerard Carruthers, University of Glasgow

This guide combines detailed literary history with discussion of contemporary debates about Scottishness. Debates concerning Celticism and Gaelic take place alongside discussion of key Scottish writers, such as Robert Burns, Walter Scott, Thomas Carlyle, Hugh MacDiarmid, Alasdair Gray and Liz Lochhead.

March 2009, 256 pp, Pb, 978 07486 3309 8, £15.99
Hb, 978 0 7486 3308 1, £50.00

ALSO AVAILABLE
from Edinburgh University Press

The Handbook of Creative Writing
Edited by **Steven Earnshaw**, Sheffield Hallam University

An extensive, practical and inspirational resource designed for students and practitioners of creative writing at all levels.

In 48 chapters the Handbook:
- examines the critical theories behind the practice of creative writing
- explains the basics of how to write a novel, script or poetry
- explores how to deal with the practicalities and problems of becoming a writer

2007, 464 pp, Pb, 978 0 7486 2136 1, £18.99
Hb, 978 0 7486 2135 4, £65.00

Texts
Contemporary Cultural Texts and Critical Approaches
Peter Childs, University of Gloucestershire

Texts is a new kind of book which shows students how to use literary theory to approach a wide range of literary, cultural and media texts of the kind studied on today's courses. These texts range from short stories, autobiographies, political speeches, websites and lyrics, through *The Matrix*, *Harry Potter* and *Big Brother*, to shopping malls, celebrities and rock videos.

2006, 192pp, Pb, 978 0 7486 2044 9, £15.99
Hb, 978 0 7486 2043 2, £59.00

The Contemporary British Novel
Edited by **James Acheson**, formerly University of Canterbury at Christchurch, and **Sarah Ross**, Massey University

Written by some of the world's finest contemporary literature specialists, the newly commissioned essays in this volume examine the work of more than twenty major British novelists: Peter Ackroyd, Martin Amis, Iain (M.) Banks, Pat Barker, Julian Barnes, A.S. Byatt, Angela Carter, Janice Galloway, Abdulrazak Gurnah, Kazuo Ishiguro, James Kelman, A.L. Kennedy, Hanif Kureishi, Ian McEwan, Caryl Philips, Salman Rushdie, Zadie Smith, Graham Swift, Rose Tremain, Marina Warner, Irvine Welsh and Jeanette Winterson.

2005, 256pp, Pb, 978 0 7486 1895 8, £16.99
Hb, 978 0 7486 1894 1, £59.00

www.euppublishing.com

ALSO AVAILABLE
from Edinburgh University Press

The Edinburgh Companion to Contemporary Scottish Literature
Edited by **Berthold Schoene**, Manchester Metropolitan University

'Will provoke and enrich debate on Scottish writing.'
Glenda Norquay, Liverpool John Moores University

'A perfect blend of expertise and enthusiasm ... In this big, bold book, Berthold Schoene has gathered all the rays of criticism into one.'
Professor Willy Maley, University of Glasgow

2007, 560pp, Pb, 978 0 7486 2396 9, £19.99
Hb, 978 0 7486 2395 2, £60.00

The Edinburgh Companion to Twentieth-Century Literatures in English
Edited by **Brian McHale**, Ohio State University, and **Randall Stevenson**, University of Edinburgh

'The moment for this book is absolutely perfect. It instructs both by its programmatic statements and by the success of its examples.'
Bruce Robbins, Columbia University

'This intriguing and informative book rides the updraught provided by the continuing popularity of guides and companions, but also performs some surprising and fascinating new mid-air manoeuvres with the form.'
Steven Connor, Birkbeck College, University of London

2006, 352pp, Hb, 978 0 7486 2011 1, £81.00

Introducing Criticism at the 21st Century
Edited by **Julian Wolfreys**, Loughborough University

Introducing Criticism at the 21st Century provides a wide-ranging guide to current directions in literary criticism. The book develops out of continental thinking and insights from poststructuralism, feminism, deconstruction and psychoanalysis and introduces new modes of 'hybrid' criticism which are emerging at the beginning of the twenty-first century.

2002, 320pp, Pb, 978 0 7486 1575 9, £18.99

www.euppublishing.com